REVISION WORKBOOK

Jurisprudence:
THE PHILOSOPHY OF LAW

CONSULTANT EDITOR: LORD TEMPLEMAN

OLD BAILEY PRESS

OLD BAILEY PRESS
200 Greyhound Road, London W14 9RY

1st edition 1997

© Old Bailey Press Ltd 1997

Previous editions published under The HLT Group Ltd.

All Old Bailey Press publications enjoy copyright protection and the copyright belongs to the Old Bailey Press Ltd.

All rights reserved. No part of this publication may be reproduced or transmitted in any form or by any means, electronic, mechanical, photocopying, recording or otherwise, or stored in any retrieval system of any nature without either the written permission of the copyright holder, application for which should be made to the Old Bailey Press Ltd, or a licence permitting restricted copying in the United Kingdom issued by the Copyright Licensing Agency.

Any person who infringes the above in relation to this publication may be liable to criminal prosecution and civil claims for damages.

ISBN 1 85836 241 5

British Library Cataloguing-in-Publication.

A CIP Catalogue record for this book is available from the British Library.

Printed and bound in Great Britain.

Contents

Acknowledgement	v
Introduction	vii
Studying Jurisprudence	ix
Revision and Examination Technique	xi
Table of Cases	xv

A: ARE MORAL JUDGMENTS PART OF THE LAW?

1	Introduction to Problems of Law and Morality	3
2	The Separation of Law and Morals	8
3	Modern Natural Law and Its Historical Background	45

B: LEGAL AND SOCIAL THEORY

4	Realist Theories	59
5	The Historical School	76
6	Critical Legal Studies	84
7	Feminist Jurisprudence	91
8	The Anthropological School	97
9	Sociological Jurisprudence and the Sociology of Law	101
10	Marxism	111
11	Utilitarianism	127

C: JUSTICE

12	Justice and the Legal Enforcement of Morality	137
13	What Are Rights?	144

D: JUDICIAL REASONING

14	Legal Personality	159
15	The Judicial Process	165

E: PREPARING FOR THE EXAMINATION

16	Jurisprudence – An Overview	187
17	University of London LLB (External) 1996 Questions and Suggested Solutions	196

Acknowledgement

Some questions used are taken or adapted from past University of London LLB (External) Degree examination papers and our thanks are extended to the University of London for their kind permission to use and publish the questions.

Caveat

The answers given are not approved or sanctioned by the University of London and are entirely our responsibility.

They are not intended as 'Model Answers', but rather as Suggested Solutions.

The answers have two fundamental purposes, namely:

a) To provide a detailed example of a suggested solution to an examination question, and

b) To assist students with their research into the subject and to further their understanding and appreciation of the subject of Laws.

Introduction

This Revision WorkBook has been designed specifically for those studying jurisprudence to undergraduate level. Its coverage is not confined to any one syllabus, but encompasses a wide range of jurisprudential topics.

However, since it is anticipated that many students will be intending to sit the University of London LLB external examinations, the questions used are primarily from past jurisprudence and legal theory papers from that course.

Each chapter contains brief notes explaining the scope and overall content of the topic covered in that chapter. There follows, in each case, a list of key points which will assist the students in studying and memorising the essential elements of the important theories. However, on the assumption that the student will already possess a textbook the details of each theorist's work have been kept to a minimum.

Additionally in each chapter there will be a question analysis which will explain and evaluate the types of questions set on each topic in past jurisprudence papers. The purpose of such a question analysis is to give an appreciation of the potential types of questions possible, different formats in questions and methods of combining two or more theories/theorists in one question.

Each chapter will end with a sample of examination questions together with skeleton answers and suggested solutions. Wherever possible, the questions are drawn from University of London external jurisprudence and legal theory papers 1990-1996. However it is inevitable that, in compiling a list of questions by topic order rather than chronologically, not only do the same questions crop up over and over again in different guises, but there are gaps where questions have never been set at all. Where a topic has never been covered in an examination question, a specimen question will have been written as an example, together with a skeleton answer and a suggested solution.

Undoubtedly the main feature of this Revision WorkBook is the inclusion of as many past examination questions as possible. While the use of past questions as a revision aid is certainly not new, it is hoped that the combination of actual past questions from the University of London LLB external course and specially written questions will be of assistance to students in achieving a thorough and systematic revision of the subject.

Careful use of the Revision WorkBook should enhance the student's understanding of jurisprudence, facilitating the study of a wide range of subject matter while at the same time enabling examination techniques to be practised.

The final chapter contains the complete June 1996 University of London LLB (External) Jurisprudence and Legal Theory question paper, followed by suggested solutions to each question. Thus the student will have the opportunity to review a recent examination paper in its entirety, and can, if desired, use this chapter as a mock examination – referring to the suggested solutions only after first having attempted the questions.

Studying Jurisprudence

The study of 'Jurisprudence and Legal Theory' and preparation for examination in the subject presents special problems for the student of law. Unlike other legal subjects there are no right answers to an issue; usually case law does not provide the solution. Instead, the student must approach the different theorists with an open mind, be prepared to criticise and evaluate and to consider law in wider social and political contexts.

The first difficulty for the student is where to begin. Jurisprudence is one of those subjects which becomes far more comprehensible when the student has completed the whole course. This will, however, be of cold comfort to the student still struggling to understand Topic One. The best advice that can be given is that a student should not rely on writings *about* the theorists – they should as far as possible read the writings *of* the theorists. In other words, stick to *primary* sources wherever possible. Only then will critiques and analyses of those theorists become meaningful. This may sound daunting. However the use of a good basic textbook such as Lloyd's *An Introduction to Jurisprudence* (latest edition) will ease the way. The student will benefit from the textbook commentary as a means of placing each theorist in an historical, social and political context and can then be guided by the extracts from original works as to the central elements of that theorist's thesis.

A mere understanding of the major theorists will not, however, be enough in itself to enable the student to obtain a good examination grade. Jurisprudence papers rarely call for straightforward analysis of theses; the student must be prepared to deal with familiar material in an unfamiliar way, to write answers comparing or contrasting more than one theorist, or even to answer a general question stretching across a whole spectrum of topics. In other words, the student should be prepared to think! A blind acceptance of what he or she has read or been told will not gain high marks. A recitation of a prepared answer on, for example, Kelsen, just because his name is mentioned in the question, will not impress any examiner. In jurisprudence, perhaps more than in any other subject, the three cardinal rules are: *read* the question; stop and *think*; *plan*.

So that the student may be in a position to do this, some hints on revising jurisprudence may be helpful. First of all, it is worth pointing out that no one could possibly read all the available literature. A pruning exercise is certainly required. Most tutors will have helped their students considerably here by producing concise digestible reading lists. The student may wish to be even more selective when the time comes to revise. But certain points should be remembered: jurisprudence is a subject where 'question-spotting' is impossible. Unusual topics are frequently juxtaposed and unusual slants on topics are common. To be too selective is therefore disastrous. The student should aim for a broad appreciation of the major schools and theorists as well as the major social, political and moral issues. Where a student *can* cut down his or her work lies in the fact that the need for rote learning is less great than in other legal subjects. Whilst the central elements of theses clearly need to be learned, the student can generally spend his time more profitably in thinking about issues and constructing his or her own views than in learning masses of detail by heart.

The last sentence perhaps explains both the appeal of jurisprudence, and the reason why it frightens the more timid. The lack of clear answers, and the need to argue for one view or another inhibits those who like to have a 'right' answer to everything. But to those prepared

Studying Jurisprudence

to challenge and evaluate what they read or are told, and to come to their own conclusions, the study of jurisprudence is one of the most valuable and interesting opportunities in their entire course.

Revision and Examination Technique

(A) REVISION TECHNIQUE

Planning a revision timetable

In planning your revision timetable make sure you don't finish the syllabus too early. You should avoid leaving revision so late that you have to 'cram'. On the other hand, constant revision of the same topic leads to stagnation.

Plan ahead, however, and try to make your plans increasingly detailed as you approach the examination date.

Allocate enough time for each topic to be studied. But note that it is better to devise a realistic timetable, to which you have a reasonable chance of keeping, rather than a wildly optimistic schedule which you will probably abandon at the first opportunity!

The syllabus and its topics

One of your first tasks when you began your course was to ensure that you thoroughly understood your **syllabus**. Check now to see if you can write down the **topics** it comprises from memory. You will see that the chapters of this WorkBook are each devoted to a syllabus topic. This will help you decide which are the key chapters relative to your revision programme. Though you should allow some time for glancing through the other chapters.

The topic and its key points

Again working from memory, analyse what you consider to be the key points of any topic that you have selected for particular revision. Seeing what you can recall, unaided, will help you to understand and firmly memorise the concepts involved.

Using the WorkBook

Relevant questions are provided for each topic in this book. Naturally, as typical examples of examination questions, they do not normally relate to one topic only. Indeed, the nature of the subject requires that you should endeavour to explore the lateral issues across topics, rather than meeting each topic as a separate compartment. For example, if you were an adherent of the Natural Law theory, it would influence your answers to questions on the nature of law, or law and morality, or law and justice, and on judicial reasoning.

Three strategies

You can choose your method of consulting the questions and solutions, but here are some suggestions (strategies 1–3).

Strategy 1

Strategy 1 is planned for the purpose of *quick revision*. First read your chosen question carefully and then jot down in abbreviated notes what you consider to be the main points at issue. Similarly, note the authorities that occur to you as being relevant for citation purposes. Allow yourself sufficient time to cover what you feel to be relevant. Then study the author's *skeleton solution* and skim-read the *suggested solution* to see how they compare with your notes. When comparing consider carefully what the author has included (and concluded) and see whether

Revision and Examination Technique

that agrees with what you have written. Consider the points of variation also. Have you recognised the key issues? How relevant have you been? It is possible, of course, that you have referred to a recent case that *is* relevant, but which had not been reported when the WorkBook was prepared.

Strategy 2

Strategy 2 requires a nucleus of *three hours* in which to practise writing a set of examination answers in a limited time-span.

Select a number of questions (as many as are normally set in your subject in the examination you are studying for), each from a different chapter in the WorkBook, without consulting the solutions. Find a place to write where you will not be disturbed and try to arrange not to be interrupted for three hours. Write your solutions in the time allowed, noting any time needed to make up if you *are* interrupted.

After a rest, compare your answers with the *suggested solutions* in the WorkBook. There will be considerable variation in style, of course, but the bare facts should not be too dissimilar. Evaluate your answer critically. Be 'searching', but develop a positive approach to deciding how you would tackle each question on another occasion.

Strategy 3

You are unlikely to be able to do more than one three hour examination, but occasionally set yourself a single question. Vary the 'time allowed' by imagining it to be one of the questions that you must answer in three hours and allow yourself a limited preparation and writing time. Try one question that you feel to be difficult and an easier question on another occasion, for example.

Mis-use of suggested solutions

Don't try to learn by rote. In particular, don't try to reproduce the *suggested solutions* by heart. Learn to express the basic issues in your own words.

(B) EXAMINATION SKILLS

Examiners are human too!

The process of answering an examination question involves a *communication* between you and the person who set it. If you were speaking face to face with the person, you would choose your verbal points and arguments carefully in your reply. When writing, it is all too easy to forget *the human being who is awaiting the reply* and simply write out what one knows in the area of the subject! Bear in mind it is a person whose question you are responding to, throughout your essay. This will help you to avoid being irrelevant or long-winded. On the whole, in jurisprudence, the shorter answers do better than the longer answers.

Examination checklist

1. Read the instructions at the head of the examination carefully. While last-minute changes are unlikely – such as the introduction of a *compulsory question* or *an increase in the number of questions asked* – it has been known to happen.

2. Read the questions carefully. Pay attention to what the examiner wants.

3. Plan your answer *before* you start to write, but in a jurisprudence examination it is wise to start writing earlier rather than later. Since the questions are always speculative you

Revision and Examination Technique

can waste time wondering what you should write. If you are well prepared your writing will flow – the good answer writes itelf!

4   Check that you understand the rubric *before* you start to write. Do not 'discuss', for example, if you are specifically asked to 'compare and contrast'.

5   Answer the correct number of questions. If you fail to answer one out of four questions set you lose 25 per cent of your marks!

Style and structure

Try to be clear and concise. Basically this amounts to using paragraphs to denote the sections of your essay, and writing simple, straightforward sentences as much as possible. The sentence you have just read has 22 words. When a sentence reaches 50 words it becomes difficult for a reader to follow.

Do not be inhibited by the word 'structure' (traditionally defined as giving an essay a beginning, a middle and an end). A good structure will be the natural consequence of setting out your arguments and the supporting evidence in a logical order. Set the scene briefly in your opening paragraph and regard it as your 'impact' paragraph. Provide a clear conclusion in your final paragraph.

Content – opinions as facts

In Jurisprudence, the opinions of academics sometimes replace the legislative and judicial authorities, which one would cite in support of an argument on another paper. As in baseball, there are a number of bases which one is expected to touch, by citing the views of the leading theorists. For example, in an essay on Natural Law these might include Dworkin, Rawls, Finnis, and Fuller.

The opinions of academic writers may then be used to explain the decisions of judges in controversial cases. For example, are there 'principles' which the judiciary resort to in order to fill gaps in the law – as Dworkin suggests? Is there 'one right answer' to any given legal problem?

Express your own views

Examiners are not in the business of 'thought control'. They expect you not merely to refer to the opinions of others, but also to express an opinion of your own. If you can argue a position, and show for example why you believe that Hart is wrong (or right), then you will be given a higher mark. So, accept whole-heartedly this opportunity also to express your own opinions on the issues.

Table of Cases

Anns v London Borough of Merton [1977] 2 All ER 492   *166*
Bourhill v Young [1943] AC 92   *230*
Brown v Board of Education 347 US 483 (1954)   *172*

C v S [1987] 2 WLR 1108   *219*

Donoghue v Stevenson [1932] AC 562   *173, 174, 175, 180*
DPP v Camplin [1978] 2 All ER 168   *96*
Dosso PLD 1958 SC 533   *24, 26*

Evans v Triplex Safety Glass Co Ltd [1936] 1 All ER 283   *175*

Federal German Communist Party v West Germany (1957)   *145*
Fisher v Bell [1961] 1 QB 394   *39, 173*

Glimmerveen & Hagenbeck v The Netherlands   *145*
Gouriet v UPW [1978] AC 435   *194*
Great Northern Railway Co v Sunburst Oil (1932)   *174*

Heydon's Case (1584) 3 Co Rep 74   *182*
Home Office v Dorset Yacht Co [1970] AC 1004   *147*

Ireland v The United Kingdom [1978] 2 EHRR 25   *146*

Jilani (1972)   *26*
Lynch v DPP for Northern Ireland [1975] AC 653   *170*

McLoughlin v O'Brian [1983] AC 410   *166, 221, 230*
Madzimbamuto v Lardner Burke [1968] 2 SA 284; [1969] 1 AC 645   *18, 24, 25, 26*
Mandla v Dowell Lee [1983] 2 AC 548   *182*
Matovu   *24, 26*
Mitchell v DPP [1986] AC 73   *18, 26, 193, 194*

Ndhlovu 1968 (4) SA 515 (RAD)   *25, 26*
Nissan v Attorney-General [1970] AC 179   *175*

Perez v Sharp (1948) 32 Cal 2d 711   *5*

R v Allen (1872) LR 1 CCR 367   *173, 182*
R v R [1992] 1 AC 599; [1992] Crim LR 207   *95, 96, 230*
R v Thornton [1992] 1 All ER 306   *230*
Riggs v Palmer 115 NY 506 (1889)   *171*
Roe v Wade 410 US 113 (1973)   *172, 230*
RRB v London Borough of Ealing [1978] 1 All ER 497   *182*

Salomon v Salomon [1897] AC 22   *160*
Shaw v DPP [1962] AC 220   *166*

Uganda v Commissioner of Prisons, ex parte Matovu [1966] EALR 514   *18*

PART A

ARE MORAL JUDGMENTS PART OF THE LAW?

1 Introduction to Problems of Law and Morality

1.1 Introduction
1.2 Key points
1.3 Analysis of question styles
1.4 Questions

1.1 Introduction

This section, whilst important in its own right, can also be seen as an introduction to the chapters on positivism and natural law below. It is necessary for the student to keep clear the separate issues here: for example, whether unjust laws are law is not the same question as whether one has an obligation to obey the law, although the two points may well overlap. The student may also find it helpful to illustrate answers to questions on law and morality by practical examples such as apartheid or the Nazi regime.

1.2 Key points

In addition to the points raised below the student should keep in mind the whole nature of the positivist/natural law debate.

a) *The connection between law and morals*
   i) Is it necessary? Fuller believes he has established an 'internal morality' consisting of eight principles.
   ii) Hart and Raz deny that this is a true morality. It could be argued that his principles are no more than a characterisation of the rule of law (which may not necessarily be an ideal anyway).
   iii) Fuller argues the existence of law to be a matter of degree.

b) *Do we have a moral duty to obey the law?*
   i) This may depend on whether one considers unjust laws to be law or not (in Aquinas's words 'lex injusta non est lex').
   ii) If one believes that unjust laws are nonetheless law the question of a moral duty to obey becomes more acute. Such a duty might be absolute (though few support this theory) or prima facie (where the duty can be outweighed by other considerations such as the harm caused by an unjust law).

1.3 Analysis of question styles

Questions relating directly to law and morality usually focus on the legal enforcement of morality, and this is often a good choice for students as the debate is topical, comprehensible and interesting. The student should also be prepared to deal with the wider issues discussed

Jurisprudence: The Philosophy of Law

in this chapter, either as part of a question on positivism or natural law, or as a question in its own right.

1.4 Questions

TYPE ONE

A common question is one that calls for an evaluation of Fuller's theory. The candidate should always consider the criticisms of Fuller's theory in the light of the whole positivist/natural law debate.

Is Fuller right to claim that there is a morality that is 'internal' to law?

University of London LLB Examination
(for External Students) Jurisprudence and Legal Theory June 1995 Q12

General Comment

A good question to attempt by describing Fuller's eight principles of 'inner morality'. A detailed discussion of his main claim is required with a description of the principles. Hart's criticism can, on this occasion, be attacked and a general conclusion that Fuller's concept has merit, in part, can be made.

Skeleton Solution

Introduction to Fuller's claim – moralities of aspiration and duty – eight principles of the 'inner morality' – Hart's criticism – conclusion.

Suggested Solution

Fuller claims, in his criticism of legal positivism, that some things taken as legal facts are merely achievements of legal aspirations. He says that law can only be said to be binding if citizens believe or act as if it is, and that a genuine working legal system cannot be understood merely by looking at the rules consciously created by law makers. His justification is the American constitution which does not mention a requirement to legislate although all American legal authority flows from it.

Whilst Fuller does not seek to prove that substantive morality is bound up with law, he identifies perils when seeking to prove a relationship between a relativist, content-based concept of morality, and a content-neutral, universal conception of law. He argues that if morality must be seen as being relative rather than absolute, then if we seek to relate morality to law, such morality must be one specific to the nature of law. He concludes that legal morality must be a particular type of morality which is found in the nature of law itself rather than an abstraction from other moral norms.

Moralities of aspiration and duty

Fuller's concept of morality has a practical criterion with goals to which the legal system should aspire, thus his morality of aspiration is largely one of degree. A morality of duty can be distinguished in terms of the rules of a substantive morality such as 'thou shalt not kill'.

Whether there is an informal morality of law presents Fuller with a problem because he is concerned to relate a morality that is linked to his content-neutral concept of law. It seems not to follow the conventional approach of asserting that law respects certain substantive moral values. Therefore, the content of the internal morality of law looks remarkably like common-sense rules of good craftsmanship. His contention is that there is an inherent logic to the subjugation of human conduct to legal rules which, if ignored, lead to failure.

Eight principles of the 'inner morality'

Fuller asserts that the eight principles of the 'inner morality' of the law are as follows:

1. A legal system must be based on or reveal some kind of regular trends. As such law should be founded on generalisations of conduct such as rules, rather than simply allowing arbitrary adjudication.
2. Laws must be publicised so that subjects know how they are supposed to behave.
3. Rules will not have the desired effect if it is likely that your present actions will not be judged by them in future. As such, retrospective legislation should not be abused.
4. Laws should be comprehensible, even if it is only lawyers who understand them.
5. Laws should not be contradictory.
6. Law should not expect the subject to perform the impossible.
7. Law should not change so frequently that the subject cannot orient his action to it.
8. There should not be a significant difference between the actual administration of the law and what the written rule says.

These criteria are in the form of the moral rules of duty. Fuller expresses them as principles or goals; generality of laws; promulgation of laws; minimising the use of retrospective laws; clarity; lack of contradiction; possibility of obedience; constancy through time; consistency between the word and the practice of law.

Fuller's evaluation speaks for itself:

'Though these natural laws touch one of the most vital of human activities they obviously do not exhaust the whole of man's moral life. They have nothing to say on such topics as polygamy, the study of Marx, the worship of God, the progressive income tax, or the subjugation of women. If the question be raised whether any of these subjects, or others like them, should be taken as objects of legislation, that question relates to what I have called the external morality of the law.'

Fuller states, by showing how the Nazi regime suffered a progressive decline in its adherence to such principles of legality, that the internal morality of law is neutral towards the law's substantive aims, with exceptions. The urge for legal clarity fights against laws that direct themselves against alleged evils which cannot be defined, such as racial discrimination. He cites *Perez* v *Sharp* (1948) where a statute which prevented the marriage of a white person to any Negro, Mulatto, Mongolian or member of the Malay race was held to be unconstitutional because the constitution required clarity.

Hart's criticism

One of Hart's more unfair criticisms concerns Fuller's assertion that beyond the satisfaction of a very minimal standard the legality of a system is a matter of degree: a legal system, some say, cannot 'half-exist'. Also, if a legal system exists only to a lesser degree, how can we decide when we do or do not have to take account of one point – how many people need to disobey a legal system for it to cease to be a legal system?

Fuller's eight principles, which loosely describe requirements of procedural justice, ensure that a legal system would satisfy the demands of morality to the extent that a legal system which adhered to all the principles would explain the all-important idea of 'fidelity to law' and command obedience with moral justification.

Conclusion

It is unfortunate that Hart's criticism has observed Fuller's main claim of a morality that is 'internal' to law. There is an important sense of legal justification where claims made in the name of 'law' are morally serious. A genuine claim for legal justification of an immoral, Nazi-style legal system must have some moral force about such a claim. Thus, when a claim is made about our 'law', it carries some moral force. It is submitted that a denial is insufficient and an explanation required — an explanation that can be found, in part, by Fuller's eight principles.

TYPE TWO

This is a fairly straightforward essay on the obligation to obey the law. The answer will be improved by reference to the difficult practical question of obedience to, for example, Nazi decrees or apartheid laws.

Is there a prima facie moral obligation to obey the law?

Written by the Editor

Skeleton Solution

Absolute obligation — prima facie obligation — are unjust laws law? — gratitude theory — promise — keeping theory — utilitarianism — duty to obey laws in a democracy — Peter Singer — fairness as compromise — participation — problem of unjust laws.

Suggested Solution

This question does not raise the issue of absolute obligation to obey the law (which few philosophers would accept) nor does it deal with non-moral reasons for obedience (such as sanctions, fear of social disapproval). It concentrates on the question of prima facie moral obligation: is there a moral obligation to obey the law which may in certain circumstances be outweighed by factors justifying disobedience? This is a rather different issue to that of whether, in Aquinas's words, 'lex injusta non est lex'. This answer will take the position that unjust laws are law, but that of course they raise special problems when considering the existence of a moral obligation to obey the law.

An argument used to support the view that there is a prima facie moral obligation is the 'gratitude' theory. This runs as follows: an individual has received benefits from the system of law and government, and thus has a moral obligation to obey the law arising out of gratitude. Smith has dealt with this argument succinctly: 'A government typically confers these benefits, not to advance the interests of particular citizens, but rather as a consequence of advancing some purpose of its own.' Viewed in this way the concept of 'gratitude' becomes meaningless, and it is clear that this theory thereby fails to establish an obligation for the individual.

A second common argument used to show a prima facie moral obligation to obey the law is that of 'promise-keeping'. This is closely linked with social contract theories; an individual owes obedience to the law in return for its protection. Clearly this argument must rest on individual

1 Introduction to Problems of Law and Morality

consent to be valid – a 'contract' must be made by one exercising free will. Since being a member of society is non-voluntary, there can be no such free will or consent. The arguments from 'promise-keeping' are thereby unconvincing.

A third possible means of showing a prima facie obligation to obey the law lies in utilitarianism. The argument here is that breaches of the law will always diminish the amount of 'welfare' in society and there is thus a moral obligation to obey the law. One might well argue that such a general claim cannot be substantiated – can driving safely through a red light on a clear road really be said to diminish general 'welfare'? Surely the effect of each breach can only be judged individually, and as such one cannot claim a general moral obligation to obey the law. This argument could be answered by the submission that a breach of law **is** always detrimental to social 'welfare' because it sets a bad example and thus threatens social cohesion. Yet as Raz has pointed out, this argument is fallacious: some offences are never known to anyone but the offender (for instance, a minor undiscovered tax fiddle) and thus set no example at all.

It has been argued that none of the above arguments convincingly establishes a prima facie moral obligation to obey the law. Yet one is led to wonder whether part of the reason for their lack of persuasion is that all the arguments cited could apply to a dictatorship or an autocracy just as well as to a democracy. And one does have an intuitive feeling that there is more likely to be a moral obligation to obey law enacted in a democratic society than law enacted by a dictator. The crucial issue is whether this intuitive feeling can be supported by convincing theory. Peter Singer, in his book *Democracy and Disobedience*, suggests that a prima facie moral obligation to obey the law does exist, not in every society, but only where the law has been enacted by democratic means. His central argument is 'fairness as compromise'. By this he means that a decision making process of equal say for each person provides a valid reason why individuals have a moral obligation to obey the law. Individuals should recognise the fairness of compromise in a society and thus obey the result of a majority decision rather than act on their own judgement. Singer also suggests that an individual who participates in the democratic process by voting is bound by a type of estoppel to abide by the outcome. Although this 'participation' theory does leave unclear the position of abstainers, it is submitted that Singer's argument for a moral duty to obey in a democracy is convincing. If one applied his theory to a country in South Africa where many are denied the vote, there would be no moral obligation to obey the law. But it then appears that Singer has left open a difficult question: Assume that a morally reprehensible group such as the Nazis are democratically elected to power, including the power to enact law. Is the democratic process itself enough to establish a prima facie moral obligation to obey those laws?

Singer does, however, have an answer to this puzzle. He suggests that disobedience to the law is justified where, despite a democratic process, there is:

1 a tendency for a minority group to be subjected to unfair laws; and

2 legal means of getting those laws changed have proved unsuccessful.

He cites disobedience to law by the Catholic minority in Ulster as an example. But his theory would appear to work equally well for the example given above. Disobedience to Nazi laws where, for example, the Jewish minority are persecuted, would be morally justifiable even if those laws had been enacted according to a democratic process. It is thus submitted that Singer's theory gives a convincing answer to the question of prima facie moral obligation to obey the law which works well in relation to genuine practical dilemmas.

2 The Separation of Law and Morals

A IMPERATIVE THEORIES
2.1   Introduction
2.2   Key points
2.3   Analysis of question styles
2.4   Questions

B THE PURE THEORY OF LAW
2.5   Introduction
2.6   Key points
2.7   Analysis of question styles
2.8   Questions

C MODERN THEORIES
2.9   Introduction
2.10 Key points
2.11 Analysis of question styles
2.12 Questions

A IMPERATIVE THEORIES

2.1 Introduction

Although Bentham is now generally considered to have postulated a more sophisticated imperative theory than that of Austin, the student should be prepared to deal with either, and to compare the two. It is also sensible to revise this section in conjunction with the modern theorists such as Hart and Raz who will provide useful standpoints of criticism of the traditional positivists. Since one of the most important issues in jurispurdence is the natural law/positivist debate, the imperative theories, like positivism generally, should be considered in the light of natural law theories.

2.2 Key points

The student should understand the similarities and differences between the theories of:

a) Bentham

b) Austin

In particular the following aspects of both theories should be studied:

c) Law as 'commands'.

d) The concept of sanctions.

e) The concept of sovereignty.

Criticisms and comparisons with other positivists can be found in Parts B and C of this chapter.

2.3 Analysis of question styles

This section will concentrate on questions relating specifically to aspects of Austin or Bentham. Such questions often call for some type of comparison between, or evaluation of, the two different theories. The concept of sanctions is often raised in examination questions and is an easy topic to deal with. Students should be prepared to use their knowledge of imperative theories in answering more general questions, some of which appear in the later parts of this chapter.

2.4 Questions

TYPE ONE

A typical question on sanctions is one calling for a comparison between Austin and Bentham. Although a degree of evaluation of the use of sanctions in their theories would be helpful, there is otherwise little necessity for reference to other theories or writers.

'A sanction is a conditional evil' (John Austin). Explain the nature and importance of Austin's idea of sanction in his theory of law and contrast it with the use made of the term by Jeremy Bentham.

> University of London LLB Examination
> (for External Students) Jurisprudence and Legal Theory 1983 Q3

Skeleton Solution

Imperative theory of law – coercive sanctions is an essential element – Austin – sanction as a conditional evil – correlative to duty – nullity as a sanction – Bentham – Sanction is coercive or a reward – close connection with obligation – power – conferring laws – criticisms.

Suggested Solution

Austin and Bentham both expounded the imperative theory of law, which explains a law as the command of a determinate person or body, an order to someone to do (or not do) something. An essential element in the theory as it was developed by both of them was that of coercive sanctions. To enforce the order, the sovereign imposed a sanction – an evil, a punishment to motivate obedience. First, I will outline the contribution made by sanction to Austin's explanation of law, and then analyse that contribution by contrasting Bentham's similar but better considered views. Finally a brief evaluation of their notions of sanction will be given.

For Austin, all laws were commands. Included in the idea of a command is the likelihood of a sanction being incurred if the command is disobeyed. The nature of this 'sanction' is that it is an evil which will be visited on the person commanded by the sovereign, if he does not comply with the wish (so the sanction is a 'conditional evil'); its importance in brief is that unless such a sanction is likely to be incurred the expression of a wish is not a command. The next question is 'how likely must it be?' and the answer cannot be a certain one, as Austin was not consistent; in the end, he seems to have settled on the smallest chance of incurring the smallest evil as sufficient to constitute a command. Although the idea of the sanction is to motivate obedience, actual fear of it is not required; just likelihood in the smallest degree.

The sanction is correlative to duty; it is the likelihood of suffering the sanction, according to Austin, that constitutes legal duty or obligation. Disobedience of the command (which by definition includes an evil in prospect) is a violation of that duty. All laws, Austin says, take this form of a command, backed by the likelihood of an evil, creating an obligation. Some laws appear not to be of this form: those Professor Hart has named 'power-conferring rules'. Such rules, which may be public or private, appear to give the power holder the legal capacity to alter the legal situation of himself or others (for example by entering a contract), and do not appear to impose any obligation on him to do so, or any sanction if he tries to do so and fails.

Austin's theory follows that of Bentham in many important respects, the main points of contrast being the greater complexity of Bentham's thought in several areas; overall the use Bentham makes of sanction is almost the same. For Bentham, 'command' is only one of four senses or 'aspects' of the sovereign's will; there are two imperative aspects (command – 'do some revision', prohibition 'do not do some revision') and the permissive aspects (non-prohibition – 'you may do some revision', and non-command – 'you may refrain from doing some revision'). Bentham in fact develops a new logic of imperatives ('deontic logic') to explain the relationships between these, but that need not detain us here. The important points to note are that the permissive aspects are related to the imperative (because they release the subject from earlier commands or prohibitions, and are therefore dis-imperative), and that in any case all 'complete' laws (or in more modern terminology individual laws) are imperative in form.

Bentham's notion of imperation and disimperation is more subtle than Austin's, then, but does not alter the basic point that laws are seen as imperative. A law contains two parts, the directive part (giving the ordered conduct) and the incitative part, the prediction of a sanction. At this stage the sanction is no more than a prediction; it takes a subsidiary law to an official ordering the imposition of a sanction in case of breach of the first law (this subsidiary law must be backed up by another and so on) to actually ensure that the prediction becomes a reality. All laws, then, have sanctions attached. As with the notion of command, Bentham's notion of 'sanction' is far richer than Austin's: a sanction can be either coercive or a reward, and if it is coercive Bentham identifies several forms (political or legal, moral and religious) which it can take. While commands with reward sanctions ('praemiary laws') are close enough to the coercive sanction type to be properly 'laws' they are distinct, rare, and they do not (as we shall see) create obligations.

As with Austin, the idea of sanction is closely connected with that of obligation. Both, in fact, subscribe to what Hart called a mixed theory of obligation. Austin's legal obligation is created when a command is issued (by the sanction) ordering or forbidding some conduct, and a sanction is likely to be imposed if the command is disobeyed. Bentham's more complete exposition of aspects of will and of sanctions, and his identification of a role for the permissions and praemiary laws, mark his theory out from Austin's; but apart from rare praemiary laws and permissions (not in any case 'complete' laws), for him too all laws are in an imperative mode, with likelihood of sanction having a central role as part of the law (although enforced by a separate law) and constituting the legal obligation.

Bentham's explanation of power-conferring laws is more convincing than Austin's. There is much detail and some ambiguity in Bentham on the subject of these laws. Over-simplifying, powers are either of *contrectation* (powers of handling persons or property), which are conferred by permissions in some way exceptional – for example, the owner's power to walk on his property is given him by a permission to do so set against the general prohibition against walking on the land, or of *imperation* (powers of changing people's legal position by making them subject to commands or prohibitions). These latter powers are 'shares in imperation', which the sovereign allows so that general descriptive laws (eg of property or contract) can be fleshed out or completed by the power holder (with details of people and terms), to enable a complete law imposing duties (eg on the contracting parties) by the imposition of a threat of sanction (damages for breach) to be made.

I could perhaps stop at this point, having attempted to both explain the nature and importance of sanction to Austin, and to contrast that to Bentham's more developed theory. However, a brief reference to some major criticisms of the command-sanction-obligation model of all laws will serve as an appropriate conclusion. Coercive sanctions are clearly central to all present developed legal systems; the mistake of the imperative theorists is to refer to sanctions in the definition of an individual law and the obligation it creates. In some cases, we think of obligations being imposed by legal rules even though no sanction is ordered to enforce that obligation; and even when there is a sanction prescribed the fact that it is not likely in a particular case (if the offender has left the country, say, or died) to be imposed is not held to alter the obligation. That such a sentence as 'he fled the country to avoid his legal duty to report for the draft' does not warp our notion of legal duty is proof of this.

There is a confusion between the idea of obligation and duty, on the one hand, and that of being forced or obliged by fear of the sanction on the other. The reason for applying a sanction is that there was an obligation; that obligation results from the authority and validity of the rule, the fact that the rules or systems from which it comes has authority over the subject. To include a coercive sanction as a necessary constituent of a law distorts our view of these matters.

Freed from such a view, we no longer have to fit power-conferring laws in the same model. Bentham's attempt to do so particularly, by making them part of a complete imperative law, is interesting; but a better approach is that they are separate types of laws, intimately connected with laws imposing duties, but having a distinct function.

TYPE TWO

Another type of question is one calling for an evaluation of Austin's general concept of law.

'Austin's theory is not a theory of the Rule of Law – of government subject to law. It is a theory of the "rule of men" – of government using law as an instrument of power. Such a view may be considered realistic or merely cynical, but it is, in its broad outlines, essentially coherent.' (Cotterrell)

Discuss.

University of London LLB Examination
(for External Students) Jurisprudence and Legal Theory June 1995 Q4

General Comment

Beware that this question does not require a statement covering all you know about John Austin. It looks for a rational discussion of what Austin sees as the scope of jurisprudence, with the gloss that Cotterrell puts on it.

Jurisprudence: The Philosophy of Law

Skeleton Solution

Austin's definition of the scope of jurisprudence – Cotterrell's main criticism – the concept of sovereignty attacked – Hart's rejection of 'coercive order' – conclusion.

Suggested Solution

Within the context of Cotterrell's statement, John Austin's theory will include a concept of law as a species of command with an analysis of sovereignty. In *The Province of Jurisprudence Determined*, Austin defined what he saw as the precise scope of jurisprudence. To him, it involved drawing a clear distinction between morality and law.

Austin's theory has been much criticised, but in essence he regards the nature of law as based on the concept of power exercised by a superior and not on ideas which are perceived to be 'good or bad', or 'just or unjust'.

Jurisprudence, according to Austin, is concerned specifically with 'positive laws' or 'law properly so called' as he puts it. Law is viewed as a species of command issued by a person or a body of people to whom habitual obedience was rendered. It was characterised by constituent elements:

1. command;
2. sanction;
3. duty;
4. sovereignty.

Law can be described as the command of a sovereign backed by sanctions.

Cotterrell's criticism

Austin's theory is criticised by Cotterrell who says it is not a theory of the 'rule of law', but more a theory of the 'rule of men'. The two separate concepts require distinction. De Smith sees the 'rule of law' as an abstract concept intended to imply that powers exercised by politicians and public servants require a legitimate foundation. Such powers are based upon an authority conferred by law, when the law conforms to certain minimum standards of justice, either procedural or substantive.

The 'rule of men' theory describes a position where deviation goes beyond what is acceptable, where executive discretionary power increases at the expense of individual freedom, and where the courts have the right to decide when legal preconditions for the loss of liberty are satisfied.

The validity of Cotterrell's view can be determined by the review of main criticisms levelled at Austin's theory. Initial criticism of Austin's theory revolved around his positivism which was denounced as 'a sterile verbalism which produced a travesty of reality' and also for an apparent 'narrowness of perspective'. Austin was accused of failing to understand the implications of his brand of positivism because his distinction between questions of 'law' and of 'morality' distanced him form an awareness of the real complexities of law within society.

Later criticism attacked Austin's 'simplistic view' of law saying he confused 'law' with the 'mere product of legislation'. Critics accused him of failing to understand that 'law' was much more than mere statutory measures because it included custom and international law which both received scant attention with his analysis. Further, Austin's analysis did not cover an adequate examination of 'judge-made' law arising from decisions of the courts.

Austin's command theory was also considered to have a linguistic looseness or ambiguity where the term 'command' has its own singular connotations. Command theory generally suggests the issue of order arbitrarily without using the word 'command' accurately when referring directly to the content of the large bulk of legislation. Austin also took criticism where the characteristics of a 'command' are absent from much contemporary legislation.

Sovereignty

Critics suggest that Austin's concept of sovereignty was 'over simplified' and incapable of an application to problems which arose from the legal structures of democratic society in particular. His view of 'the sovereign as possessing unlimited powers' was thought to have no validity within a parliamentary constitution. The indivisibility of a sovereign's power also created difficulties for those who sought to apply it to the analysis of a federal state.

Bryce says that Austin may have blurred the difference between a 'de facto' sovereign and a 'de jure' sovereign; a 'de facto' sovereign receives the habitual obedience of his subjects, whilst a 'de jure' sovereign is a law enacting institution. British constitutional law clearly distinguishes the Queen as sovereign from the Queen in Parliament. Austin had concentrated specifically on the form of 'law' and its outward manifestations relating to a sovereign and had given insufficient weight to the functional aspects of sovereign power in society.

Professor Hart has made serious criticism of Austin's theory when he rejected any model of law which was based merely on 'coercive orders'. Hart's justification was that 'coercive orders' were inapplicable to a large section of the modern legal system which confers public and private legal powers. Hart identified the mode or origin of law as being substantially misunderstood if it was seen as merely having emerged from 'orders plus threat'.

Conclusion

It can be concluded that Austin's analysis of 'law' in terms of a sovereign who is habitually obeyed as an omnipotent ruler exempt from all legal imitation does not account for the continuity of legislative authority which is the main characteristic of a modern legal system. In such circumstances, the sovereign cannot be identified either with a modern legislature or the electorate itself.

It is submitted that Cotterrell's contention that Austin's theory is more a theory of the rule of man rather that law flows logically from the substantial criticism levelled at Austin, most recently by Hart.

B THE PURE THEORY OF LAW

2.5 Introduction

The pure theory of law was developed by Kelsen, and has been said by Lloyd and Freeman in *An Introduction to Jurisprudence* to be the most 'illuminating analysis of the legal process' this century. Kelsen shared many characteristics with other positivists – for example, his insistence on sanctions as being central. But the most crucial and outstanding element of Kelsen's analysis is his norm theory: that an 'ought' statement is derived from another 'ought' statement or norm, until one ultimately arrives back at the grundnorm. In revising Kelsen students should consider his theory in the light of positivism generally. It might also be useful to consider comparisons with other types of theories such as Realism.

2.6 Key points

a) *Why is Kelsen's theory 'pure'?*

   i) It aims to explain law free from the taint of other social sciences, sociology, and particularly, morality.

   ii) Kelsen makes a distinction between the prescriptive and the descriptive – one of his criticisms of Austin and Bentham was that they mixed prescriptive and descriptive propositions.

b) *The hierarchy of legal norms.*

   i) A norm is prescriptive of conduct, and is an 'ought' statement.

   ii) Each norm or 'ought' statement is validated by a higher norm, and the higher norm by a still higher one.

   iii) The chains of norms stretch back to the basic norm or grundnorm which is the presupposed ultimate rule. It provides the criteria by which one may assess whether any particular norm belongs to the legal system.

c) As with the imperative theories, the pure theory of law stresses the importance of sanctions. For Kelsen, law consists of norms backed by coercive sanctions. There are many criticisms of a sanction – based view of law.

d) *The important relationship between validity and efficacy.*

   i) Norms are valid where they have ben made by the correct procedure. Validity can be traced back to the grundnorm. A valid norm is binding in legal terms in that it guide behaviour.

   ii) Efficacy means that people do actually behave in the way that the legal norms prescribe.

   iii) Validity and efficacy are thus separate: but if the system as a whole ceases to be efficacious then the validity of individual norms is lost.

e) Kelsen addressed the issue of revolution. For him, if a new order takes over and becomes generally efficacious, then that new order will be valid and a new grundnorm presupposed. It has been argued that his theory gives a judge no assistance in revolutionary situations (see question Type 3 below).

2.7 Analysis of question styles

Kelsen and his pure theory of law crop up in a number of different guises. Although specific questions on parts of Kelsen's theory are sometimes asked, it is more common to find a more sweeping question on positivism (see chapter 2.C for examples). It is also possible to be asked a question comparing Kelsen with a theorist from a quite different school, for example, a Scandinavian Realist.

2.8 Questions

TYPE ONE

This is a very straightforward question on Kelsen's concept of the *legal* norm. Provided that the student knows his or her material and structures it well, a question like this should result

2 The Separation of Law and Morals

in a high mark. Relevant intelligent criticisms of Kelsen's theory will make the answer more sophisticated.

Explain what you understand Kelsen to have meant by his notion of a norm.

University of London LLB Examination
(for External Students) Jurisprudence and Legal Theory 1985 Q9

Skeleton Solution

Law as directives to officials to apply sanctions – norm is prescriptive – 'ought' – norm guides behaviour – concept of sanction – efficacy of legal system – norm as standard of evaluation – the basic norm – presupposed – provides criteria of validity for other norms – also criterion of identification.

Suggested Solution

'Law is the primary norm which stipulates the sanction' says Kelsen. In other words, 'law' properly so called, consists of directives to officials to apply sanctions where certain specified conditions obtain. Thus, a typical law for Kelsen would be in the form 'if conditions X and Y obtain, then, O Judge, apply the sanction'. For example, where property belonging to another is dishonestly appropriated with intention permanently to deprive, the law would be the directive to the magistrate or judge to apply the stipulated sanction (a fine or sentence of imprisonment).

At first sight this seems a curious definition to adopt. Most people would regard the obtaining conditions ('thou shalt not steal') as the legal prescription and not the directive to the official. Nevertheless Kelsen remains of the view that the prescribed conduct merely forms an antecedent if-clause to the proper law which is the directive to the official. Sometimes a secondary norm has been inferred to overcome this apparent difficulty with Kelsen's account. The secondary norm would be the prescribed conduct which is conditional to the application of the primary norm. But, as Harris points out, this adds nothing to the information conveyed by the primary norm. To say that X is under a legal duty to do 0 is the same as saying that if X does not do 0 then the law will stipulate a sanction.

Law therefore consists of norms addressed to officials. A norm is *prescriptive* of conduct and is expressed in 'ought' form. In Kelsen's terminology to say that law is the primary norm which stipulates the sanction amounts to the statement 'if X is the case, then Y ought to happen', Y being the directive to apply the stipulated sanction.

Kelsen's account of the notion of a norm is at times obscure. He confirms the conventional wisdom by stating that the meaning of a norm is 'ought' and amplifies this by explaining that a norm entails that an individual ought to behave in a certain manner. It follows, as Raz explains, that a norm serves as a standard to guide the behaviour of the norm-subject. If a norm prescribes certain conduct then this prescription will serve as a guide to the individual embarking upon such conduct. For example, a person knows not to park his or her car on double yellow lines, because this conduct is prohibited by the legal norm in question as 'if a person should park his or her car on double yellow lines, then, O Judge, apply the stipulated sanction'. This example illustrates an important aspect of the use of norms in Kelsen's legal theory, namely to explain how the law lays down standards which individuals can use as guides to their behaviour.

A second feature of Kelsen's use of norms is that they also serve as reasons for behaviour.

This feature is consequent upon the guidance aspect discussed above – if a norm is to serve as a guide to the behaviour of the norm-subject then it must also serve as a reason for his adopting the prescribed behaviour as opposed to some other course of action which may occur to him. In this context the concept of sanction is crucial. For Kelsen, every legal norm must be 'backed' by a sanction otherwise the law cannot guarantee the necessary motive for compliance. Thus, the norm which prescribes the conduct in question is the same norm which stipulates the appropriate sanction that the official should apply in the event that the norm-prescribed conduct is not followed.

Two points should be noted here. First, Kelsen is not saying that the threat of sanction is the only motive for obedience, but that it is the standard reason provided by the law. Indeed, legislators themselves are unlikely to desire that obedience should be motivated solely by fear of sanction, but the sanction ensures compliance.

Secondly, the question of the threat of sanction operating as a reason for compliance with the norms depends upon the efficacy of the legal system as a whole. This is a particularly difficult area of Kelsen's theory but in this context the efficacy of the legal system will bear upon the effectiveness of the threat of sanction as a reason for compliance with the norm-prescribed conduct. If (i) the likelihood of application of sanction is diminished because the legal system is generally inefficient and (ii) this is known, then its function as a reason for compliance correspondingly diminishes.

A third aspect of the concept of a norm is to be derived from Kelsen's claim that the norm functions as 'a scheme of interpretation'. By this is meant that a norm serves as a standard or yardstick by which the conduct of individuals may be evaluated. The norm itself determines whether behaviour is legal or illegal, and this function is best illustrated by the judicial use of norms. The same legal prescription which regulates the conduct of individuals in society also serves as the yardstick by which such conduct is measured by the judiciary. In the above example the norm which informs people not to park on double yellow lines is the same norm which tells the judge what sanction to apply and under what circumstances.

Of course, it is not only the judiciary which use norms as standards of evaluation. Ordinary people frequently use norms to evaluate other people's conduct or indeed their own past behaviour. Kelsen's point is that a norm serves as a dual standard for guiding and evaluating the behaviour of those subject to the norm.

Fourthly, Kelsen's treatment of the validity of norms requires to be noted. This is a necessary component of any theory which seeks to represent law as a system of norms. The specific aspects of norms discussed above would apply equally to other normative systems such as games or morals. In Kelsen's theory the legal validity of norm is accounted for by the basic norm.

Much academic literature has been devoted to the nature of the basic norm. Kelsen is unhelpful in this regard – he says that the basic norm exists in the juristic consciousness and is valid because it is presupposed. For present purposes it suffices to say that the basic norm is necessary for the existence of a legal system. A legal system must consist of legally valid norms and in Kelsen's theory the criterion of validity is provided by the basic norm which authorises all the other norms of the system. In essence the basic norm is the superior norm which validates the historically-first constitution of a legal system. The First Constitution validates general norms (say, Acts of Parliament) which in turn validate specific norms (say, local traffic regulations). Of course, in the United Kingdom the judiciary and Parliament are from historically different sources of law. Moreover, there is no written constitution as such,

2 The Separation of Law and Morals

but all sources of law lead to the basic norm which is the ultimate source. The legal system may therefore be represented as a pyramid of norms leading up to the basic norm. Each individual norm can trace its validity up through other norms until it reaches the basic norm.

Furthermore, the basic norm provides the criterion by which to identify the norms of the legal system. If a norm can be traced through the 'chains of validity' until it reaches the basic norm then it is a member of the legal system. In both this respect and as regards validity the basic norm performs the same role in Kelsen's theory as John Austin's Sovereign or Hart's Rule of Recognition.

TYPE TWO

Again these are specific questions about Kelsen's pure theory of law and, in particular, his theory of legal validity. They centre around the 'purity' of his theory – what does this mean, and why is it a useful enterprise? – and the general nature of his *Grundnorm*. These questions call for a more critical and evaluative approach than the preceding one: unless the student is prepared to come to his or her own conclusion on the issue, high marks will not be forthcoming.

1) Does the fact that Kelsen's basic norm is 'a fictitious norm' (Kelsen: *The Philosophy of As-If*) mean his theory is a logical contradiction?

University of London LLB Examination
(for External Students) Jurisprudence and Legal Theory June 1995 Q7(a)

General Comment

This Kelsen question has a specific intention because it requires the student to analyse his concept and debate whether the creation of the basic norm is in fact a contradiction or not when viewed logically. Whichever side you opt for, the examiners are looking for a clear understanding of Kelsen's theory with more recent comments on it. Explain what you find good, bad or indifferent about this idea.

Skeleton Solution

General definition of Kelsen's concept of a 'norm' – how the basic norm can be enforced – does it matter whether his theory is a logical contradiction? – conclusion.

Suggested Solution

Hans Kelsen's 'Pure Theory of Law' is a theory of positive law. It provides that legal activity can be traced back to an authoritative standard such as a 'norm' or an 'ought'. The adjective 'pure' illustrates Kelsen's belief that matters such as ethics, politics, ideology, sociology, religion and history merely obscure an analysis of what the law is. Kelsen holds that a scientific theory of law requires the analysis of law to be restricted to the 'norms' of positive law.

A 'norm' means that something ought to be, or ought to occur. A legal norm is an 'ought' according to Kelsen which provides that if certain conduct is performed, then a sanction should be applied to the offender. The legal system is thus coercive with its norms based on the threat of force.

It must be stressed that Kelsen's use of the term 'ought' does not raise questions about what the law ought to be in terms of relative moral notions. Kelsen merely considers that if the basic norm is valid, then the law ought to be obeyed.

He suggested that norms ought to be interpreted objectively and should be distinguished from mere subjective acts of will. Thus, a norm is valid when it is authorised by an even higher norm.

He described norms in the following way:

'The command of a gangster to turn over to him a certain amount of money has the same subjective meaning as the command of an income tax official, namely that the individual at whom the command is directed ought to pay something. But only the command of the official has the meaning of a valid norm ... Only the one order ... is a norm-positing act, because the official's act is authorised by a tax law ...'

To be valid and binding, therefore, a norm must be authorised by another norm which in turn is authorised by a higher norm within the system. The hierarchy of legal norms which form a legal system can ultimately be traced back to the grundnorm or basic norm of the legal system. By definition, the validity of the basic norm cannot depend on any other norm and it therefore must be presupposed:

'because it cannot be posited, that is to say: created, by an authority whose competence would have to rest on a still higher norm.'

Kelsen formulates the basic norm as follows (see *The Pure Theory of Law* (1967) (Norm and norm creation)):

1. Coercive acts ought to be performed under the conditions and in the manner which the historically first constitution and the norms created according to it prescribe.

2. The basic norm exists only in the juristic consciousness and is therefore a fiction. It is not, however, chosen arbitrarily. It is selected by reference to whether the legal order as a whole is efficacious. Efficacy is not a sufficient condition of the validity of a legal order, but it is a necessary condition.

3. The norms of a legal order are valid until their validity is terminated. This may occur in accordance with the rules of the legal order – the principle of legitimacy, or by revolution. In the case of revolution, when the basic norm of the system no longer attracts general support, it may be supplanted by some other basic norm.

4. The principle of legitimacy is limited by the principle of effectiveness. When the new laws of the revolutionary government are effectively enforced, says Kelsen, lawyers presuppose a new basic norm.

These aspects of Kelsen's theory has been applied by courts in various jurisdictions which have undergone revolutions: the Ugandan coup of 1965 (*Uganda* v *Commissioner of Prisons, ex parte Matovu* (1966)); the Rhodesian (Unilateral Declaration of Independence) in 1965 (*Madzimbamuto* v *Lardner-Burke* (1969)); and the revolution in Grenada: (*Mitchell* v *DPP* (1986)).

Writing in the *Cambridge Law Journal* (1971), Harris draws attention to the role of judges in enforcing a new basic norm:

'It is true that Kelsen's theory does not directly authorise a judge to make any particular decision. But indirectly it suggests that, when legal science gives a clear solution to a case, the judge ought to adopt that solution and this is true when, soon after the occurrence of a revolution, the question arises: has the grundnorm changed?'

Kelsen's theory, applied in the case of revolution, suggests that there would appear to be an unavoidable overlap between legal and political science. All revolutions are politically motivated.

2 The Separation of Law and Morals

The new basic norm follows the political initiative. The new basic norm and the political status quo are thus interdependent.

Kelsen concedes that a presupposed norm contradicts reality, and that this objection can only be met by supposing an imaginary authority whose act of will has the basic norm as its meaning. However, in so supposing, the basic norm is now defined as the meaning of an act of will that does not exist. It is submitted that this must be a contradiction in terms.

Writing in the *Juridicial Review* in 1980, Kelsen goes further by suggesting that with this fiction, the acceptance of the basic norm becomes contradictory to accepting that the constitution whose validity is grounded by the basic norm is the meaning of the act of will of a supreme authority over which no higher authority can be admitted:

'Thus the basic norm comes to be seen as a genuine fiction in the sense of the Vaihingerian philosophy of As-If. A fiction in this sense is characterised by its not only contradicting reality, but also containing contradiction within itself.'

Kelsen's theory is a logical contradiction, but does that matter? In *Law and Legal Science* (1979), Harris suggests that Kelsen, by calling the basic norm a 'fiction' in the As-If sense, merely reiterates the view that such a mental construct is needed in order to understand and explain the logic of legal science.

Therefore, the basic norm has two principal functions. First, it helps to distinguish between objectively valid demands and subjectively invalid demands, as, for example, between the demands of a robber and those of the law. Secondly, it provides an explanation for the existence of a legal order. In Kelsen's language, the basic norm is a transcendental epistemological postulate, ie in order to make sense of what we know, we have to get outside our experience and make clear our assumptions. Kelsen illustrates this point by stating that 'objective reality' can only be understood in the context of concepts such as time and space. These concepts do not exist; it can be argued that time and space are less realities than concepts. They are merely tools with which to make sense of the world. Similarly, with the law, concepts such as 'norms' are necessary, even if they are fictitious.

2) Is a 'pure theory' of law either possible or desirable?

University of London LLB Examination
(for External Students) Jurisprudence and Legal Theory 1990 Q2

Skeleton Solution

Kelsen's aim – positivists – concern with normative structure – importance of background considerations – scientific status and scope – objectivity and subjectivity – anti-behaviourist – validity and efficacy – Basic norm – nature of norms – presupposing the Basic norm – 'might is right' – circularity – directions to officials – sanctionist perspective – all encompassing delicts.

Suggested Solution

Few would agree that a pure theory of law was either possible or desirable. Such a view flatly contradicts the work done by Hans Kelsen in formulating a theory of law which he named 'The Pure Theory of Law'. Kelsen followed in the footsteps of the legal positivists in trying to separate from the field of legal reasoning all foreign elements, such as sociology, morality and justice. He felt that, with this accomplished, it would be possible to view and analyse the essential structure and nature of the law. Like the legal positivists, Kelsen considered law as a means of regulating human conduct in a unique manner. Thus law was separated from other social forms of control and regulation. It is in Kelsen's work that this aim receives its clearest, and arguably, most extreme expression.

Assuming that Kelsen is successful in his aims, would such a theory be desirable? Kelsen recognises that in reality law exists against a background of sociology, justice, morality etc, but feels that there is an area of normativity which is distinctly legal. He feels it is possible to elucidate the *structure* of law without having regard to the *content* of a legal regime's laws. However, he himself realised that there could be powerful objections to viewing law as merely a structure. In certain contexts the background to legal rules and reasoning is important, eg a legislator, or a judge, faced with having to make new law may find it best to exercise his/her respective judgements on the basis of justice, morality, economic efficiency, as well as other 'background' considerations.

In distilling a pure theory of law, Kelsen also sought to elevate legal theorising to the level of a science. He wanted to present law as a body of scientifically verifiable elements using a negative methodology ie the exclusion of imponderable variables (which he felt were constituted by the background considerations). In one important area Kelsen attempted to extend the sphere of science into the realm of normativity. Following Hume (and other positivists), he recognised a distinction between the world of 'ought' and that of 'is'. Legal rules were 'oughts' but despite this, he felt that, unlike morality, legal rules required some form of objective validity. A person made to pay compensation by virtue of a legal rule must see the rule and the utilisation of various institutions of law as objectively justified.

As a result of this aim, Kelsen clearly states that the normative field of law can be studied and represented as a science. Hence the legal structure can be seen not as the product of the subjective wills of the powerful, but as an objective, verifiable fact. Legal positivists would, in the main, agree that such a scientific status accorded to the sphere of law is highly desirable.

Earlier we assumed that Kelsen had been successful in putting forward a pure theory of law. His critics have claimed that a pure theory is impossible and pointed to its shortcomings. It might be said that a theory of law that ignores how people behave as a result of rules and judicial decisions is inadequate. If, as Kelsen suggests, law is a hierarchy of norms in which higher norms authorise lower norms, then Kelsen envisages a legal structure as being valid even when most people openly disobey the rules.

This is harsh and inaccurate criticism, which ignores the subtlety of Kelsen's theory. He asserts that his normative jurisprudence is concerned with questions of validity – what authorises an official to impose a sanction against a citizen – what gives the law its authority to coerce? As such he claims that questions of efficacy (are the rules obeyed, are they successful in securing the aims intended etc?) is the field of study that belongs to the socio-legal theorist.

Kelsen makes a minimal claim; to present the conceptual structure of law. He is influenced in this conceptual search by Kant. Kelsen believed in a theory of knowledge in which events that happen in the physical world can be changed by the conceptual categories which are applied to them by the human mind. One of these conceptual categories is legal norms. Therefore, Kelsen claims that his theory explains how people translate a subjective physical act, or an act of will into an objective, and legally valid act that has meaning. An example will illustrate this: a series of norms indicate what I ought to do in order to pass my wealth to those I favour after my death. One such norm being that my intention must be witnessed. In obeying the norm I see my subjective will or desire transformed into the objective legal concept of a valid testamentary document.

This long digression is the key to Kelsen's concern with validity. This translation process must always exist as a possibility, irrespective of whether people obey the norms. However, Kelsen is inconsistent. He acknowledges that, although not concerned with efficacy as far as individual or small groups of norms are concerned, a legal structure *as a whole* must be effective in order to be valid. Kelsen, therefore, admits that at some level his theory must be tainted with "impurity"; that of empirical behaviourist analysis. It would seem that a pure theory of law is not possible.

The spectre of impossibility raises its head in regard to the ultimate normative authorisation of the legal structure. We can view Kelsen's conception of the structure of law as a pyramid of norms. A norm is an ought proposition (eg one ought not kill), it may also be facilitative (eg A's estate may on death devolve on B on the basis of a will). It must exist in a field of other norms because each norm has a dual aspect. It authorises another norm but must be itself authorised by a still higher norm. In response to the problem of infinite regress, Kelsen argues that at the top of the pyramid sits the most general norm – the 'basic norm'. This is the ultimate normative authorisation and is not authorised by any higher norm.

The basic norm is a logical necessity. Without it a citizen who incurs a sanction as a result of a breach of a norm could forever unravel the authority behind the use of coercion. The norms would also lose their objective validity; they could be seen as the subjective whims of the State of some ruling class – not the neutral mechanism that law claims to be. Why should a citizen obey another's will? The basic norm converts ordinary expressions of 'oughtness' in law.

Kelsen secures the basic norm at a cost; the purity of his theory. He claims that the consent of the basic norm is that *one should obey the historically first constitution*; this norm authorises the norms contained in that particular constitution. However, is Kelsen not engaged in questions involving impurity ie historical enquiry? Furthermore, Eekelaar has shown that in times of revolution judges will obey the constitution that is backed by power. This is because it is power that ensures that the laws made under the basic norm will have effect. It would be undesirable that Kelsenite theory should justify the maxim 'might is right'. Kelsen's theory would grant legal authority to whichever régime has sufficient power to ensure that its constitution is respected.

There is a problem of circularity. The basic norm is presupposed by the fact of a pre-existing legal structure. This structure needs to have meaning for its acts. Yet, how can a structure of legal norms come into existence without the basic norm being presupposed first? The presupposition appears circular and exposes Kelsen once more to claims that a pure theory of law is impossible.

Closer inspection of the pure theory reveals some more undesirable consequences. Kelsen viewed legal norms as directions to officials as to what they should do when the conditions specified in those norms were met. Thus he claimed to define law as a body of norms that stipulate the conditions under which officials impose sanctions. Law is, therefore, to be viewed from a sanctionist perspective; we can find out what the law is by observing what sanctions have been imposed. Law is no longer a guide to general conduct; ordinary citizens have no legal duties nor obligations. Few would agree with this picture of law or see it as desirable to have a legal structure that only imposed duties and directed the conduct of a few.

Secondly, Kelsen calls acts which incur sanctions (ie breaches of legal norms) 'delicts'. This blurs the distinction normally made between civil and criminal law. Kelsen would claim that the reasons behind the distinction should be relegated from the purview of the legal scientist because they are non-legal.

Ultimately, although Kelsen's theory is illuminating in emphasising the normative structure of law, the price is a minimalist and unacceptable function for law. The basic norm remains unclear (with Kelsen later claiming that it was not a factual presupposition but a fiction). We may also question the desirability of a description of law that divorces it from its wider underpinnings.

'There is a great danger that if we take the watch to pieces and analyse each part separately, we shall never attain the overall picture which shows us how it works.'

However, as an exercise in logic Kelsen's method is absorbing, but at the end of the day we might wish to agree with Laski; that what is required is an exercise in *life*.

3) Is Kelsen's pure theory of law pure?

> University of London LLB Examination
> (for External Students) Jurisprudence and Legal Theory June 1991 Q2

Skeleton Solution

Kelsen's positivist aim – law as a field of norms – validity of law – problem of overall efficiency – basic norm and problem of infinite regress – Eekelaar – paradoxical necessity of impurity.

Suggested Solution

In his aim of presenting a 'pure' theory of law that separates the legal structure from external considerations, such as morality and social science, Kelsen must be said to have presented us with an impure theory of law. Furthermore, the impurity of his theory would seem to be a result of the purity he actually seeks. This paradox can be seen after Kelsen's theory has been examined.

As a legal positivist, Kelsen claimed that law could be analysed as it actually existed, apart from what it 'ought' to be. He also felt that modern legal systems had a certain unique structure that could be isolated from the particular and varying content of such systems. For him the study of the structure of law was a study of legal *science*; the law could be studied by virtue of the existence of certain scientifically verifiable facts. To distil these facts all imponderable variables had to be excluded; these were non-legal considerations, like morality, sociology and history, that might be relevant to the content of a particular system but not to its essential, universal structure.

Using this methodological approach Kelsen identified the legal structure as a field of norms, thereby accepting that law was a normative practice. These norms gave legal meaning to otherwise ordinary human acts. They were expressed in terms of 'ought' and 'may' and had a dual aspect in that they were authorised by a higher norm whilst themselves authorising lower norms. It was by virtue of these legal norms that human subjective wills were given objective legal validity. For example, the many norms that stipulate how to form a legally valid contract convert the externally observable act of agreement between the parties into a legally valid contract.

From this picture of legal systems, Kelsen envisaged the legal scientist to be interested in questions of validity. Therefore, a legal scientist investigated whether a particular norm, or

2 The Separation of Law and Morals

set of norms, belonged within the structure of legal norms. Those norms which did not so belong, or were contradictory, were not to be considered as part of the legal structure; they were *invalid*. Validity resulted from the authorisation received from yet a higher norm, which in turn received its validity from a yet higher norm and so on.

Kelsen asserted the central importance of validity to the extent that he claimed that questions concerning whether or not the legal rules (norms) were complied with, or enforced, were outside the field of legal enquiry. It was this concern for validity which led Kelsen to import impure elements into his theory of law.

Kelsen's concern with the validity of norms meant that the possibility that a norm or group of norms was generally disobeyed or unenforced did not affect the question of its legal validity. Although he accepted the ineffectiveness of particular or small groups of norms, he asserts that there must be general compliance; the legal system *as a whole* must be obeyed. At this point questions of *efficiency* become important to Kelsen.

Such a concession can be criticised on two grounds. Firstly, if general compliance is required, Kelsen would be forced to study the behaviour of citizens, which he earlier claimed to reject as being outside the field of legal analysis. Yet Kelsen seems forced to make this move, since few people would agree that a legal system which no one obeyed was valid. Secondly, the *logic* of Kelsen's methodology provides no grounds to justify this move. He concerns himself with efficiency in order to avoid an unrealistic view of law but at the cost of the avowed purity of his theory.

Validity also results in problems concerning the 'basic norm'. Kelsen posits the basic norm ('Grundnorm') as the ultimate norm that authorises all the norms below it but is itself not normatively authorised. The basic norm is required to stop the problem of infinite regress. This is basically a problem of validity. If we ask the question 'why do we obey law X?', we cannot continue infinitely in reference to higher norms which give validity to law X. At some point there must be an ultimate response to our questioning, a norm whose validity is unchallengeable. Kelsen argued the basic norm was a logical necessity. It could be claimed, on the contrary, that logic requires an infinite regress. If this is so, Kelsen has avoided the full logical rigour of his theory only by yet further tainting it with impurity.

More impurity can be seen when Kelsen gives content to the basic norm, not least because despite his interest in the structure of legal systems, he is forced to give content to a particular norm in order to secure the structural view. The major impurity concerns the actual content of the basic norm, which Kelsen claims to be that *one should obey the historically first constitution.*

The problem is that the basic norm urges citizens to comply with a constitution that came about by virtue of *non-legal* means. This must be the case because if the constitution came about by the exercise of a legal procedure, the norms constituting that procedure would have to be hierarchically authorised. These norms would be open to challenge and the problem of infinite regress would re-appear. If Kelsen claims that the validity of a legal system is based upon the first constitution, then legal validity must be based upon non-legal factors.

Eekelaar has highlighted this problem with the example of judges who must decide whether or not to recognise new revolutionary regimes as legitimate (ie valid). He claims that in such situations judges will invariably hold as legitimate constitutions backed by force – might equals right. Even if we claim that judges will not simply authorise the wishes of the most powerful group, it must be admitted that judges will be forced to weigh up non-legal considerations (eg politics and morality) in setting up a first constitution's validity. Although such a situation would seem unlikely in most countries with liberal legal systems, it is important to note that on the level of theory Kelsen cannot exclude these impure considerations from a theory that claims purity as its main virtue.

In conclusion, Kelsen's pure theory of law is pure only if certain impure assumptions are accepted. Questions of validity, or what could be called legitimacy, cannot ultimately be resolved solely by resort to legal considerations. Areas which Kelsen claimed to be outside the field of legal enquiry must therefore be investigated. Paradoxically, legal science must involve itself with issues of morality, politics and sociology if it is ever to succeed in being a legitimate institution. Kelsen's purity necessitates impurity.

TYPE THREE

These are questions on Kelsen's theory of revolution (to be found on pp117–121 of his *General Theory of Law and State* (1945)).

What role, if any, might Kelsen's pure theory of law play in the question of the determination of the de jure validity of a government which has gained control by illegal means?

> University of London LLB Examination
> (for External Students) Jurisprudence and Legal Theory June 1993 Q5

General Comment

This is yet another question which requires careful attention to what is being asked. (It sounds obvious when put like that, doesn't it?). Nevertheless, it is extremely common for candidates to suppose that this is an excuse to say everything they know about the topic of 'Kelsen and revolution' and, in truth, in practice, it means either parroting Harris's excellent chapter on Kelsen in his *Legal Philosophies*, or providing an ill-understood summary of it. The candidate, obviously, at university level must have developed some sort of attitude to these cases and to Kelsen's theory: only then will good marks be obtained. A major point to remember, too, is that Kelsen's theory is a positive theory (indeed, that is all that is meant by 'pure' – questions of legal validity are purely legal and not moral, that is all). Because of this, you should ask yourself how *any* positivist would consider his theory as having a 'role' to play in a revolution. Considering this point would help enormously. Also, be a little bold. Don't assume the judges were right in employing Kelsen; don't assume Kelsen's theory is of help; don't 'assume' anything, and work out your own answer for yourself. Everybody finds difficulty in this difficult area and if you parrot other people's thoughts that will be rapidly obvious to the examiner. The suggested answer below will take the tack of working out what any positivist would think and then work out what Kelsen's positive theory might say in particular.

Skeleton Solution

Description of a relevant revolutionary situation (Rhodesia) – consideration of how a theory might 'play a role in determining validity' – consideration of positivism's possible role – application to Kelsen – consideration of how *Dosso*, *Matovu* and *Madzimbamuto* cases were decided – consideration of how Kelsen was used in these cases – conclusion that Kelsen, and any other positivist's theory, provides a practical solution by saying that any determination of de jure validity is *not* to be *legally* determined, only politically or morally.

2 The Separation of Law and Morals

Suggested Solution

A typical sort of revolutionary situation in a legal system arises when a government is completely thrown over by a rebel government which has control, purports to annul the old constitution and introduces a new constitution. Typically, the judges appointed in accordance with the old constitution are asked to pronounce on the validity of the new constitution and thus on the validity of the rebel government's actions. This is what happened in the famous Rhodesian case of *Madzimbamuto* v *Lardner-Burke* (1969). Mrs Madzimbamuto sought habeas corpus for her imprisoned husband on the ground that he was detained in accordance with regulations made under an illegal constitution created by the Smith Government in 1965 which declared the 1961 Constitution to be no longer valid. At first the court decided that the 1965 Constitution was indeed illegal (and thus the Smith Government was only a de facto government) but that these particular regulations had to be upheld on the basis of a common law principle known as 'state necessity', that is, they were needed to maintain civil order; finally, however, three years later, in the case of *Ndhlovu* (1968), the courts decided that, because the Smith Government was firmly in power, it had therefore acquired de jure status. (The Privy Council, of course, did not agree, but by that time it was no longer the final court of appeal in Rhodesia, from the 1965 Constitution's point of view, so Mrs Madzimbamuto was unsuccessful in obtaining her husband's release.)

How might a theory of law assist in these matters? Austin would suggest looking to see where the power is located, which seems clear enough except that in *Madzimbamuto* the problem was that it was not clear early on whether the Smith Government would remain in power; further, the issue was complicated by the fact that the judges had some political sway to 'turn' the revolution so that their decision could only be creative of a state of power and could not merely report on it. So it is not clear that Austin's theory would be of immediate help. What about Hart? He is fairly clear in his discussion of his rule of recognition in Chapter six: this is that the rule of recognition simply 'changes' in revolutionary situations. This is not of immediate help to a judge since it is not clear to judge by what criteria he is to bring about change.

However, both Austin's and Hart's theories are similar in being positive theories which separate law from morality. They would, therefore, be clearly against the sort of argument that goes: the Smith Government is an illegal, racist government and therefore must not be accorded validity (which was Dendy Young J's reason for resigning from the Rhodesian judiciary at the UDI in November 1965); nor would positivists approve of the contrary argument: the Smith Government is the best government morally for Rhodesia, so therefore it must be the legal government (MacDonald J's apparent reason for according validity in the Appellate Division of *Madzimbamuto*). So how would Kelsen react to an illegal revolution? One would expect him to take the positivist line that moral and political considerations were irrelevant, as too would be sociological or historical reasons which are not the same as legal reasons.

Kelsen is very specific about legal revolutions in his *General Theory of Law and State*. The important point is that effectiveness alone is not sufficient for validity; this is a clear statement that he regards any idea of a de facto government or legal system 'ripening' into a de jure one: Why does Kelsen maintain this? Because his theory is not going to allow the derivation of an 'ought' from an 'is'; legal 'oughts' cannot be derived from the historical facts – the 'is'; this argument, drawn from Hume, was the basis of his grundnorm theory, namely, that legal norms could only derive their validity from an assumption that actions ought legally to be done in a particular way. The grundnorm is no more (and no less) than this. (How do we know that a person has assumed a basic norm? We look first to see whether there is a set of 'by and large' effective norms (effectiveness is a necessary condition – a sine qua non – of validity) because Kelsen is clear that legal systems must exist other than in the imagination; second, we look to see whether a person acts, talks, writes, etc, and thereby shows that he/she accepts it as law. Then we can say that, for that person, it is law.

How would this apply to revolutions such as the Rhodesian one? Well, in the early cases (the General and Appellate Divisions), the judges did not think that the facts of effectiveness were established; therefore, their decision not to accord de jure validity was right in Kelsen's terms. For this decision, Kelsen was helpful. It is the same sort of point that Hart made when he said that Roman law was not valid because it was no longer effective. After a while, in *Ndhlovu*, the judges began to act as if the new regime had gained de jure validity; now we could use Kelsen, in much the same way as we would use Hart, to say that the judges had changed their point of view (in Kelsen's case, to say that the judges now 'assumed' a new grundnorm; in Hart's case, to say that the judges now 'in fact' showed that a new rule of recognition had come into being). But neither Kelsen's nor Hart's theory would tell a judge what to do, that is, *whether* to make the assumption, or change the rule of recognition. And, of course, that is what you might expect, given that they are both positivists.

Now let us look at what happened in the revolution cases as far as actual judicial reference to Kelsen's specific theory was concerned. In *Dosso* (1958), the Pakistan Supreme Court simply 'applied' Kelsen because the new government did not have a rival to power (there was also reference to Kelsen's odd theory of international law, which need not concern us here); in other words, in *Dosso*, the Kelsenian doctrine was just equated to an Austinian 'might equals legal right' doctrine. That, of course, runs absolutely counter to everything that Kelsen ever stood for! Kelsen's precise criticism of Austin was that effectiveness alone was not sufficient; the injunction appears time and again in his works and, most particularly, in his explicit theory of revolution. In *Matovu*, *Dosso* was 'applied' despite this case now being a Ugandan one! And the error further continues right through the *Madzimbamuto* cases in the form of a pseudo-'Kelsenian' doctrine that historically, de facto governments ripen into de jure ones. (And this error continues right up into Lord Reid's majority speech in the Privy Council case of *Madzimbamuto*, despite his finding against Lardner-Burke, a fact seized upon by the judges in *Ndhlovu*!)

We can conclude, then, that Kelsen's theory was incorrectly applied in the revolutionary cases. If it had been 'applied' correctly, it would have informed the judges that where there was no legal solution (because, in Kelsen's terms, the old grundnorm could no longer be assumed) only a political, moral or ideological decision could be made to 'join' the revolution; the judges should not, to use the phrase most frequently use to criticise the early revolution cases, 'dress their political decisions up in legal garb.' We might, too, add the further suggestion that perhaps Kelsen's positivist solution is not the best since the grundnorm cannot account very well for such principles, employed in the revolutionary cases, particularly later ones like *Jilani* (1972) and *Mitchell* (1986), as the doctrine of state necessity.

C MODERN THEORIES

2.9 Introduction

This section focuses on Hart (who is particularly important for examination purposes) and Raz, and the extent to which they have advanced the positivist debate. It should be noted that

2 The Separation of Law and Morals

Hart actually eschews the term 'positivist' yet he sees no necessary connection between law and morals. His *The Concept of Law* is undoubtedly one of the leading contemporary jurisprudential works. It is clearly and elegantly written, and the student would be wise to read it. Apart from putting forward his own theories, Hart provides an excellent standpoint of criticism of other positivists. No student should ignore Hart. Raz's theory attempts to take the debate a stage further, by meeting the criticisms levelled at Hart.

2.10 Key points

a) *'The Concept of Law'* – Hart's great contribution to jurisprudential debate
   - i) The union of primary and secondary rules form the centre of a legal system.
   - ii) There is an internal and an external aspect to rules (and this distinguishes a rule from a mere habit)
   - iii) Law is different from 'orders backed by threats' – there is a contrast between being obliged and being under an obligation.
   - iv) No evaluation of Hart is complete without consideration of Dworkin's *Law as Integrity* which is dealt with in Chapter 14.

b) Raz has sought to advance upon Hart's theory in *The Concept of a Legal System*. The student should consider Raz's theory in the light of criticisms levelled at Hart.

c) In studying Hart and Raz, one should be aware of their criticisms of Austin, Bentham and Kelsen (see chapter 2, sections A and B).

2.11 Analysis of question styles

It is not uncommon to find specific questions on Hart. Indeed, there has been a compulsory question in the University of London external LLB examination on Hart for some years. The student should be familiar with *The Concept of Law* and at least some of the more common criticisms of Hart's theory. Most examination papers contain an 'across-the-board' question on positivism or some aspect of it, which will require knowledge and evaluation of a variety of theories and philosophies. Examples of such questions are given in question Types 3–5 below.

2.12 Questions

TYPE ONE

These are questions specifically about Hart's *The Concept of Law* which should certainly not be attempted by a student who has never opened the book! The examiners never ask for just a description of Hart's theory. The sting is the requirement for a discussion of his methodology, and practically all questions on Hart seek some informed comment on this.

1) 'My aim in this book has been to further the understanding of law, coercion, and morality as different but related social phenomena.' (Hart, *The Concept of Law*).

   How successful has Hart been in achieving his aim?

   University of London LLB Examination
   (for External Students) Jurisprudence and Legal Theory June 1993 Q1(a)

Jurisprudence: The Philosophy of Law

General Comment

This question is a very wide one and for that reason candidates are advised not to produce an 'all they know about Hart' type answer because the examiners will pay more than usual attention to an attempt to *answer the question*. The question asks for an account of Hart's purpose in writing his work on legal positivism and calls for a detailed assessment of whether Hart has met up with his own standards.

There is an infinite number of ways it could be done. Here is a suggestion: first, a brief description of his theory, second, a consideration of why he produces it which entails a discussion of the points outlined in Hart's famous *Preface*, and the 'three recurring issues' outlined in chapter 1, with others relating to his general methodology, and third, a consideration of how well he attains his purpose.

However, there are other possibilities. For example, one could examine whether the command theory, in the end, is all that different from Hart's theory. Hart, after all, tries to distance himself from it by referring to the difference between coercion and law; but he is still a positivist and his explanation of law refers to an authority that is as barren of moral authority as Bentham's and Austin's sovereign.

Skeleton Solution

Consideration of question – three recurring issues – Hart's methodology – the legal as opposed to pre-legal world – the rule of recognition – his theory of law briefly described – the wider conception of law and its advantages – consideration of the virtues of positivism.

Suggested Solution

The discerning of Hart's purpose is not easy as his book suggests at least two. These are the describing of an entity which he obviously regards as law 'out there' in much the same way as an historian would describe some event that 'had occurred' or a scientist might describe some properties of something that exists in the real world. Hart does, after all, describe his work as 'an essay in descriptive sociology', by which he meant, presumably, that his work was to be just descriptive of the world, in Dworkin's 'plain fact' sense (see Guest, *Ronald Dworkin*, chapter 5, for example).

But a second purpose in his work expresses a desire that seeing law as separate from morality is good from a moral point of view, because then people would not confuse what the State demanded with what it was morally right to do, as perhaps was inherent in the allegedly moral excuse of the Nuremburg tribunals – 'I was just obeying (legally valid) orders'.

How do we find these two strands in Hart's work? He refers early on to 'three recurrent issues' in Jurisprudence: the distinction between coercion and law; the distinction between moral and legal obligation; and the question of what constituted a social rule. In what sense are these 'important' issues? I suggest that they are important for him because he is not just interested in description but justification as well; he wants a theory that draws a distinction between the bank robber ('obliging' a victim) and a legislature who can create 'obligations'. Further, he obviously thinks that it is of practical importance to distinguish moral obligations from legal obligations since, as a positivist, he thinks that there can be laws so immoral that we have no duty to obey them. Thirdly, he regards an explanation of the nature of a social rule as important, given his extended discussion in chapter 7, to explain the law-making discretion judges have in making decisions within the penumbra of law.

2 The Separation of Law and Morals

It seems, then, that Hart's methodology may combine elements of description and justification: the purpose of his theory is to draw a map of law as well as to commend it to us as a way of solving practical problems: keep law and morality distinct and the three recurring issues will be answered.

There is further, and stronger, evidence of his two purposes in the distinction between his pre-legal and legal worlds. He commends, by dignifying with the label 'legal', a view of law in which courts, legislatures and rules of certainty, created by the three secondary rules, exist to 'cure' the 'defects' of the 'pre'-legal world. Here there is clear evidence of Hart's justifying purpose to produce a theory of law that helps society. And the rule of recognition is the most important. It cures uncertainty and makes the chief virtue of a legal system the certainty with which it identifies what is and is not law.

The theory of legal positivism he finally produces then distinguishes law from morality so that, as he says in chapter 9, the fact of legal validity 'is not conclusive of the question of obedience'. This is very important for Hart because this theory endorses a 'wider conception of law' which includes 'morally iniquitous laws' unlike the 'narrower' conception, the natural law conception, which excludes them. (In fact, the use here of two possible 'conceptions' of law sits a little unhappily with the title of Hart's work, which is, after all, the *Concept of Law*. This title is much more consistent with the 'plain fact' strand isolated earlier in his work; there is a concept of law 'out there' and there is no room for alternative accounts.)

How successful is Hart in these two purposes? Positivism does describe law, in the UK anyway, in a significant way. The sort of clear law that solicitors and law students love is the clear law that speaks with certainty in a 'black and white' way. On the other hand, Hart doesn't seem to account very well for the way in which barristers argue and judges decide in what Dworkin calls the 'hard cases', where there is uncertainty. But Hart could reasonably reply that this law is not important law. Rather, it is penumbral to what centrally should be thought to be law. This attitude is central to his method of definition, after all.

What about the second, justificatory strand to Hart's work? This places the principle of 'justice as certainty' at the very heart of the theory; remember the criterion of legal validity, the rule of recognition was to 'cure' uncertainty. But I suggest that legal certainty is only one of a number of desirable virtues for a legal system; flexibility is another, especially in constitutional cases, or cases of tort, where the justice of the instant is far more important than the justice of 'having one's reasonable expectations' fulfilled. In fact, the virtue of certainty really only reaches its height in Chancery, land law-type cases.

To sum up; Hart's purposes are two-fold and in each he succeeds to the extent of describing and justifying a legal system from the point of view of either an historian uninterested in the minutiae of hard cases or a Chancery solicitor interested in giving precise predictions to her clients. Overall, however, he fails to give a satisfactory account, both descriptively and normatively, of cases of which we are all experienced where the question of what the law is remains uncertain.

2) To what extent, if any, can Hart's *The Concept of Law* be described as 'an essay in descriptive sociology'?

University of London LLB Examination
(for External Students) Jurisprudence and Legal Theory June 1994 Q1

General Comment

This question asks for an overall consideration of Hart's book and his concept of a legal system. While he claims that his work is an essay on descriptive sociology, the question needs an evaluation of the extent to which his own view is right. The answer requires more than a mere description of the social phenomenon of law. It is of use to create a model of how Hart sees a legal system and not just an acknowledgment that Hart's own description of his work is an adequate explanation.

Skeleton Solution

Hart's characteristics of the human condition – social habits/rules – primary/ secondary rules – the essence of a legal system – conclusion.

Suggested Solution

Professor Hart views his concept of a legal system from the perspective of a positivist when legal institutions, and other phenomena linked to the law, are studied exactly as they are. His methodology is to consider law apart from morality and to subject it to systematic analysis. He states in his introduction that 'notwithstanding its concern with analysis the book may *also* be regarded as an essay in descriptive sociology; for the suggestion that inquiries into the meanings of words merely throw light on words is false'. It is clear that Hart does not limit his own description of the work because he sees law as a social phenomenon involving reference to the characteristics of the human condition.

Hart expresses his concept of the essential features of a legal system by listing characteristics in the following ways:

1. human vulnerability – where each person can be subjected to undesired physical violence;

2. approximate equality – where each person makes necessary mutual forbearance and compromise;

3. limited altruism – where each person has tendencies to aggression which require control;

4. limited resources – where each person requires food, shelter, clothing which are in limited supply; and

5. limited understanding and strength of will – where each person's understanding of long-term interests cannot be taken for granted.

Hart's conclusion is the need for rules to protect people, property and promises and it is this issue of rules with their features and inter-relationships which is the mainstay of his interpretation of a legal system

The method Hart employs is to argue the need for the existence of two circumstances. First, a variety of 'valid obligation rules' must be present and generally obeyed by citizens in a society; and second, officials within such a society must accept, in addition, certain rules of 'change, adjudication and responsibility'.

Hart sees a society with social habits and social rules. Habits can be seen, possibly, as customs – such as people in a group having coffee together every Saturday lunchtime. If one group member does not attend, no element of fault will be attached to him. On the other hand, social rules, if broken, lead to criticism through fault. It can be considered a point of emphasis where support and awareness for the significance and acceptability of a rule are the 'internal aspects of that rule', while the external aspects involve someone from outside being aware of its existence. Social rules are subdivided into social conventions and rules constituting obligations, with the latter overlapping with moral duties. Here, moral duties become a significant and

2 The Separation of Law and Morals

important portion of society's moral code, although breach does not necessarily result in punishment.

Primary and secondary rules

The legal rules relating to obligations are either primary or secondary rules. Primary rules can be seen as obligations under criminal law or tortious liability arising from a civil breach. Secondary rules embrace 'defects' to the primary rules. Defects of uncertainty, of static rules and of inefficiency require remedies and Hart explores such remedies not merely on a sociological model but by embracing a wider concept of 'law' as a system and for individuals.

For the defect of uncertainty, Hart devises a secondary rule of recognition to combat the lack of authoritative procedures for settling disputes so that the rule 'is a rule of the group to be supported by the social pressures it exerts'.

The static rule defect is remedied by a rule of change which allows specified people to make changes in their legal positions. The third defect of inefficiency is remedied by a rule of adjudication where authorised people are given power to determine whether an individual has breached a primary rule or not.

Secondary rules are a supplementary system and have been viewed as parasites on the primary rules. This, possibly, is where the measurement of Hart's label 'descriptive sociology' becomes extended because secondary rules provide that citizens in a community may, by doing and saying things, introduce new rules. Such rules could modify older rules or control the operation of primary rules such as the giving of additional public or private powers to citizens by applying secondary rules. Hart sees the union of primary and secondary rules as constituting the 'law'.

For a legal system to exist, more than descriptive sociology is required to explain a basis upon which conditions must be present to satisfy an answer to 'does a system exist or not?' Hart concludes that rules, particularly the rule of recognition, must be obeyed and that secondary rules must be accepted by society's officials as 'common public standards'. General obedience in practice by members of a society to its rules must be present together with an acceptance by a society's officials.

Hart is under no illusions when examining the existence of a legal system based on his model. To say that such a system exists is to offer a 'Janus-faced statement' which looks at the obedience of (and acceptance of rules by) ordinary people together with an acceptance by a society's officials of the secondary rules as common standards of official behaviour. It is, therefore, more than a simple sociological or adjectival regard being used to recognise a legal system; it is an appraisal by society's officials of their own and each other's performance which extends beyond the mere descriptive label. To this extent, Hart was using 'descriptive sociology' as only a partial commentary of his overall thesis.

3) 'What surely is most needed in order to make men clear sighted in confronting the official abuse of power, is that they should preserve the sense that the certification of something as legally valid is not conclusive of the question of obedience, and that, however great the aura of majesty or authority which the official system may have, its demands must in the end be submitted to a moral scrutiny.' (Hart, *The Concept of Law*).

Discuss.

University of London LLB Examination
(for External Students) Jurisprudence and Legal Theory June 1993 Q2

Jurisprudence: The Philosophy of Law

General Comment

This quotation is at the very heart of Hart's book; in some ways it is the paragraph that sums up the whole purpose of his writing it, which was to provide a theory of the fundamental difference between law and morality so that people in society would behave in morally better ways. There are, as always in jurisprudence, an infinite number of answers. One way might be just to go straight to the crux: what sort of society is Hart advocating? (and this is the tack taken below). But another way would be to do some cross-referencing with other legal philosophers at this point; it is always worthwhile to do this. Not only do they supply interesting insights, it is a way of showing the examiner how much you know! For example, this question, carefully done, could use as a platform a discussion of the Hart/Fuller debate. Fuller was concerned about positivism's inability, as he put it, to explain the concept of 'fidelity to law'; that was what his 'eight principles of the inner morality of law' was about. Hart, on the other hand, wanted a strict divorce of the question of the identification of what is valid law from the question of obedience. Another tack would be to concentrate on the question of the Nazi informer case and Hart's insistence that the best solution is to have retrospective law in order to preserve the principle of nulla poena sine lege (no punishment without law). The answer below takes the question by the horns and asks: What sort of society does Hart want? But it also draws upon the other two approaches.

Skeleton Solution

Make clear what the question means – description of Hart's theory – the 'wider conception' of law – the sort of society this would be, contrasting it with a natural law type society of fundamentalists – comparison with Fuller's approach – conclusion that Hart's theory of law is underlaid by a strongly individualistic liberalism – suggest that this is at odds with his linguistic analysis and avowed 'descriptive sociology of law'.

Suggested Solution

Hart means in this quotation that the point of his distinguishing law from morality (more exactly: questions of legal validity from questions of what it is morally right to do) is to drive a wedge between personal conscience and what the State demands in the name of law. That is, a citizen of a state should be able, always, to say, 'Yes, this is the law, but it is too evil to be obeyed.' He achieves this in his theory through the creation and use of his rule of recognition. This rule is the one which supplies the ultimate criterion of legal validity which is, in the end, 'official' recognition. While Hart is not specific about what 'official' means, it is clearly intended to have, and it is suggested, does have, an intuitive appeal. Basically, in the end, law is that which is identified by whoever has official power or authority.

This theory is that of the 'wider conception of law' referred to by Hart in chapter 9, whereby morally iniquitous laws are to be thought of equally as morally good or neutral laws. Why does Hart think that it is so important to look at law in this way? He thinks that what the State demands must always be subject to scrutiny and he is concerned about official abuses of power. What sort of society is he against, then? What sort of society is it that adoption of a positivistic way of thinking will help to protect us from? We can imagine such a society; it will be one where the State is all powerful, although not necessarily an unpleasant dictatorship. It is one where people don't actually think that there is any difference between what the State says and what it is morally right and wrong to do. We can imagine a fundamentalist society; or a medieval religious state. These would be states, or communities, where one religion is

2 The Separation of Law and Morals

equated with one morality and that the pronouncers of the 'right way' are the legislators. It would be a society in which morality and law are so intertwined that people don't think to themselves, 'That is what the State says I must do and I must keep my thoughts to myself,' but, 'That is what the State says and so *it must be the morally right thing to do*'. In fact, in such a society, there would probably be no need to have separate words for 'religious', 'legal' and 'moral': they all mean the same thing.

What is wrong with such a society? People have differing views. It is a very community-minded society, and that has its good sides; the picture advocated by Hart paints citizens as individuals, making their own minds up about what to do. Is that wise? Would that be a good state of affairs? On the other hand, Hart's society values the independence and freedom of thought of citizens; doing things in a 'common way' is traded off for individual freedom of opinion (and maybe expression).

It is very useful to compare Lon Fuller's approach to law. He combines, in a much looser but more passionate way, requirements of community with those of individualism. Fuller thinks that legal systems necessarily have a moral content, brought about by the attention paid to the eight principles of the 'inner morality of law'. Despite Hart's strong attack that these eight principles are analogous to such things as 'the poisoner's art' of the carpenter's trade that is 'neutral' on the question of producing 'hospital beds or torturers' racks', there is a moral element that runs through them. This is that the eight principles assert implicitly the principle of procedural fairness that rulers should proceed carefully with those they rule; they should be general, prospective, open, fair, stable, not require the impossible and so on. This suggests an intermediary between the rather depressing picture painted of the 'one way for everyone' communitarian approach of the fundamentalist type legal system and the, perhaps, excessive individualism of Hart's approach. The rulers command obedience in Fuller's legal system but they must do it in a fair way, one which recognises individual moral divergences in its citizens.

To sum up: Hart's theory of law is a theory of individualistic liberalism, consistent with the strong democratic underpinnings of Western legal systems. Put this way, Hartian positivism (and perhaps Austinian and Kelsenian positivism) is a moral theory justifying a particular relationship between the citizen and the State. This is a long way from his initial aim to provide a 'description' of law, based on following linguistic practices!

4) Explain the distinction which Hart draws between 'primary' and 'secondary' rules. On what grounds does he make this distinction? What purpose does it serve? In what sense, if at all, is it correct to say that law is a 'union' of 'primary' and 'secondary' rules?

University of London LLB Examination
(for External Students) Jurisprudence and Legal Theory June 1992 Q1

Skeleton Solution

Introduction: Hart's *The Concept of Law* – law and legal system – meaning of primary rules – meaning of secondary rules – distinction between primary and secondary rules – purpose of distinction – evaluation – clubs – international law – Dworkin.

Suggested Solution

Hart's *The Concept of Law* proposes a theory of law which, to a certain extent, equates 'law' with 'legal system' in that it focuses on the difference between primitive or pre-legal societies and societies which may be described as having a legal system. It is in relation to this aspect of the theory that the distinction between 'primary' and 'secondary' rules and the notion of the union between the two arises.

Hart attempts to explain how a legal obligation can be recognised and distinguished from, for example, human conduct which is the result of mere habit. In Hart's view a habit will be the result of common behaviour but a rule, unlike a habit, will have some 'internal aspect' which renders a particular type of conduct in some sense obligatory. This internal aspect of obligation is the identifying feature of Hart's 'primary' rules. Rules which are necessitated by the nature of man as a partly selfish, partly cooperative creature with a will to survive in a world of limited resources may fall into this category. Such rules might, for example, forbid killing, stealing or deception and are described by Hart as 'the minimum content of natural law'.

Hart suggested that primary rules may exist in pre-legal societies. However, in such societies the process of changing the content of the rules will be slow, adjudication upon the rules will be unregulated, and it may be difficult to distinguish legal rules from other social rules. In order to facilitate the three functions of change, adjudication and recognition of primary rules of obligation, Hart proposed the existence of secondary rules. Secondary rules of change would allow society to adjust the content of primary rules in a relatively efficient manner. Rules of recognition would allow the identification of the form and content of legal rules more quickly than in pre-legal societies where one would have to 'wait and see' if a particular rule were to be accepted as such. Rules of adjudication would provide for officials who could enforce the rules and punish wrongdoers. For example, Hart suggested that in England the supreme rule of recognition might be 'Whatever the Queen in Parliament enacts is law'.

Primary rules can be distinguished from secondary rules on the grounds that the latter are in a sense parasitic upon the former. Primary rules regulate conduct of individuals in society, whereas secondary rules regulate the primary rules themselves and are the concern of officials of the state rather than individuals generally. The purpose of the distinction in the context of Hart's theory is to provide a means of identifying advanced social systems. Hart was concerned to move away from the view, expressed by Austin and others, that law was the result of the command of the sovereign. For Hart such a theory could not explain why individuals would obey the commands of the successor to the sovereign, nor could it explain why old laws could remain laws today. Mere rules of obligation, which were characteristic of the 'command theory', could not, in Hart's opinion, explain these phenomena. It was for this reason that Hart proposed the existence of secondary rules and, in particular, the rule of recognition.

In Hart's view, it is the 'union' of primary and secondary rules which provides the basis for a legal system. If rules of behaviour, primary rules, are generally obeyed, and rules of change and adjudication are generally accepted as common public standards of behaviour by officials, then Hart thought a legal system could be described as being effectively in force.

Although the logic of Hart's theory is compelling it leaves certain questions unanswered. For example, Hart's theory does not adequately deal with the difference between social institutions such as clubs, which have both rules of obligation and 'secondary' rules of change, recognition and adjudication, and the state. Furthermore, international 'law' fails to meet Hart's test for an advanced legal system in that it does not have a central organ of adjudication with compulsory powers, has no method for changing rules other than by agreement (tacit or express) of states, and has no clear rule of recognition. Although the question of international law as law is an oft-debated subject, few would argue that it is not some form of legal system, albeit different from systems of municipal law. Perhaps the essential difference derives from the fact that the 'subjects' of international law are states, which are not in a position of

2 The Separation of Law and Morals

'approximate equality' as Hart considered man to be. This is a distinction which Hart recognised. One must question whether the union of primary and secondary rules is the essential characteristic of all advanced legal systems or whether, on the contrary, there may be different criteria applicable in certain situations.

Finally, it is worth bearing in mind that the very basis of Hart's theory, in company with the theories of legal positivists generally, is that law is solely comprised of rules. This premise has been criticised by Dworkin for failing to recognise that there may be other principles which may legitimately be described as forming part of the law. Dworkin identifies as standards which are not rules the policies and principles which may be referred to by a judge in a 'hard case' in order to reach a decision. Policies are defined as community goals, such as a goal that car accidents should be decreased. Principles are defined as standards to be observed generally, such as 'a man may not profit from his own wrong'. Any conclusion as to the validity of the description of law as the union of primary and secondary rules must question in the first place whether, as Dworkin argues, rules alone are simply not enough.

5) '... the rule of recognition exists only as a complex, but normally concordant, practice of the courts, officials, and private persons in identifying the law by reference to certain criteria. Its existence is a matter of fact. (Hart, *The Concept of Law*).

Discuss.

University of London LLB Examination
(for External Students) Jurisprudence and Legal Theory June 1993 Q3

General Comment

This is straightforward but difficult; the sort of question which you do if you can do it but don't touch if you cannot. If definitely needs a very clear and accurate account of Hart's rule of recognition; that means an account of what it is, why Hart postulated it, examples of such rules, an account of what Hart means by 'officials' and 'fact', and the role the rule of recognition plays both in identifying particular laws as well as legal systems. A good answer would suggest possible parallels with Kelsen's grundnorm and explore criticisms of the idea, along the lines, for example, taken by MacCormick, Finnis and Dworkin.

Skeleton Solution

Reason for rule of recognition, to 'cure' uncertainty – role of identifying valid law – internal point of view of officials – 'Officials' left unexplained in Hart – difference between ultimate and supreme criteria of validity – role in identifying legal systems – comparison with Kelsen's grundnorm – MacCormick's account of the attitude officials should take to the rule – Finnis's account of the 'central sense' in which officials morally accept the rule of recognition – Dworkin's criticism of the 'master rule' whereby 'hard cases' are left unexplained.

Suggested Solution

Hart's rule of recognition arises out of his analysis of law whereby he envisages the step from a pre-legal to a legal society. It is only 'legal' when the secondary rules, one of which is a rule of recognition, are added to the primary rules. The rule of recognition has a clear purpose. It is to remedy the defect of uncertainty; it has therefore to make clear to everyone what the law is and it has the quality sought by those who call themselves 'black-letter lawyers'.

Hart's analysis arises out of his criticism of the command theory of law, which referred only to habits of obedience, which idea he thought could not account for the *normative* quality of law. Rules imply standards of behaviour which justify criticisms for deviation (and praise for conformity). Whose standards? Those who adopted 'an internal point of view' towards some particular sort of action. In the case of the rule of recognition, the standards are those of the officials of the system; they adopt the internal point of view – an official attitude – towards certain criteria of legal validity.

The idea is basically simple. Hart is saying that when we find out what is law, all we are doing is some research into the question of what judges (the obvious officials) accept (adopt an attitude towards) as counting as valid law. We know how to do that; we learn it in our first year as law students by learning the sources of law. For example, we learn that statutes are valid law *because* they are accepted in the courts as law (ie they are accepted by the officials as law). We learn, too, that while the 'ultimate' criterion is *what officials accept* there is, within that acceptance, a ranking of subordinate and superior criteria, with, at the top a 'supreme' criterion of validity. In the UK's case, that supreme criterion happens, as a matter of fact, to be 'What Crown-in-Parliament enacts is law'. Hart's theory is also relatively straightforward about identifying legal systems. That a legal system exists is a 'Janus-faced statement' (Janus was the Roman god who could look out of the back of his head at the same time as looking forward) which looks backward to the proposition that the legal system is generally effective (ie is obeyed) and forward to acceptance by the *officials* of a rule of recognition. Hart doesn't think that is a necessary condition of the existence of a legal system that the citizens accept, for example, that 'what Crown-in-Parliament accepts is law' and, on reflection, that seems a reasonable thing to say, given that it is the officials who can wield enormous power and simply compel - Austinianlike – the obedience of the populace.

Hart's rule of recognition is identified factually; its existence is, as he says emphatically throughout *The Concept of Law*, a question of empirical fact. In other words, we can find out what the criteria of legal validity are in his theory in a rather straightforward way; we simply look and we see, as a matter of observation. It follows from this that what the criteria in the rule of recognition are is an uncontroversial question – because the question is just one of empirical fact.

A useful comparison may be made here with Kelsen, whose 'master rule' was emphatically not to be found as a matter of fact but as a presupposition of 'juristic consciousness' (and so, assertions that all positivists believe the law is 'posited as a matter of fact' are wrong, since Kelsen, an arch-positivist clearly did not believe that). But Hart thought that an extra presupposition that the factual test, the rule of recognition, was itself valid, was at best a luxury at worst an obfuscation, rather like assuming the Paris metre bar to be 'assumed to be' validly one metre long.

The major criticisms of the rule of recognition focus on the attitude the officials should take to the criteria of legal validity. It is crucial for Hart's theory that judges should not be specified to have a moral attitude (eg approval of democracy, or whatever) towards the criteria of legal validity. Why? Because if so, then 'valid legal rule' would mean 'judges have endorsed morally (somewhere along the line) and that would be a natural law theory'. And in later life, Hart continually reconfirmed his belief that, for validity, it was necessary that judges have any particular attitude.

MacCormick, while a positivist like Hart, thought it was going too far not to specify what he calls a 'volitional attitude', one which showed commitment to the law, as opposed to a 'cognitional attitude', one which just showed awareness of the criteria of validity. Some kind of purpose had to be displayed, he thought. This point sounds reasonable because, after all, judges do display a kind of commitment to the rules they are applying from day to day; it is volitional acceptance because it provides a reason for their decisions. On the other hand, would Hart dissent from this view?

But Finnis and Dworkin go further; both think that it doesn't make sense to think of law – which governs most of actions in society – as being neutral, with judges only giving the kind of commitment that one might give to the rules of chess. Finnis employs Hart's 'central sense' form of definition; what, he asks, is the central sense in which we should view a judge's commitment? Not self-interest in the form of money or status, surely. Finnis goes for full-blown moral acceptance of the rule of recognition; it only makes sense, for him, to talk of legally valid rules in the context of a system which is assented to morally. Dworkin is as explicit; laws only make sense if they are justified by sound principles of morality. It is not enough to justify placing people in prison, or taking money from them, by reference to a factual test itself – there must be a deeper underlying justification for the assertion, for example, that 'What Crown-in-Parliament enacts is law'. In the latter example, he says that the reason for respecting statutes as law, and allowing them to be part of the justification for judicial decision-making, is democratic. Crown-in-Parliament, like the US Constitution, are not empirical facts, but complex justificatory ideas.

It is difficult to say who is right. Hart's positivism is fuelled by his liberal idea that states and citizens are best kept apart in matters of legal validity; Finnis and Dworkin disagree. One can see the arguments on both sides. On the other hand, there is considerable pull in the idea, so forcefully mooted by Fuller, that thinking of law as a neutral entity (an 'amoral datum' in Fuller's terms), really does not accord with the sense in which we understand law as a living, justificatory complex, through which we understand such clearly moral ideas such as justice and fair play.

TYPE TWO

This is the kind of question requiring a knowledge of many 'positivist' theorists. Although Austin's work provides the focal point, the meat of the answer lies in the importance of rules, and it is here that a knowledge of Hart (and Raz) is helpful. Like so many questions, the student is required to come to his or her own conclusion – the approach to this answer is necessarily analytical and evaluative.

What are the strongest points, in your view, of the command theory of law?

> University of London LLB Examination
> (for External Students) Jurisprudence and Legal Theory June 1993 Q4

General Comment

This is not a question whereby you write 'all you know' about Austin (and, remember, 'all you know' may be exactly what 1,000 others like you 'know' from having read the same piece in Harris, say – do pity the poor examiner who may be just as cynical as you!). This question is asking for something different, namely, a justification of the command theory, and the implicit warning is that the candidate should not feel that he/she has to produce the long list of criticisms of the theory that Hart produces (again, that same list, gleaned from secondary sources, will be identical to the lists of many other candidates). Obviously you have to explain the theory; that is the easiest bit. Note that the question does not specify either Austin and Bentham, and a comment should be made about that; it is a question about the essentials of the theory, namely, what is common to both Bentham and Austin. There would be nothing wrong with taking from the point of view of Bentham's command theory or Austin's command theory or, indeed, an amalgam of both, provided you specify what you mean by 'command theory'. Essentially, the question is: what advantages are there in the idea that the law is to be thought of as coercive only, or as 'orders backed by threats'?

Skeleton Solution

Description of command theory, ironing out and mentioning differences between Austin and Bentham – description (in this case) of Austin's theory – list of strong points: law 'really' about power; explanation of power-conferring rules as reflexive of duties; idea of judges acting on behalf of sovereign; idea that sovereign cannot bind itself; compactness of idea of 'independent political society'; idea of sanction as real, as opposed to merely provided for (cross reference to Kelsen); idea that no law if no sanction; idea of the indivisibility of sovereignty; idea of 'habit of obedience'; idea of law as 'plain fact' 'out there' (cross reference to Dworkin) – conclusion that Austin's theory has a basic good core of sense.

Suggested Solution

The command theory is generally referred to as a theory of law which, in the end, is about the direction of human action in society by force; this is what is in common with the theories of the famous authors of the theory, Bentham and Austin. There are subtle differences between these jurists, both in method and detail; for example, Bentham thought that reward in the form of 'alluring motives' could ensure compliance, unlike Austin, and Bentham, too, thought that sovereigns need not be legally illimitable, laws being restricted in scope, rather, by a 'limited disposition to obey' by the populace. Austin took a scientific view of the description of law; definitely for him, law existed 'out there' waiting to be described. Bentham, on the other hand, probably thought that the idea of law had to be thought of as commands because only then would the 'greatest happiness of the greatest number' be assured.

These differences are, however, relatively minor. What is important is the idea of the command and, in this essay, I shall concentrate on Austin's particular theory. This falls into two parts; the definition of a command and the definition of the sovereign. The command consisted of a wish, an expression of that wish, and a sanction. It was not a 'command plus a sanction'; for him, the term 'command' included the sanction. Already, one can see the subtleties in the idea. First, there is not a law (because all laws for him were commands) if there is only a wish in the sovereign's mind; in other words, there had to be expression of that wish. This idea is very like the idea, in Fuller, of that principle of 'inner morality' of law, of promulgation. It is no use, in other words, for a sovereign to say, in legal justification, 'you should have *guessed* what I was thinking'; Austin's theory makes it clear that there has to be expression of the wish for it to be law. And there is subtlety in the idea of the sanction being part of the command. After all, how can we say that a person 'commanded' another, if in the end there is no threat? The sergeant-major commands his men by virtue of the fact of his authority, and what real sense can we give to his authority if at no stage can he place a corporal on detention or whatever?

The second part of the command theory is the sovereign; positive law (which was Austin's main concern) was not just a command, but the command of a particular person (or body of persons) called the sovereign. This was a factually existent thing; not at all like Kelsen's grundnorm, nor the same kind of entity as the rule of recognition (which exists as a fact, but a much more complex kind of fact). This particular person is unique in that he does not habitually obey anyone else (although he might occasionally) and is himself obeyed by the 'bulk of the population'. This notion of 'sovereignty' is appealing in many ways. It is usefully clear; it identifies the legal system for us very easily; indeed, Austin thought that he had solved the problem of defining what an 'independent political society' was by this means; if the sovereign obeyed no-one and was obeyed by most people, then all the people plus the sovereign was one identifiable entity. This idea, too, has great appeal; how do you distinguish states? How, for example, do you make sense of the current state of Bosnia? It is natural, when asked whether there is an independent state there, to ask questions such as: Who rules? Are they under the power of anyone else?

Armed with the idea of law as the command of the sovereign, Austin thought that he had 'the key to the science of jurisprudence'. But there have been criticisms; one is Hart's famous attack on the idea of a command as explaining only the duty-imposing rules, whereas law (as evidenced by the way people speak) consists in large part of power-conferring rules. In fact, this criticism of Hart gives a much more benign appearance to the law than Austin's. After all, power-conferring rules suggest the law is not just like the criminal law, but allows us to marry, make contracts, write wills, form companies, and so on. It is reasons like this that make, to many, Hart's theory much the more attractive of the two, especially so since Hart's theory fits in with linguistic practices.

However, Austin can easily be defended; he obviously, like Bentham, thought that the 'key' was the sanction. But he did not think that there were no power-conferring rules; rather, he thought that law was *fundamentally* about power, and his theory of law is constructed carefully to bring this fact out. Hart skates along the surface of law, in other words, not bringing out the underlying truths. True, we can marry, make contracts, and so on, according to Austin, but these sorts of activities *only make sense* on the understanding that ultimately marriages will be backed up, contracts will be enforced, wills will be carried out and so on. In the end, legal right means legal *might*. How is all this possible, though? Austin has a reflexive view of legal powers; a person has a power to do something by virtue of the sovereign's 'tacit command' that other people obey that person in the area of competence tacitly allocated to that person. Austin explained judge-made law in this way: the judge had the power – the jurisdiction – to apply law by virtue of the sovereign's command for people to obey him. So, if an executor did not carry out the terms of a valid will, which had been granted probate, the judge had the power to make the appropriate order, invested with the power of the sovereign. There is a lot of sense in this; after all, what are legal powers unless there is a 'sting' to them? Also, given the reference to the sovereign's power here, much sense is given to the idea that the judge should not usurp the function of the legislature (see Lord Diplock in the famous flick-knife case of *Fisher* v *Bell* (1961)), because the judge will only have the power where the sovereign has 'tacitly commanded', and that means that the judge has to put himself in the position, in the case of interpreting statutes, whereby he imagines what the sovereign *would* have commanded *had* he been aware of the circumstances. And even the criticism, made by a number of people, including Hart, that the idea of 'tacit' command is flawed, is not wholly convincing. To use Hart's own example, we can imagine a sergeant telling one of his men to take over, adding 'do what I'd do in any situation that arises'. This is a simple idea; it just means that if the delegated man has to make a judgment in special circumstances, he is empowered only to do 'what his sergeant would have done'. In fact, 'do what I'd have done' makes perfectly good sense, and so why not with the idea of tacit command?

There are a number of other strengths of Austin's theory which can also be mentioned. The compactness and clarity of the idea of the sanction's being a real one is attractive. How many of us regard parking meter offences as really only creative of a 'legal obligation to obey' in Austin's sense? Rightly or wrongly, people regard their 'obligation' to put money in the meter as a situation (if we must refer to linguistic niceties – see Hart) of 'being obliged'. If there were no traffic wardens about, and thus no 'likelihood of an evil being visited upon us', then it seems that escaping paying is fair game: this aspect of Austin's theory has a pleasing touch of reality to it. It includes the idea of a sanction's actual existence, not just its merely being provided for in every law, as Kelsen requires, or even, in Hart's theory, not being a necessary condition of a law's validity, but as vaguely connected as the requirement that, for a legal system to exist, it must be 'by and large' effective, which may imply that sanctions are being applied at some stage.

The indivisibility of sovereignty is, again, another pleasing strength to Austin's theory: what sense could we give to the UK legal system if there were two rulers, each governed by different rules giving conflicting responses? This indeed is a worry, real or perceived, of those in the UK against closer cooperation with Europe. Further, despite what Hart says, it is not clear that, for the 'bulk of the population', conformity to laws is no more than a mere inbuilt, conditioned 'habit of obedience'; the case of obedience to parking regulations is a good common example of this sort of behaviour. And, to add one more, there is good appeal in the idea that the law exists 'out there' to be described; how else could we make sense of the way we interpret many of our laws? There is no controversy, no-one disagrees, it accords with the way we all think, to say that (for example) if there are no witnesses on what otherwise would be a will we can, just by looking at the Wills Act 1837, s9, assert that this is an invalid will.

To conclude: Austin's theory has a robust appeal to common sense while at the same time producing an underlying general account of what law is, basically about physical power to apply sanctions. Criticisms that say that this is not in accordance with the way we speak underplay the emphasis that the theory intends to place on the 'cutting edge' of law, and various other criticisms can be shown to be not as powerful as they first appear.

TYPE THREE

Sanctions is a topic which crops up fairly regularly (sometimes also in the guise of laws as 'orders backed by threats'). Sanctions are, of course, central to imperative theories and to the pure theory of law, but Hart provides a convincing critique of this approach. It is always important to note the distinction between being obliged and being under an obligation.

'It is because a rule is regarded as obligatory that a measure of coercion may be attached to it; it is not obligatory because there is coercion.' (Goodhart).

Consider the theories of Austin and Kelsen in the light of this statement.

University of London LLB Examination
(for External Students) Jurisprudence and Legal Theory June 1994 Q10

General Comment

This question requires the cross-referencing of theories between effectiveness and validity when discussing political philosophy in general and legal philosophy in particular. Austin equated might with legal right whilst Kelsen (and Hart) took the view that there was an additional element of authority arising from a commitment to an 'internal attitude'. Austin's command theory, including the idea of a sanction inside the command itself and not merely commands backed by sanctions, needs to be compared with a critical discussion of Kelsen's grundnorm.

2 The Separation of Law and Morals

Skeleton Solution

Coercion – Austin and Kelsen compared – the grundnorm – conclusion.

Suggested Solution

Norms, to Kelsen, were not commands but depsychologised commands. Austin, who relied on the idea of a command as an expression of will, ignored the normative character of legalising rules because he believed in reliance on each other and not on an active will. On the Kelsen model, for example, where the norm is that the judge orders the payment of damages by a defendant, then damages ought to be levied under coercion, if necessary, on the principle of enforcement of a judgment. It is neatly contrasted between the authorised demands of a tax collector and the unauthorised demands of the gunman, exemplified by Hart.

With sanctions, Austin saw the primary norm as the 'do not murder' part, while Kelsen saw the primary norm as a directive to apply the sanction. Kelsen agrees with Austin that coercion is one of the essential features of law but he rejects Austin's reliance on motivation by fear.

Austin is seen to have failed to capture what has been described as the 'dynamic quality of law'. He ignored the dynamic process of law whereby there is the creation of law occurring throughout the hierarchy of norms and which derive validity from the constitution.

Austin saw the law and state as separate entities, called dualism. To Kelsen, they were the same thing with the state merely the personification of the legal order and the sovereign merely the order's highest organ. Austin, however, made the error of basing the validity of his legal order (or sovereignty) on a factual situation such as habitual obedience. He ignored the logical objection to basing the validity of a norm on anything but another norm.

The grundnorm

Kelsen's model of a legal system comprises an hierarchy of norms where each norm is 'validated' by a prior norm until the point of origin of legal authority is reached with the basic norm: the basic norm becomes, or is, the grundnorm. The structure of 'norms' excludes moral, political and social values and is concerned with the actual working of active functional legal norms. Kelsen describes it thus:

'... the basic norm ... must be formulated as follows: Coercive acts sought to be performed under the conditions and in the manner which the historically first constitution, and the norms created according to it, prescribe.'

Initially, Kelsen treated the grundnorm as the basic element of national or municipal life and this remains essentially so. In later work, Kelsen considered a broader view, examining the relationship between public international and national or municipal law, postulating an international grundnorm ranking higher than the municipal grundnorms of particular states, though such a view does not affect the grundnorm when viewed at national level.

Austin, writing at a time when international law was institutionally much less developed, relegated the system to the sphere of 'positive morality'. Hart, however, identified that international law approaches the closeness of a 'legal' status without actually achieving it, with Kelsen reassessing the grundnorm internationally.

Austin's view that public international law is not 'law', but instead 'positive international morality', when he wrote that Grotius, Pufendorf and others had fallen into 'a confusion of ideas', where 'they have confounded positive international morality, or the rules which actually

Jurisprudence: The Philosophy of Law

obtain among civilised nations, ... with their own vague conceptions of international morality as it ought to be' is a misunderstanding by Austin as to the claims of Grotius and others.

In the early nineteenth century, as today, there is no international sovereign commanding public international law. The United Nations operates sanctions for the international community covering economic sanctions and military action, as seen in Iraq and Bosnia. Morrison has criticised Austin, writing that if Austin had investigated whether a particular sovereign with whom he was concerned recognised the system of international law, 'he might have been led to a much more standard view of the basis of authority on international law than the snap conclusion he made'.

A subtle contrast can be illustrated here by concluding 'does public international law serve the same ends in the community of nations which positive law (or Austin's laws 'properly so called') plays nationally?' It has been argued that Austin's exclusion of public international law as 'law properly so called' appears to have an unduly narrow definitional focus.

TYPE FOUR

A question which relates positivist theories to modern events, and which requires reference to natural law and theories of justice.

The National Salvation Front in Romania executed the President of Romania and his wife after a secret trial and in accordance with a decree issued by the Front after the President was deposed.

Consider whether this action could justifiably be criticised as contrary to law.

University of London LLB Examination
(for External Students) Jurisprudence and Legal Theory June 1990 Q10

Skeleton Solution

Legal and moral validity – legitimacy and legality – historical facts – Eekelaar – Hart – Fuller; inherent nature of law-form and content – Dworkin; integrity – institutional fit – social facts and morality.

Suggested Solution

Why should citizens accept the decrees of the National Salvation Front as law? Is a fundamental principle breached by virtue of a secret trial? These two questions seem central to the problem at hand. However, we may feel that the question is drawn too narrowly. It is worth stating at the outset that even if a secret trial and an execution are justifiable because they are in accordance with the law, for some theorists that does not mean that the grounds of criticism are exhausted. Hart and other legal positivists would wish to assert that such acts can still be subject to our *moral* opprobrium. They would wish to keep the valid existence of laws and the moral evaluation ('censorial jurisprudence') separate. As a result the National Salvation Front's actions may be beyond criticism because they are legally valid but, at the same time be said to be morally iniquitous; and therefore worthy of criticism on these grounds.

Returning to the justifiability of legal criticism. Two issues would seem to affect our ability to criticise the National Salvation Front's actions. These are a) how is the legitimacy of a new political and legal regime recognised? and b) the legality of secret trials and executions. Different theories can provide different responses to these issues and in turn different

2 The Separation of Law and Morals

justifications for criticism. Some theorists such as Austin, Hart and Eekelaar would see the issue of legitimacy as being resolved by reference to historical facts.

Austin claimed that the legitimacy of a legal regime was no more and no less than a brute social fact. Whoever had political power decided what the law was to be. His imperative theory of law envisaged a person or body that was politically unrestrained. In Austinian terms, if the National Salvation Front was not in the habit of obeying orders from any other source it would be a legitimate legal authority. Austin would answer the second question about legality by stressing the irrelevance of the content of the National Salvation Front's decrees. As long as it wielded power by virtue of the historical fact of sovereignty, then secret trials and executions would be *in accordance with the law*, Austin would claim.

Eekelaar claims that in deciding what is a legitimate regime it is the judiciary that makes the choice. They decide by reference to certain accepted principles including,

'The principle that it is in the public interest that those in de facto impregnable control should be accorded legal recognition.'

Laws are useless unless they are given effect. Eekelaar asserts that only judges can give this effect to the laws of a regime. The judiciary will act on the above principle by recognising the regime that has historically seized political control. They will recognise this regime as a referee recognises the victory of the first person to cross the line in a race. Once a regime has political control the judiciary will see it as part of their function to make the laws emanating from that regime have an effect upon the outside world.

Similarly, Hart would rely on another form of historical acceptance. The internal acceptance by the officials of the decrees of a new regime. This corresponds to the rule of recognition; the rule which provides for the identification of legitimate legal authority. Hart does not explain *how* we should decide the legitimacy of the officials which is a weakness in his theory. As a result he provides no solution to a situation where the National Salvation Front may have installed its own officials after the revolution. Hart and Eekelaar seem to ignore the practicalities of revolutions which Austin addresses. In practice a new regime will (at least initially) employ coercive measures which will initially ensure their acceptance. However, Hart and Eekelaar may be correct in asserting that the longevity of this legitimacy will depend on historical factors other than power. For Hart and Eekelaar the legality of the secret trial and the execution are dependant upon forms of official acceptance.

Perhaps we could interpret 'contrary to the law' as contrary to the *spirit* of the law? This interpretation would affect our assessment of the legality of the National Salvation Front's actions. Fuller claims to present the inherent nature of all laws; the spirit of laws. He claims that, by virtue of their function, laws must aspire to meet certain ideal requirements. If the National Salvation Front had failed to meet requirements such as non-retrospectivity, clarity and the possibility of compliance then Fuller would claim that its decrees were illegal and that the secret trial and execution were illegal. Fuller's illegality is based upon a view that certain forms of law are 'ultra vires' the inherent logic of law. The National Salvation Front may still hold a secret trial and execute the President as long as, inter alia, the law is clear, non-retrospective, consistent and capable of being obeyed. One drawback of Fuller's theory is that it is more concerned with the universal form of law as opposed to its particular content. As a result Fuller may be of limited value in resolving the issue of the legality of the National Salvation Front's decrees.

Dworkin would see a secret trial as breach of a conception of law based upon principled integrity. This inherent integrity manifests itself in doctrines such as natural justice, due process and the open administration of justice. Dworkin might claim that the execution runs counter to a principle that runs through the Romanian legal system, which although as yet unpronounced in any judicial announcement, can nevertheless be present. If this is the case, the President's execution is a violation of the legal system's 'integrity' because it would be acting in an unprincipled and incoherent manner.

On the other hand, if secret trials and executions have been an essential feature of the Romanian legal system which has been based on some principle (eg the state has the right to use coercive force in any manner in order that it may protect itself from subversive elements), the National Salvation Front may be said to have acted with integrity. Viewed in this light a decree that continued this principled tradition would meet Dworkin's threshold requirement of institutional fit. However, what of the other requirement, that of justification? Does the decree form part of a picture that presents the legal regime as the best it can be? Essentially, is the State's use of coercion justified? Dworkin would acknowledge that this is a question of interpretation that requires a deep enquiry into the politico-legal values of Romanian society and the claims made by its political and legal institutions to justify their activities. If the National Salvation Front's justifications match those which they claim to be the values of their new regime, Dworkin would claim that they were acting with integrity, and as such in accordance with the law.

There seems to be a division of opinion between those that see legal authority and state coercion as mere brute facts or matters of judicial acceptance and those who see these issues as resolved by a resort to questions of morality and principle. For the latter, the historical fact the National Salvation Front may have seized power and become accepted by Romanian officials is an insufficient response. They would stress that the questions of whether the National Salvation Front can legitimately exercise the State's coercive machinery and whether the new laws adhered to certain fundamental legal principles must still be answered.

3 Modern Natural Law and Its Historical Background

3.1 Introduction

3.2 Key points

3.3 Analysis of question styles

3.4 Questions

3.1 Introduction

The central tenet of natural law theories is that there is a set of principles or moral values which are discoverable by man's reason, and according to which all things ought to behave. There is a necessary connection between law and morals. Those moral values or principles are universal, unchanging and absolute. The student will realise at once the dichotomy between these natural law theories and those of positivists; natural law and positivism must be studied in conjunction. Natural law in general is also important for the law/morals debate, especially that between Hart and Fuller.

3.2 Key points

a) *The historical development of natural law*

   i) The Greeks – Aristotle, Cicero.

   ii) The Scholastics – Aquinas.

   iii) The secularisation of natural law.

b) *The central propositions prior to Finnis*

   i) There are objective moral values that can be discovered by the use of reason on the realities of the human condition.

   ii) These are universal, unchanging and absolute.

   iii) Any law violating these moral values is not a law.

c) *Finnis' restatement*

   i) His seven basic goods are 'self-evident'. He thus avoids the illegitimate 'is-ought' derivation of traditional natural lawyers.

   ii) A validly made, unjust law is still law. The natural law/positivist dichotomy is thereby narrowed so that the issue of obligation to obey the law becomes all the more important.

3.3 Analysis of question styles

Natural law is a popular topic, but it is not easy to predict the form a question will take. It is often necessary to have a broad grasp of a variety of theorists, and to understand the areas of dispute with positivists. The student is inevitably asked to do more than reproduce the theories of natural law – a critical approach is vital.

3.4 Questions

TYPE ONE

This question calls for a broad knowledge of the historical development of natural law in addition to an evaluation of the tenacity of the theory in its various guises.

'The doctrine of natural law has existed continuously for almost twenty-five hundred years in various forms' (Brendan F Brown).

University of London LLB Examination
(for External Students) Jurisprudence and Legal Theory June 1986 Q7

Skeleton Solution

Greeks to Romans – right through to Second World War – restatement by Finnis in 1980s – attractions of doctrine – objective test of right and wrong – based on use by man of his reason – flexibility – even in face of philosophical attack.

Suggested Solution

Natural law thought has spanned the centuries, from the Greeks to the Romans, through Aquinas and the natural rights theories before the French Revolution and right through to a revival since the Second World War and a strong restatement in 1980 by John Finnis of the traditional viewpoint. In this essay I will try to isolate the reasons for the endurance of the natural law viewpoint: what strengths does the doctrine have which can explain its longevity?

The greatest strength is the attraction of the central ideas of natural law. Without going into the differences between the views of the main natural law writers, we can say that natural lawyers claim that by the use of man's reason certain principles can be reached from a study of man and his nature. These natural law principles govern how man and human societies should act and be organised respectively.

This is, of course, a vastly over-simplified statement of the position but we can use it to point to two major 'attractions' of the doctrine. First, it produces an objective test of right and wrong; second, it is based on the use by man of his reason. I will look at these in turn.

Many of the arguments concerning natural law centre on whether there are any such things as objective principles or values or, in other words, whether there is any objective test of what is right and wrong. The attractions in terms of clarity and certainty of an objective notion of right and wrong against the uncertainty of the subjective notion are obvious. Over the centuries, organised religion has been mainly based on the objective notion (although allowing 'subjective defences' to individuals in calculating their guilt and innocence) and so has the law (although again often requiring intention – but not knowledge or acceptance of the particular law – as a prerequisite to guilt); indeed, it would be difficult for law to be organised on any other basis; how could the law allow as a defence to criminal liability the plea that the law in question did not accord with the individual's subjective notions of right and wrong?

Natural law does not just present a series of principles for individuals to live by; rather, it also claims that human laws should accord with those principles. A further attraction of the objective nature of the principles is that they provide a very strong and clear criticism of human

3 Modern Natural Law and Its Historical Background

laws which fall foul of them. In this century, natural law has enjoyed a considerable revival since the Second World War. It is thought that this revival results from the fact that writers such as Radbruch were dissatisfied with the inability of positivist theories of law, which deny that there is a necessary conceptual link between law and morality, to provide a basis for an effective criticism of iniquitous Nazi 'laws'. Radbuch, Fuller and others denied that these 'laws' were in reality laws at all, because they transgressed the objective natural law principles. It must be said that in Finnis' restatement in *Natural Law and Natural Rights*, such laws would not be denied the title 'law' but would instead be dismissed as 'corruptions of law' – in a dismissal fairly similar to Hart's (positivist) view that they should be treated as laws but criticised as being immoral and unjust.

The second major attraction of natural law theory is that the principles emerge by the use of man's reason: in fact, the whole universe and God himself is, according to Aquinas, governed by reason. The principles are, therefore, reasonable; what is more, a man is left in control of his own destiny, since he can use his reason to discover the principles that apply to him. Natural law is, in this way, a philosophy of action. This can clearly be seen in Finnis' work; one of his seven self-evident values towards which men work is practical reasonableness, ie the exercise of reason in terms of action, deciding what to do. A practically reasonable man will spend time developing a life plan, by which he will achieve his desired mix of the self-evident goods. This is an inspiring viewpoint.

Natural law, then, has been enduring because of the attraction and strength of these two central ideas. Another reason for its longevity is its flexibility. The quotation in the question mentions the 'various forms' of natural law and through the centuries natural law has developed and shown different traits.

The traditional natural law viewpoint, that of Aquinas, is generally supportive of government. There is a wide discretion for governments to make laws, so long as natural law principles are not infringed. Indeed, even if there is some infringement, a generally just government should be supported for reasons of stability.

In the seventeenth and eighteenth centuries a 'natural rights' variant of natural law theory developed. Not only are there natural law principles but also 'natural rights'. Objective rights which people have and which governments and other people must not abuse. If governments do abuse them then, according to (for example) Locke, revolution is justified. Thus natural law can be revolutionary as well as supportive of governments: a cynical view might say it was being 'all things to all people', but I think it is just showing a flexibility to cover very different circumstances. The natural rights idea has proved to be an enduring one also, again perhaps because of the attraction of its objectivity and certainty.

Natural law has also shown its flexibility in the face of philosophical attack. In the early part of this century, natural law views were not often expressed, mainly because of the devastating attack by Hume who criticised what he saw as the derivation of an 'ought' (natural law principles) from an 'is' (facts of man and nature). As I have mentioned above, natural law enjoyed a post war revival despite this attack and Finnis' *Natural Law and Natural Rights* contains a detailed refutation of Hume's argument. Natural law starts, according to Finnis, from the self-evidence of the seven basic goods and does not start from facts about nature or man; hence, there is no derivation from an 'is'.

Jurisprudence: The Philosophy of Law

TYPE TWO

An evaluation of Finnis' highly influential restatement of natural law. This is the type of question where an understanding of the relative positions of natural lawyers and positivists is so important.

'A theorist cannot give a theoretical description and analysis of social facts unless he also participates in the work of evaluation, of understanding what is really good for human persons, and what is required by practical reasonableness.' (Finnis)

Discuss with particular reference to the modern debate between legal positivists and natural lawyers.

University of London LLB Examination
(for External Students) Jurisprudence and Legal Theory June 1994 Q11(b)

General Comment

The debate between natural lawyers and legal positivists does not necessarily require intimate acquaintance with John Finnis. Start with a definition of legal positivism and compare the different versions.

Skeleton Solution

Definition of legal positivism – Finnis: 'human goods' – natural law and its critics – conclusion: the unreal basis.

Suggested Solution

Legal positivism declares that morality is irrelevant to the identification of what is a valid law. Hart defines it as meaning 'the simple contention that it is in no sense a necessary truth that laws reproduce or satisfy certain demands of morality, though in fact they have often done so'. Forerunners of legal positivism, such as Aristotle and Aquinas, asked practical questions and supplied answers about the way in which we view laws.

Professor John Finnis attempts to reconsider the fundamentals of natural law on a contemporary basis. While his philosophy is inspired by Aquinas, his methodology has been termed one of analytical jurisprudence, with its consideration of the legal order and its general purposes. *Natural Law and Natural Rights* emphasises the need for a jurisprudence which explores legal realities while considering the significance of human needs and values. It is accurate to describe Finnis as making no concession to the theories of legal positivism or relativism.

Finnis calls for a system of rationally-based law which will recognise the basic values of human existence which he models 'human goods'. Such 'human goods' can only be secured through appropriate laws and legal procedures. He sees 'human goods' as 'the forms of human flourishing' which are necessary for the full development of individuals, such as: life, knowledge, play, aesthetic experience, sociability, practical reasonableness and religion. However, Finnis does not derive his analysis from Catholicism and he does not build a theory of natural law from rigid dogmatic theologies. While the natural law has been said to emerge from the very nature of people as God's creatures, Finnis has a different view of the nature and purpose of the legal order.

In the debate between natural lawyers and positivists, 'pleasure' does not appear as a basic

3 Modern Natural Law and Its Historical Background

human good in the Finnis list. However, he analyses 'practical reasonableness' in a manner which allows him to delineate principles enabling a person, such as a legislator, to distinguish 'social' from 'unsocial' thinking. Such an individual must follow a 'rational life plan' and he must pay equal regard to each basic human good. Finnis sees the individual as recognising that others will participate in attaining such goods and he has two requirements for such a person: he ought not to waste his opportunities by inefficient action; and he must not act contrary to his conscience.

Finnis is not without his critics, who have indicated that the list of 'human goods' is little more than a highly-subjective addition to the interminable number of recipes for human perfection, such as the Confucian formulae for happiness. Activities such as 'knowledge' and 'sociability' are very wide terms which make detailed analysis very difficult. MacCormick commented that Finnis had moved well beyond the 'medieval scholasticism' which had dominated discussion of the 'law of nature'. Weinreb, however, argues that Finnis has assisted the jurist 'to recognise the level of agreement about human ends and how to achieve them, and he has provided a shelter from the wind of moral relativism'.

Other philosophers, like Hume, years before the modern debate, criticised the unreal basis of natural law drawing attention to its confusion over 'ought' and 'is', while Bentham attacked natural law as metaphysical nonsense.

The logical positivists, such as Carnap, see natural law propositions as worthless because of their incapacity to be verified. It is submitted that this is the very point Finnis starts with because the irreducible basic values of our existence are found in 'human goods'. Other commentators, like Ross, see natural law as an umbrella for many different doctrines, with the consequent difficulty of attaching specific meaning to it. While natural law seems to depend on soundly based intuition to some, it is viewed as an inadequate basis for a theoretical construct by others.

TYPE THREE

These are both questions based on a quotation which calls for an evaluation of the natural law doctrine. They are useful examples of how a student may be expected to arrange familiar material in an unfamiliar way: in such situations a student will have to *think* before putting pen to paper.

1) Natural law has been described as 'a harlot at the disposal of everyone' (Ross). Does natural law deserve this reputation?

University of London LLB Examination
(for External Students) Jurisprudence and Legal Theory June 1987 Q2

Skeleton Solution

Context of natural law – lex injusta maxim – historical factors behind the maxim – consideration of Finnis' restatement of natural law – criticism of Finnis – positivists' critique.

Suggested Solution

Whether natural law deserves the description given to it by Ross that it is a harlot at the disposal of everyone would depend in my opinion on which context natural law is viewed. Where the view expressed by Ross comes from is clear. It is the perception of natural law clear from the criticism of Hume that the maxim attributed to Aquinas lex injusta non est lex can be applied as a harlot in whatever way the person using it wishes.

For Aquinas the maxim was used by a political superior to the legislative decrees of his political inferiors. In the Europe of the Middle Ages the Pope was the political superior of the Princes and Kings. It was the Pope who would determine, according to criteria of religious doctrine, whether the laws of the kings and princes were valid. The maxim was misinterpreted in two ways by Hume and those adopting his criticism. In the post Papal supremacy era there was no body politically superior to the legislative power in the various states and indeed it was the supreme legal power to legislate that became known as sovereignty. It would follow that it would then be the task of the political inferiors to determine whether the law of their political and legal superior was just or not. This was clearly objectionable from the Imperative theorists' point of view. The invalidity of deriving an ought from the natural world was demonstrated by Hume when he denied to the natural lawyer the use of the deductive syllogism through his disproof making use of inductive reasoning.

I would take the view that the answer to the quotation must depend on which theory of natural law one is looking at. In his restatement of natural law John Finnis in *Natural Law and Natural Rights* takes the view that the criticism levelled by Hume against the natural law doctrine was unfair. Finnis insists that Hume and the early positivists had ulterior motives for their attack on the lex injusta maxim. Finnis insists that the attack launched by the positivists was directed at the wrong concept. For Finnis emphasis needs to be placed on the meaning not of 'justice' but of the word 'law'. Finnis believed that absolute values are possible and hence he is described as a natural law theorist, unlike the positivists who share Hume's ethical non cognitivism. Finnis described how in his view it was possible to arrive at these absolute values through what he calls the seven basic goods. He would then say that a law that does not meet up to this standard is still law but that it lacks the moral authority to bind the conscience of men. This is not too far from the position adopted by some positivists vis-a-vis Nazi law. Finnis concentrates on the word 'lex' rather than 'injusta' and speaks of the focal and penumbral meaning of the word 'law'. Within Finnis' view then it would appear that if one were prepared to accept that there are such things as absolute values or, in the alternative, whether it were possible to ascertain what those absolute values are then a natural law theory becomes possible. If, however, one were to take the view that this was not possible then it would follow that any attempt to call upon supposedly absolute values would be to adopt what has been described as a 'moral blue pencil'. The use to which the pencil could be put would be determined by the person using it and hence the analogy with a harlot. It is not the pencil but the person who is using it that will determine the use to which it is put.

There has been much criticism of Finnis directed not surprisingly at his derivation of the seven basic goods which he described as self-evident. The criticism is that he may have left other goods out and included certain goods that are not necessarily basic. The effect of this, if accepted, would be to undermine Finnis' restatement on the grounds that he has selected his own subjective values rather than 'found' absolute values and that his theory then will be used as a harlot at the disposal of those who want to argue that there is no obligation to obey particular laws or a particular legal system.

The positivists *do not* think morality should not be part of the law: they merely insist that the determination of the content of the law be separated from the assessment of its justness. Their critique against the natural law schools was that they fused and confused these two distinct questions in order to censor unjust law. If they held that an unjust law was not law then there would be no need to obey. It was not law. What Finnis is saying is that it is law but

3 Modern Natural Law and Its Historical Background

lacks the power to bind our conscience into obedience. The effect is the same although the route is distinct.

I would therefore tend to agree with Ross that natural law theories are used as harlots and that they have so left themselves open to such use by confusing what the positivists regard as two distinct questions.

2) 'Natural law, in this sense, seemingly symbolises a belief in uniform rules or in principles which prevent the intrusion of the variable personal element into the legal realm. There is an opposing view typically expressed by Roscoe Pound who once wrote of "the purely personal and arbitrary character of all natural law theories" ' (Jerome Frank). Explain which of these attitudes is closer to your own view of natural law and why.

University of London LLB Examination
(for External Students) Jurisprudence and Legal Theory June 1984 Q4

Skeleton Solution

First view – not complete – purpose or telos – reason – 'uniform rules or principles' – large area of discretion remains – introduction of variable personal element – Finnis' self-evident goods – two views not necessarily contradictory.

Suggested Solution

A convenient approach to this answer will be for me to consider first, in turn, the two views of natural law set out in the question, since my comments on those views will serve as an introduction to my own views to which I will then turn.

The first 'sense' or view of natural law is set out in the first sentence of Frank's quotation. I think this view heads in the right direction as an explanation of a natural law position, but it not complete and is, therefore, inaccurate. There are, of course, many writings and writers in the 'natural law school' and it is not possible to sum up in a few sentences just what they meant by natural law.

In essence, though, I think that a natural lawyer believes that mankind has – in common with all other parts of the creation, of existence – a purpose or telos. However, man has an attribute setting him aside from the rest of creation: he can reason. If he uses this reason to consider how it will be possible for the purpose of man to be fulfilled, certain principles governing human behaviour will emerge. These are the principles of natural law. You will note that I do not include a divine element in this explanation; whilst most natural lawyers – notably Aquinas, and in our own times Finnis – do believe that natural law is part of a divine plan, it is not necessary to believe in God to be a natural lawyer; the theory stands (or falls) on its own.

So far, the first sense seems to fit the bill: natural law does symbolise belief in uniform rules or principles, which are objectively derivable by reason. Do these principles 'prevent the intrusion of the variable personal element into the legal realm'? The answer is yes – and no. The principles will dictate certain specific rules – not to kill or injure, for example – and to that extent the 'variable personal element' is excluded. However, there will still be a large area of discretion for the law-maker to lay down rules on areas not covered directly by the principles.

Indeed, so long as he lays down rules for the common good his discretionary decisions are supported by natural lawyers: traditional natural law was a conservative force which supported governments. It is true that none of the law-maker's rules may breach the principles of natural law – indeed a law which does so is lex injusta (an unjust law) which is not a law at all (the famous maxim of Aquinas 'lex injusta non est lex'); such laws may justify revolution, as later natural rights theorists argued. The fact remains that in law-making, natural law allows for a large – albeit controlled – measure of discretion of the variable personal element. This element will also, of course, occur in the law enforcement and judicial processes.

Turning to Pound's opposing view, it is easy to see why it might be thought that natural law theories are purely personal and arbitrary. While purporting to be based on objective facts, any fully developed natural law theory must discuss the purpose or telos of human life, and must reason from this to specific principles. Surely both the chosen purpose and the reasoning process are subjective, so that all such theories are 'purely personal and arbitrary'?

My own view is that this type of argument is used to prove too much. I accept that because of the choices involved, no natural law theory can be proved nor be said to be objectively 'correct'. However, this does not render natural law theories 'arbitrary'. There is much force in Finnis' argument that there are various goods – purposes – which are self-evidently good and therefore should be pursued. It is not susceptible of proof, but neither is it arbitrary, to say that knowledge is such a good, or friendship, play etc. At the least, very good reasons can be given as to why one should pursue knowledge and friendship as against money or pure pleasure.

I do not think that the two views as stated in the question are necessarily contradictory; it would be perfectly possible to hold to the first sentence as a descriptive account of a natural law view and to the second as one of criticism of such views. The personal element in the first sentence refers to the law-maker, while the 'purely personal character' refers to the personal views of the theorist (as against the objective truth).

Having pointed out that the two sentences are not contradictory, I would say that the first sentence is closer to my own view both as a description of natural law views and as an idea – that of uniform rules and principles – which I would be prepared to accept. I would not accept that the principles of natural law are objectively verifiable and therefore 'true' in that sense; but I would accept that there are strong reasons to accept many of the principles included in natural law theories as proper guides to human conduct. In this sense, natural law theories are rational, based on reason, and not purely personal and arbitrary. However, to go back to the first sentence, these principles do not accord to natural law theory and will not in fact exclude the variable personal element: not only because natural law is not universally accepted but also because, even if it was, the exact principles chosen would be a matter of dispute and personal choice. Further, the principles that were in fact chosen in a given legal system would probably allow for a large element of personal discretion from law-makers, police and judges.

3) 'Given survival as an aim, law and morals should include a specific content.' (Hart).

Discuss, with particular reference to Hart's minimum content of natural law.

University of London LLB Examination
(for External Students) Jurisprudence and Legal Theory June 1991 Q1

Skeleton Solution

Hart's theory – positivist view of natural law – form/is v substance/ought distinction – empiricalism v normativity – lack of empirical basis – uncertainty of consequences – other human aims; Fuller – wider interpretation of 'survival'; Finnis' theory.

3 Modern Natural Law and Its Historical Background

Suggested Solution

Hart's 'minimum content of natural law' was posited by him as being the product of a sociological and empirical enquiry as to what basic function a legal system must perform in order to ensure human survival. In turn, human survival was seen as the ultimate *'telos'* (purpose) of human existence. Following on from this, Hart concluded that by virtue of six invariable characteristics of the human condition (human vulnerability, limited resources, limited altruism, limited understanding, limited will power and approximate equality) *all* legal systems must have a *specific* content. In other words, the law must ensure a minimum level of protection, otherwise human survival would be impossible. Although Hart does not provide us with any specific substantive rules, he does state that this minimum content of natural law would have to protect persons, property and promises.

Hart was at pains to reduce the concession he had made to natural law, hence the term 'minimum'. This is hardly surprising given his declared aim of presenting law from a positivist viewpoint. Hart, like other legal positivists, felt that the law could be looked at as a mere structure, or form, without the need to describe it as including certain universal principles, such as justice. Legal positivists criticised natural lawyers for failing to keep separate the universal form of law from its varying content, or substance. Positivism sees the law as having a specific and universal form, whereas its substansive content was variable.

The implications of this view were that, for example, laws promulgated under the Nazi German regime, although iniquitous and immoral in *content*, nevertheless still bore the structure of laws and were therefore legally valid. Another way of seeing this distinction between form and substance is to see legal positivists as claiming to analyse law as it *'is'*, as opposed to making normative claims as to how it *'ought'* to be.

By conceding that law had a specific content it would prima facie seem that Hart has contradicted his positivist claims. However, he stresses that this specific content does not entail certain higher or fundamental principles with which all laws must comply. The specific content of law is merely dictated empirically by the universal nature of the human condition. Theoretically, therefore, should the six fundamental conditions Hart mentions alter in the future, the declared minimum requirements of the law needed to ensure human survival would also be subject to change.

A number of criticisms have been made of this minimal inclusion of natural law within Hart's anti-natural law theory. Firstly, Hart claims that the concept of what law is is provided by an 'exercise in descriptive sociology'. Likewise, he claims that his minimum content of natural law is empirically necessitated. D'Entreves has argued that there is a lack of any empirical basis for Hart's view of the human condition. It may therefore be said that Hart has merely made an intuitive assumption; if this is true he can be justly accused of making the very normative (instead of factual) assumptions so criticised by legal positivists. On the other hand it is true to say that his minimum conditions are, on common sense grounds, largely true.

Secondly, there is some vagueness in Hart's theory. It is uncertain what protective laws would flow from his premises concerning the human condition. For example, limited resources may justify a claim that the law should protect those resources in limited supply but there are many societies in which the exploitation of resources is encouraged. Even when such protective laws exist, Hart's theory is of no help in the debate as to *how much* protection to allow, as in the environmental questions that concern us today.

Finally, in allowing for a minimum level of natural law, Hart may be forced to concede to more radical natural law claims. Fuller has stated that the ultimate aim of human beings is *communication*, rather than survival. He asserts that it is through our ability to communicate that we acquired the knowledge that has in turn ensured our success in competition with other, often stronger, animals. Proceeding from this premise, Fuller claimed that a universal 'anatomy' or 'inner morality' of law existed. This was in the form of certain essential procedural requirements within the structure of any efficiently functioning legal system. It could be stated that such requirements, such as the non-retrospectivity of laws, are Fuller's own minimum content of natural law. The difference between Hart and Fuller lies in their description of human existence and its aims. Both use the same methodology of making normative assumptions concerning the ultimate aim of life.

If we concede, however, that survival is the central aim of human existence, it might then be claimed that Hart's account of natural law is too minimal. A natural lawyer such as Finnis, might give a wider interpretation of survival as being synonymous with human *flourishing*. This notion forms the basis of his assertion that all legal systems must provide the conditions under which citizens can attain so called 'basic goods' with which they can flourish.

Whether we stick with Hart's claim as to the central position of survival as a human aim, or challenge it as not being empirically proven, his minimum content of natural law can be attacked as being too minimal. Furthermore, his theory is open to allegations of uncertainty and, most fundamentally, internal incoherence; in that it seems to undermine the central tenets of legal positivism to which Hart purports to adhere.

4) What are Fuller's principles of the 'morality of law'? Why does he posit them? Are there any practical problems which might be resolved by recourse to these principles?

University of London LLB Examination
(for External Students) Jurisprudence and Legal Theory June 1993 Q11

General Comment

This is a giveaway question to someone who has studied Fuller properly, which means reading his book *The Morality of Law*. (This book is readily available and enjoyable to read; it is not difficult and rewards the student with many insights. For goodness' sake, don't spend hours of your time trying to piece together what Fuller said from four or five swotbooks; read the book itself in a full afternoon. It will stick in your mind).

First, state what the eight principles of the 'inner morality of law' are. Do this fully; merely stating them is parroting and each one has its own ramifications and interest. Then consider why it is that he posits them. These reasons may be gleaned from his remarks in response to Hart in the famous Hart-Fuller debate, although you might consider the general question why people devise theories of law in the first place, in order to pep up your answer (and reference to Finnis would be useful here). Then consider what practical problems could be solved, given the light of Fuller's overall purpose (which is to explain, remember, the human 'purposive' element in law). You should come to some sort of conclusion that rules of procedural fairness have very good point and go back to illustrating four or five of the principles of the 'internal morality of law' applying.

Skeleton Solution

The eight principles – why Fuller posits them – Finnis's attitude to this kind of theorising – Hart's response in talking of the virtues of positivism (from the Hart/Fuller debate and his

3 *Modern Natural Law and Its Historical Background*

review of Fuller's *The Morality of Law*; see also Fuller's reply to Hart's criticisms in the revised edition of *The Morality of Law* – how the rules of the inner morality of law have virtue as 'procedural rules of fairness' – conclusion that Fuller's views have a number of virtues.

Suggested Solution

Fuller was a natural lawyer, strongly opposed to the positivistic insistence that law and morality were distinctly separate; he therefore thought that there was a logically necessary relationship between any statement about what the law was and some correct moral statement. For example, to say that such and such a law was part of a legal system, was to say that a legal system concurred with a certain degree of morality. The test case is that of the Nazi legal system. Since it did not have a moral core, it could not correctly be called a 'legal' system, and thus any rules that emanated from it could not properly be called 'laws' and could have no moral obligatory effect. This view strikes an intuitive chord in us; there was clearly great evil in the Nazi legal system. 'Laws' that purportedly authorised sadistic murders and torture in inhumane 'camps' don't seem properly to be called 'law', which idea we appear to associate with justice, fairness, or at the very least, some basic level of human decency. Here Fuller is at his strongest in his attack on Hart, because it is quite clear that Hart regards his own theory as able to provide criteria according to which Nazi law, however 'iniquitous' is nevertheless law (and Hart's reason was that seeing the law in this way would provide useful and essential clarity, certainty and objectivity). According to Fuller, Hart's positivism presents law as an 'amoral datum'; as a piece of scientific matter, not to be endowed with any sense, as Fuller puts it, of 'human striving and purpose' in which the great ideal of 'fidelity to the law' can be explained. This idea is attractive but how does Fuller get to it?

He says that a large part of the necessary conditions to be in place in order to say that a legal system exists consists of the eight principles of what he calls the 'inner morality of law'. The greater degree of conformity that a set of rules purporting to govern society has to these 'principles', the closer to a fully working legal system – which to him means one that commands moral fidelity from citizens – the set of rules becomes. These principles of 'inner' morality are contrasted with the 'external' morality, which is the morality 'that makes law possible', and is a simply understood idea through the relatively straightforward idea of the community, or its officials, accepting the basic constitutional arrangements from the moral point of view.

What are these 'inner' principles? Laws must be *general*, that is, they must apply to classes of people, and to classes of acts, and not to individuals only (see Austin's extension of the meaning of command, in *The Province of Jurisprudence Determined*). This makes sense; a legal system in which laws applied to some individuals and not to others would be open to the charge of arbitrariness. Laws must also not be *secret*; if they were, this would lay the way open for corruption since there would be no public check on what the officials were doing. Laws must not, generally, be *retrospective*, for otherwise there would again be unfairness, since people would not know what was expected (although Fuller thought that the occasional retrospective law could be useful to right a former injustice). Laws must be *clear*; otherwise, people would again not be able find out what was expected of them. Law must not require the *impossible*; so, for example, it would be wrong for laws to lay heavy responsibility on those who lack the capacity to bear such responsibility, such as infants or the mentally disordered. So, too, would it be wrong to institute too many laws that impose strict liability. For similar reasons, Fuller thinks that laws ought not to require people to have to do *contradictory* things; for example, it would be silly to have a law that required people to have their number plates changed on a national holiday, when garages were not free to trade. Law also must not be subject to *frequent change*; this would result again in people being in a secure position about how to plan their lives (which is a fairness issue). This admonition against frequent change is particularly apt in the case of property law; if the Law of Property Act 1925 was altered dramatically, year in and year out, people would not be secure in their property rights. Finally, Fuller's eighth principle was that there should be a *congruence between official pronouncement and official action*. The sort of thing Fuller was getting at is the situation where what the law says in the books is quite different from what actually happens in practice; an example is the Statute of Frauds which for centuries was 'applied' by the courts in a way that was quite unrelated to the wording of the statute.

Fuller thinks that the Nazi 'legal system' abused most of these eight principles and therefore could not be properly called law and, consequently, the 'obligations' that these laws purported to create were unreal. The practical upshot is that claims such as 'I was only obeying orders' made no coherent claim for moral excuse from blame for atrocities done in the name of law. But it is useful to consider Hart's response. Hart thought that the eight principles were good principles of legal craftsmanship, but in no way guaranteed that the legal system would be moral. He says that it is possible for us to envisage a society in which all eight principles are adhered to, but where there is a fairly evil legal system in place (eg possibly in South Africa). He says that any activity could have 'principles of craftsmanship' extrapolated from it which would not necessarily guarantee that the use to which the thing crafted was put was a moral one; for example, he imagined principles of the 'inner morality' of poisoning (eg use odourless poisons, poisons that don't induce vomiting, etc) which could aid murder, or principles of 'good' carpentry that would be neutral between the production of hospital beds and torturers' racks!

This fairly devastating attack by Hart can be shown to be misguided by Finnis's account of moral reasoning securing, in legal theory, the moral basis behind the reasons that legal theorists such as Fuller and Hart have for producing their theories. Fuller is motivated by the moral concerns of 'moral consistency and fair play between governors and governed'; these principles of craftsmanship can therefore be seen to be part of the ideal of a legal system which, for Fuller, lies in adherence to principles of procedural fairness. Possibly he doesn't succeed in spelling out the principles in full enough detail, and perhaps his list is not sufficiently long; nevertheless, this view is that if lawyers pay attention to the nitty gritty of procedural fairness, in the end the law will 'work itself pure' and substantive fairness will finally be achieved. This view is a distinctly American view and finds echoes in the work of Dworkin and some others.

If we accept this view, we find that Hart's concerns for clarity, certainty and objectivity, to be achieved by his insistence on a rule of recognition, empirically determinable, are not dissimilar. Hart wants a clear wedge between the citizen and the state; in other words, he wants an 'above the board' public distance between them. One way to achieve this is, of course, in conjunction with the requirement for use of rules of procedural fairness. For these reasons, it can be seen that Fuller's eight principles of the inner morality of law do, contrary to what Hart claims, have a strong connection with the moral requirements of law and legal systems.

PART B

LEGAL AND SOCIAL THEORY

4 Realist Theories

A AMERICAN REALISM

4.1 Introduction

4.2 Key points

4.3 Analysis of question styles

4.4 Questions

B SCANDINAVIAN REALISM

4.5 Introduction

4.6 Key points

4.7 Analysis of question styles

4.8 Questions

A AMERICAN REALISM

4.1 Introduction

American Realism can be seen as a reaction to the theoretical school of formalism. Realism attempts to be more pragmatic than theoretical; the important issue is how law works in practice. It is hardly necessary to say that the student would be foolish to revise American Realism in isolation from Scandinavian Realism. Questions on the Realist 'school' are common, calling for a broad knowledge of the similarities and differences between various theorists. (The student should consider whether there really is a 'school' of Realism at all.)

4.2 Key points

a) *Rule-scepticism*

   i) There is more to law than the logical application of rules.

   ii) Rules are merely predictions of what the court will do.

   iii) Factors such as the background and upbringing of judges are more important in the settling of disputes than rules.

   iv) Llewellyn and his 'law-jobs' theory.

b) *Fact-scepticism*

   i) The certainty of prediction which Llewellyn espouses is impossible in relation to lower courts.

   ii) The fact-finding process is inherently uncertain.

   iii) Jerome Frank.

Jurisprudence: The Philosophy of Law

c) *Jurimetrics and judicial behaviouralism*

   i) Jurimetrics is the scientific investigation of legal problems using computers and symbolic logic.

   ii) Judicial behaviouralism involves research into the patterns of judges' behaviour (see J A G Griffith's *The Politics of the Judiciary*).

   iii) Note the connections with American Realism.

4.3 Analysis of question styles

Although it is possible to be asked about a specific American Realist, such questions are rare. It is more likely that general questions on Realism will be asked, some of which will require discussion of both American and Scandinavian Realists. Examples of the latter question type appear in Part B of this chapter.

4.4 Questions

TYPE ONE

A straightforward critical analysis of one theorist is called for here.

Discuss critically Llewellyn's 'law-jobs' theory.

University of London LLB Examination
(for External Students) Jurisprudence and Legal Theory June 1987 Q9

Skeleton Solution

Llewellyn – realist – rule sceptic – identify the law jobs – functional analysis – ignores dimension of power – period style – fact sceptics criticism – over generalisations.

Suggested Solution

Llewellyn, one of the mainstream American Realist Rule Sceptics saw the basic function of law to be twofold. That it aid the survival of the group and that it engage in the quest for justice, efficacy and a richer life. To assist the law in fulfilling these functions the institution of law has a number of law jobs.

He saw an institution in terms of an organised activity which is built around doing a job. The important aim is to ensure that these jobs are well performed. These law jobs are then the basic functions which the law has to perform. He lists these law jobs in *My Philosophy of Law* as:

1 The disposition of trouble cases which he likened to garage repair work with the continuous effect of the remaking of the order of that society;

2 The preventative channelling of conduct and expectations so as to avoid trouble and looks not only at new legislation but at its purpose;

3 The allocation of authority and the arrangement of procedures which mark action as being authoritative;

4 The net organisation of society as a whole so as to provide integration, direction and incentive;

5 Juristic method as used in law and the settlement of disputes.

4 Realist Theories

The analysis of these is found in his *The Normative, the Legal and the Law Jobs: The Problem of Juristic Method* (1940) in which he identifies the bare bones aspect of law jobs and that these law jobs are implicit in the concept of a group. The first of these he sees as the most important yet he does not tell us about their interrelationship. He suggests that these law jobs are universal, yet this quest for universality has, as Lloyd and Freeman observe, led Llewellyn to concepts of a high level of abstraction.

Llewellyn was concerned to find the best way to handle 'legal tools to law job ends'. Although he suggests that his framework provides a general framework for the functional analysis of law, he suffers from a defect common to other functionalists in that he overlooks the dimensions and structure of power.

In his concept of juristic method developed in his *Common Law Tradition* he outlines his theory of craft. Here he identifies his period style of judicial reasoning. He identifies two polar positions within this period style and says that judges will fall within that spectrum. At the one pole is his Grand Style in which judges are less strictly self constrained by the rules of precedent and in his Formal Style the judge considers himself bound by the rules of precedent entirely. In the Grand Style the judge will follow what Llewellyn calls a 'situation sense' in order to ensure that a reasonable result is achieved. By identifying a judge's propensity then it may be possible to achieve the aim of the American Realists; namely the prediction of the outcome of the case. If we know what approach a judge takes we may be able to predict how he will approach a particular dispute.

Llewellyn has made an important point, namely that law is not just about rules and that the prediction of the outline of cases is an important and useful function. However, law is not solely concerned with the prediction of what the court will do about a particular dispute. It is also about behavioural guidance to individuals.

A fellow American Realist, although from the fact sceptic aspect, Judge Frank took the view that Llewellyn's work was focused on the appeal courts and took no real account of the work of the trial courts where it was not the application of the rule that was important in predicting the outcome but the uncertainty about the fact- finding process that was the key.

A strong criticism levelled at both the rule sceptics and the fact sceptics is that they engage in over- generalisations in order to make a valid point. Furthermore the judges do use rules to explain their decisions and the judge is judge by virtue of a rule that says he will decide disputes. These are relegated to virtual unimportance in Llewellyn's law jobs theory. To this extent that analysis is defective.

TYPE TWO

A broader, more evaluative question based on a quotation. The student must be careful in such questions to tailor his or her answer to the quotation rather than merely discourse on 'American Realism' for 45 minutes or so.

'The English lawyer, in reading the Realists' own assessments of their achievements, finds it difficult to avoid feeling that nothing very startlingly fresh has emerged beyond ... what the reasonably progressive and socially-minded lawyer might already have accepted as axiomatic.' (Lloyd: *An Introduction to Jurisprudence*). How far is this an accurate assessment of the contribution made by American Realists to jurisprudence and legal theory?

Written by the Editor

Jurisprudence: The Philosophy of Law

Skeleton Solution

Reaction to formalism – pragmatic – rule sceptics – rules as predictions – fact sceptics – jurimetrics – judicial behaviouralism – some good points – extreme and over-generalised – but have prompted many to think.

Suggested Solution

The American style of Realism has been viewed by many as a reaction to the school of formalism. Whilst formalism concentrated on a priori reasoning, American Realism was pragmatic, asking the question: How does law work in practice? Although this was the main preoccupation of all American Realists, there was in fact, considerable divergence between their approaches. Thus they are often divided into 'rule sceptics', of whom Karl Llewellyn was notable, and 'fact sceptics', such as Jerome Frank. The purpose of this answer is to examine whether the techniques and theories of the various American Realists did in fact throw up anything new, or whether much of what they said would be self-evident to any 'reasonably progressive and socially-minded lawyer'.

For Llewellyn, rules were merely 'pretty playthings'. This attitude of the rule sceptics led them to deny that rules were more than predictions of what the court would do. When it came to the settling of legal disputes, other factors such as the background of the judges were operative factors. In this respect one might note the views of Griffith in *The Politics of the Judiciary* that the conservative homogenous background and education of English judges has had great influence on their decisions.

Fact sceptics such as Frank were even more extreme in their denunciation of rules. Frank believed that certainty of prediction could only ever be achieved in the appellate courts. In lower courts, the uncertainty of the fact-finding process is the reason why decisions are unpredicatable. Like the rule sceptics, Frank pointed to the personal values, etc, of judges as one cause of uncertainty, together with the unpredictability of juries and witnesses. American Realism led to more sophisticated techniques of examining court decisions. It influenced jurimetrics, by which a gathering and processing of data has taken place. It also prompted the surge of interest into judicial behavouralism – research into what judges actually do, and why. But at the end of the day, the question remains: has American Realism produced anything 'startlingly fresh'?

It seems fair to say that both rule sceptics and fact sceptics have made some good points. They have brought out in the open some of the hidden factors in judicial law making, as well as emphasised that judicial decisions are not necessarily a matter of certainty. Frank has a point that fact-finding can be affected by the inherent values of judge and jury. Although all these points have been criticised on the grounds that they are over-generalised, the question which concerns us is whether they are purely axiomatic. It can be argued that in fact they are not: we are so used to talking in terms of rules and precedents that the operation of less apparent factors can be easily forgotten. Perhaps a 'reasonably progressive and socially minded lawyer' would regard the Realists' points as self-evident if he stopped to think about them – but it is just as likely that he would not stop to think at all. On these lines, it must be said that the Realists' influence towards more sophisticated techniques of assessment of judicial decisions can only be a good thing.

Beyond that, one might indeed argue that nothing very new emerged from American Realism. Indeed, much of what was good was spoilt by the tendency towards extremism and over-

4 Realist Theories

generalisation. Furthermore, as Lloyd has pointed out, there is a great deal of traditional law (eg the rules of contract formation) which are not well-suited to a 'Realist' reassessment on the basis of new, sophisticated techniques.

Despite the above, I feel that the quotation in the question is a little too dismissive of American Realism. Realists made some good points, and whether they are axiomatic or not is not really the important issue – what matters is that they are only axiomatic to those who stop to think about them, and without American Realism the number of people prepared to do that might have been a great deal smaller.

TYPE THREE

This queston focuses on judicial decision-making. Although it concentrates particularly on American Realism, a student with a broader jurisprudential knowledge (eg what would Dworkin have to say about this issue?) will score much higher marks.

'The process by which judges arrive at their decisions on questions of law is a topic of endless fascination and analysis' (Frederic Reynold). Discuss with particular reference to the writings of American Realist jurists.

University of London LLB Examination
(for External Students) Jurisprudence and Legal Theory June 1986 Q6

Skeleton Solution

Rule-sceptics – how to predict judicial decisions – judicial behaviouralism – Llewellyn's law-jobs' – Dworkin – 'grand' or 'formal' style? – fact sceptics – appellate court – Hart.

Suggested Solution

The many schools of jurisprudential thought which focus on the judicial decision-making process and the success of such books of *The Brethren* (on the US Supreme Court), Paterson's book on *The Law Lords* and Griffith's *The Politics of the Judiciary* show that, while not as interesting in the public mind as their decisions in the criminal arena, the way in which judges decide questions of law is (in the words of the quotation) 'a topic of fascination and analysis'.

This might come as a surprise to those who think that judges merely follow existing legal rules and extend them (where necessary) by analogy. The American Realist 'school' were in the forefront of the argument that this is not the case. Those of the Realists who were the so-called 'rule sceptics' denied that rules were the main determinant of judicial decisions. Other factors – the judge's prejudices and beliefs amongst them – influence how a judge behaves. Hence, it is not possible to predict how a judge will decide by looking at the 'paper' rules set out in legal texts; rather, a study of judicial behaviour might provide enough material to establish the 'real' rules by which judicial decisions could be predicted accurately.

One result of this view was the encouragement of studies into judicial behaviour –'judicial behaviouralism' as it is known. In this country, Griffith's book (mentioned above) is the best example. He looks at decisions in various areas and concludes that they result from the fact that the judges are trying (albeit unconsciously) to protect the 'Establishment' of which they are members.

Another result was Llewellyn's study of 'law-jobs' and of the 'crafts' of the lawyers engaged in carrying out those jobs. Llewellyn was a leading American Realist, and it was therefore natural that he identified the disposition of trouble cases as the primary 'law-job'. Similarly, for a Realist the most important 'craft' is the juristic method of decision-making. Although Realists deny that legal rules are the main determinant of decisions on points of law, Llewellyn does suggest that the predictability or 'reckonability' of decisions is high. This is because of various attributes of the system and in particular because it will be known whether the judges of the time favour the 'grand style' or the 'formal style' of decision-making.

These two 'styles' reflect a more general and wide-ranging debate in legal literature. Do judges decide cases strictly on following a logical, rules-based approach (Llewellyn's 'formal style') or do they favour a wider approach ('grand style'), taking into account policy considerations and the general context of a particular case? Dworkin, for example, has put forward a fully argued theory that judges not only do but should decide on the basis of the existing legal rules. Recently in *Law's Empire*, he has made the claim that his theory is *interpretive* of existing social practices amongst judges. Interestingly, Llewellyn believes that judges are not exclusively wedded to either the grand or the formal style; sometimes one, sometimes the other is most popular. Also, even the formal style does not guarantee complete predictability – the judges can manipulate past precedents by distinguishing cases and using other devices and so not arrive at the expected decision.

As I said above, Llewellyn's distinction between the two styles mirrors a wider debate on the way in which judges decide points of law; authors such as Levi, Cardozo and Hart have made useful contributions to this debate.

It must not, however, be thought that the concentration on the judicial legal decision-making process is universally share or applauded. Even within the American Realist school, Jerome Frank rejected this concentration as misplaced. He coined the terms 'rule sceptic' and 'fact sceptic'. He criticised the rule sceptics such as Llewellyn for looking at appellate courts; he was a fact sceptic who considered that the focus of study should be first instance cases and, therefore, decisions of fact rather than of law.

The importance of the judicial process for making legal decisions must not blind us to the fact that much of the law's life is not with the appellate court. As Frank points out, most cases do not concern disputed points of law at all; and much of the life of the law and of lawyers consists of arranging affairs so as to avoid ever reaching a court. Also, it has been shown by Hart and others to be a mistake to look for an understanding of obligation and legal rules in predictions of the decisions of courts.

The legal decision-making process certainly is one which has been the subject of 'endless fascination and analysis', but this should not mesmerise us into over-emphasising the importance of that process.

B SCANDINAVIAN REALISM

4.5 Introduction

The Scandinavian school of Realism was more philosophical than the American school, with a broader interest in the legal system as a whole. The Scandinavian Realists rejected the 'metaphysical' and subscribed to the view that a statement was only meaningful if it could be proved by empirical evidence. The student might like to consider how much of the Scandinavian Realists' theories were based on empirical evidence. The psychological was used to explain laws; the normative effect of law exists as a psychological effect, and concepts like right and duty are explained as psychological feelings. In studying Scandinavian Realism the student should be astute enough to note the similarities and differences in comparison with American Realism.

4.6 Key points

a) *Hagerstrom*
   i) Hagerstrom is regarded as the 'spiritual father' to the Scandinavian Realists.
   ii) The concepts of 'right' and 'duty' only have reality in terms of their actual effect in society.

b) *Olivecrona*
   i) The legal rule has two elements – the 'ideatum' and the 'imperatum'.
   ii) The 'ideatum' is the conduct laws are meant to produce.
   iii) The 'imperatum' is the way the ideatum is expressed.
   iv) Olivecrona has been criticised for his lack of empirical research and for his overstatement of the importance of 'force' in the law.

c) *Ross*
   i) Ross also attempts to use psychology to explain the normative effect of laws, but his explanation is superior to those of Hagerstrom and Olivecrona.
   ii) The similarities with Hart's *The Concept of Law* should be noted.

d) *Is there a 'school' of Realism?*
   i) Both American and Scandinavian Realists tried to explain law in terms of 'cause and effect' and both emphasised research and empirical evidence.
   ii) Despite this, the Scandinavians concentrated on the verification of concepts like 'right' and 'duty' in a psychological way, whilst the Americans sought to show that legal decisions were not predictable if one merely looked at the logical application of legal rules.
   iii) The student should consider which, if either, of the American or Scandinavian brands of Realism is more convincing and illuminating.

4.7 Analysis of question styles

Scandinavian Realism is a popular examination topic, and questions can range from an evaluation of a specific Realist to a discussion on the Realist 'school' generally. The student will become aware that certain questions on 'Realism' are clearly more relevant to one branch of Realism than the other (for example, Question Type 3 below). In answering such questions the student must be sure to justify the concentration on one branch.

4.8 Questions

TYPE ONE

This question on Olivecrona calls for a comparison with Kelsen. Although this might seem a strange pairing, it provides a good exercise in thinking across topics.

Jurisprudence: The Philosophy of Law

'Kelsen and Olivecrona base their accounts of the nature of law on some kind of imperative element, but they differ very much in their basic conceptions of law as to the way in which the basic elements of law are to be arranged and explained in order to produce an adequate account of its nature' (John Finch). Discuss.

University of London LLB Examination
(for External Students) Jurisprudence and Legal Theory June 1983 Q9

Skeleton Solution

Legal rules as imperative – acceptance of constitution by officials – law as system of coercion – principal difference: why and how laws bind – but their arrangement of basic elements of law is closely comparable.

Suggested Solution

Finch's brings me to consider the relationship between two theorists whom I have not compared before; on reflection, however, I think it incorrect. I hope to show that not only do Kelsen and Olivecrona agree as to an imperative element in law, they also show marked similarities in their discussions of the arrangements of a legal system. That there are important differences is clear; using the terms of the question it is only slightly over-simplifying to say that the argument I shall put forward is that in giving an account of the nature of law, they arrange the same basic elements of law in a similar way, but that they explain those elements differently.

They certainly do share the conception of legal rules as imperative. Moreover, they both suggest that this imperative element is unusual in that it derives not from the wish of any person or persons necessarily, but from the proper procedures of the system. Unlike Austin (criticised by both for supporting this element of a sovereign's volition 'commanding'), Olivecrona calls rules of law 'independent imperatives', and Kelsen 'depsychologised commands' to express this idea.

They have more in common than just that. For a start both see law's effect as emanating from acceptance of the constitution (authorising the creation of the laws) by officials. For Olivecrona, legislation is effective because it passes the procedure for promulgation of legislation authorised by the constitution. Officials of the system are interested to see that the necessary formalities have been carried out (although they are often prepared to accept the work of other officials); individual citizens are just concerned to follow rules given the appellation 'law' by the authorities. Legislators then, by virtue of their office under an accepted constitution, pass laws by following the rules thereof. Turning to Kelsen, his approach is more complex, it is true, but the basic points are there: legislation is valid, for him (we leave the difference between his 'validity' and Olivecrona's 'effective' until later; of both at this stage perhaps we should say the legislation 'takes effect') when it is passed following the procedure laid down by a higher norm, which eventually (in a chain of such norms) is authorised by the basic norm. This 'basic norm' is the presumption – by jurists – that the first constitution is valid: this first constitution in turn validates later constitutions including the present one; and that in turn lays down procedures for law-making by (inter alia, perhaps) the legislature. So, it is acceptance of the constitution (to put it simply) that accords effect to the legislation passed by the authorised procedure. The similarity to Olivecrona is striking (although Olivecrona concentrates on officials and on jurists – including judges, presumably).

Acceptance of constitution, proper procedure, legal rules. We have seen that for Olivecrona and

4 Realist Theories

Kelsen these rules resulting from the system are independent imperatives; we must now look at their joint view that law is a system of coercion, and that individual laws have coercive sanctions attached. Olivecrona says the law needs an organisation prepared to back up its rules by overwhelming force if necessary; law is properly seen as rules about the exercise of that force, and therefore as primarily addressed to officials informing them when to use such force. His 'primary' rules are to officials, and only the 'secondary' rules inform subjects how to behave; sometimes the latter are implicit, as when the legislation simply imposes a punishment for certain conduct. In the same way, Kelsen sees the law as a coercive system, and laws as including a coercive element. As with Olivecrona (particularly in his later work), he does see that the aim is to prescribe individuals' conduct by use of the sanction; again he considers that the 'primary norm' is the one that orders the sanction and so is addressed to officials; the norm which tells the subjects of the law what to do is secondary. This view of a law can be criticised, since it emphasises coercion and punishment rather than obedience, and particularly obedience out of respect for the law, not fear. Further, it seems to distort the function of those laws which confer powers on individuals and officials. These are seen by Kelsen as part of chains of norms with a sanction at the end (so, for example, the power to legislate is exercised to bring about general norms; the power to contract when used satisfied one of the conditions for the stipulation of a sanction – ie danger – by a judge); by Olivecrona, even civil laws are enforced sometimes by fines and imprisonment, and ultimately all civil laws – including contract etc – are backed by sanctions.

We can say then that Kelsen and Olivecrona's arrangement of the basic elements of law is similar: acceptance of a constitution causes acceptance of laws passed in the proper manner; both the system and these laws are coercive (Olivecrona possibly less insistent on each law being coercive), and the laws are primarily addressed to officials to stipulate sanctions.

However, Kelsen and Olivecrona's theories are by no means the same; the principal difference being the explanation of law – on the question of why and how laws bind. A foreshadowing of this was mentioned earlier, with Kelsen's 'valid' as against Olivecrona's 'effective'. Olivecrona followed the Scandinavian line of thought rejecting duties, rights etc, as 'metaphysical entities'. They only corresponded to reality on a psychological level. A duty was a feeling of being bound; the binding quality of law – its normativity, or 'oughtness' could be explained only as an aspect of the world of cause and effect. Because the constitution was accepted, law-makers appointed under it when they passed laws 'played on the minds' of the subjects, who as a result felt bound to obey. (Once a subject was what one might call legally grown-up, this process happened automatically, without fear of sanctions playing a direct part.) Logically then there was no duty if the subject did not feel bound; although officials would still feel bound to punish him.

Kelsen's theory is based on law being normative, and therefore in language at least being distinct from the world of 'causality', of cause and effect, and rather in the world of 'imputation' (if X, then Y ought to happen', as against 'if X, then Y happens). In his legal systems, rules are 'norms', which are *valid* because authorised by superior norms. Rules passed by legislatures are valid because passed under proper procedures authorised by a still higher norm, a constitution. It follows from this that one 'ought' to obey a legal rule even if one does not feel bound; if a sanction is stipulated for not doing so, one is under a 'legal duty' irrespective of fear of the sanction. For the 'validity', the first constitution must be accepted (by presupposition of the basic norm) and the system must generally work: social factors do have a role.

It is clear then that Kelsen's explanation of the nature of law – in terms of normativity within a system following acceptance of it and its general effectiveness – is not the same as Olivecrona's explanation – in terms of the psychological effects produced by an acceptance of the constitution. This should not stop us realising that the order in which they arranged the basic elements of law is closely comparable.

TYPE TWO

This question calls for special reference to the Scandinavian Realists. The student should note that this does not mean *exclusive* reference, and that a broader approach is required.

'Bentham said that: "Right is the child of law: from real laws come real rights." I would say that the opposite is the case, for it is not law which creates order, but order which generates law' (Fawcett). Discuss with special reference to the writings of the Scandinavian jurists.

University of London LLB Examination
(for External Students) Jurisprudence and Legal Theory June 1986 Q4

Skeleton Solution

Meaning of 'order' – civilisation – idea of justice – peaceful society – Scandinavian Realists – 'cause and effect' – law determines the moral order – Bentham and utilitarianism – order moulds law.

Suggested Solution

This is a difficult question, because it is not clear precisely what Fawcett means by the word 'order' as used in the quotation. I shall first look at one sense of that word and show that this cannot have been Fawcett's intended meaning; I shall then move to other senses which fit Fawcett's statement and contrast that statement in these senses with the thoughts of the Scandinavian Realists, which on this point can be considered with those of Bentham.

If by 'order', Fawcett was referring to civilisation, a certain level of culture and development in a society distinguishing it from a primitive society, his statement is incorrect. Studies by legal anthropologists over the last 60 years or so have revealed conclusively that once 'primitive' societies are studied from a viewpoint which attempts to avoid ethnocentrism on the part of the researcher, they can be seen to have 'laws' and procedures for enforcing them. Hence, their development into civilisation or 'order' is preceded by the existence of law; law is not generated by order in this sense. The study by Moore in *Law as Process* of the modern history of the Chagga tribe is a fine illustration of this point.

Fawcett was not, then, referring to civilisation. If instead he was referring to 'order' in the sense of some idea of justice, his statement – and particularly the reference to Bentham's views on rights – makes more sense; if, on the other hand, he was referring to order in the sense of a well-behaved, peaceful (one is tempted to say 'law-abiding', but that would beg the question) society, I can see his point but his reference to Bentham is puzzling.

Let us take the second of these possible meanings first. It is the most obvious and usual meaning of 'order', but I do not see that Fawcett can possibly have it in mind. Certainly, Bentham's comments on rights were not dealing with anything to do with 'order' in this sense; and it is difficult to see how the sociological comment that law is generated by a peaceful, well-behaved society could be justified.

I think, therefore, that Fawcett is talking about 'order' in the sense of 'justice', or just, moral behaviour, and claiming that considerations of morality and justice generate law rather than vice

4 Realist Theories

versa. This seems at first glance to be an obvious truism; surely murder, for instance, is made illegal because it is immoral and taxation and the welfare state are legislated for because of considerations of justice?

The Scandinavian Realists would, however, profoundly disagree with this analysis. Rejecting such 'metaphysical' notions as rights and duties, they sought to explain law in terms of cause and effect, in the real world. One of the leading Scandinavian jurists, Olivecrona, wrote that far from moral standards being embodied in law, rather the law largely determines the moral order. The regular use of force and sanctions result in moral standards by a process of 'internalisation', akin to the way in which a child learns correct behaviour as a result of being disciplined for wrong-doing when young. On this view then, it is the law which generates order, which causes people to behave in accordance with standards considered moral or just.

Although Bentham's comment on rights set out in the quotation is couched in different language, it is to similar effect. He rejects the idea of objective standards of right and wrong, natural rights, as 'nonsense upon stilts'. Rights do not generate law; rather, the only real rights are those which are given by law, generated by it.

However, the comparison between Bentham and the Scandinavians and the contrast between him and Fawcett should not be taken too far. He thought that there was a rational standard – utilitariansim – which should be used in the generation of laws. This can be seen as a moral standard, certainly a standard of justice, from which laws should be generated. Although Fawcett contrasts Bentham's views with his own in the quotation, I think that Bentham would have sided with him in denying that order is generated by law: the order, the (for Bentham) utilitarian standard, actually moulds law.

I agree with Fawcett on this and disagree with the Scandinavians. Law is based on the chosen moral, just order and is not the generating force behind that order.

TYPE THREE

The type of question which purports to be about the Realist 'school' in general, but only makes sense if focused on Scandinavian Realism.

In what ways may the 'Realists' be regarded as having developed a 'psychological school of jurisprudence'?

University of London LLB Examination
(for External Students) Jurisprudence and Legal Theory June 1983 Q7

Skeleton Solution

'School' – group of theorists united by a common theme – American Realism – sociological not 'psychological' – Scandinavian Realism – reject the metaphysical – legal phenomena can be explained by the idea of psychological occurrence – similarities with Kelsen and Hart – they have formed a 'school'.

Suggested Solution

The concept of a 'school' of thought is a notoriously hazy one: if we are to measure the Realists against it, a working definition would be of assistance. A school is a group of theories/theorists united by a common theme or idea in a particular area of thought; I am sure better definitions exist, but this one will do for our purpose. Do the Realists, then, form a psychological 'school' in jurisprudence, within the definition?

There are two variants of Realism: American and Scandinavian. The suggestion of a psychological school seems to fit the latter but not the former, so readily. I will therefore briefly consider the Americans, and then concentrate more fully on the Scandinavians. They do share some things apart from their joint name: both are 'Realist', in the sense of trying to look at law in a way stripped of mystique and metaphysics, to see how law actually works in society.

The answers given are, however, very different. American Realists are concerned to show and justify scepticism about traditional explanations of the judicial process in terms of judges making decisions by following rules laid down by the legal system. Their attack takes two forms. 'Fact scepticism', seen in the writings of Jerome Frank, for instance, indicates the importance of the fact-finding processes at first instance level; decisions in individual future cases cannot be predicted accurately because everything depends on how judge and jury find the facts in issue; such findings are influenced by, amongst other things, the results they will lead to. 'Rule scepticism' (espoused by Llewellyn, but criticised by Frank) refers rather to the appellate level. Influences such as the judge's background are said to be as important as if not more important than the legal rules that govern the case. These rules at best are predictions of what the courts will do; they are not statements of law. A statute, according to Gray, is not law until enforced and applied by the courts.

This version of Realism is not psychological at all, rather sociological; social and background factors influence and determine results in particular cases. Studies and research into these factors and into predicting legal decisions are encouraged. Indeed, one of the major criticisms of the Americans' view of rules as predictions is that in terms of the judges who apply them, it is psychologically incoherent. How can a judge apply a rule, if it is only a prediction of what he will do? Why does he justify himself on the basis of such 'predictions'?

For a psychological school, we must then look at the Scandinavian brand of Realism; here indeed we see ample evidence of a psychological approach to legal questions. The basic approach of the Scandinavians is that legal concepts such as rights and duties, ownership and obligation, are commonly used in a metaphysical way referring to a non-existent sphere of reality outside the real world of cause and effect; law must be understood strictly within that world, and rights, duties etc., must be explained in it. The Scandinavians found the explanation of these concepts in psychological occurrences – a duty might be seen as a feeling of compulsion, and a right as a feeling of power. They took their inspiration from the work of Hagerstrom; the major figures who applied this sort of analysis to the law were Olivecrona and Ross. From this basic outline, we can certainly find justification for calling these writers a school, united by the idea of psychological occurrence as an explanation of legal phenomena.

As with other schools, however, detailed analysis differs from one to another; and also as with other schools a consideration of their work might well lead to the conclusion that apart from the major theme of psychology, their views were not in the end novel or unique.

In fact, the best known Scandinavians who concentrated on law, Olivecrona and Ross, both bear similarities to positivist jurisprudents like Kelsen and Hart. Olivecrona sees laws as 'independent imperatives', statements that are imperative in form (you shall do X) but are not actually the result of a wish by anybody. These imperatives seem to produce a binding quality. Olivecrona tries several possible answers to the question of what this binding quality is, and rejects them all; law is binding or valid because it is felt to be so. This explanation of the normative quality of law is the psychological one; legislation is binding because the procedures in the act of promulgaton are those laid down by an accepted constitution, ceremonies such as marriage have legal consequences for analogous reasons.

Olivecrona is ambivalent, it seems, on whether laws are addressed to officials or individuals; in his most strongly expressed view they are addressed to officials, and concern the use of force applied by judges and others to ensure that prescribed patterns of conduct are followed. This all follows from Olivecrona's psychological point of view; that his view is similar to Kelsen's can be seen from question Type 1 above.

The most acceptable 'psychological theory' and explanation of normativity seems to be that of Alf Ross. Valid law is a scheme of interpretation of what happens in those areas we call legal; we can understand (and predict) the actions of a judge if we see that he follows the norms of that scheme of interpretation, because he considers them binding. There are two aspects of a valid norm; it is followed in practice and it is felt to be binding. The reason the judge feels it is binding is his allegiance to the sources of law in the constitution which he accepts.

For Ross as well as Olivecrona, law is addressed to officials. The only logically necessary norms are those which tell officials when to apply sanctions (law again seen as rules about force), since these imply the norms of conduct which citizens must comply with. Psychologically, there are *two* sets of norms, though; those informing the law subjects of that desired conduct have – psychologically – a separate existence.

Even this quick sketch of Ross's theory is revealing. The importance of psychology throughout is evident – norms are felt to be binding because the judge gave mental allegiance to the constitution; individuals consider that they are addressed by a set of norms, etc. Also, the similarity to Hart is apparent; although Hart would reject the idea that law as rules about force is properly seen as addressed to official, he does see (see Notes to *The Concept of Law*) the parallel between Ross's feelings of compulsion and his own internal aspect; that this is especially important to officials in the legal system is apparent to both of them.

What does all this tell us? I think the Scandinavian Realists can be said to have formed a 'school' – as defined above – in relation to their emphasis on the psychological process as the explanation of legal concepts. This appears to be a novel way of considering legal phenomena, but we should emphasise that the novelty is one of viewpoint and not substances and thought. Olivecrona and Ross both accept and attempt to explain the notion of normativity; they do so from the psychological viewpoint, but the fact that this is tied to the acceptance of a system by judges above all, which system enacts procedures for the particular laws, is now a commonplace of Western jurisprudential thought.

To the extent that my definition is a satisfactory one, the Scandinavian Realists form a psychological 'school' of jurisprudence.

TYPE FOUR

These questions are aimed at Realism in general and are perhaps more difficult. Certainly they require thought and planning by the student, as well as a consideration as to whether there is a Realist 'school'.

1) 'The juristic task is to observe the facts of human behaviour including judicial and other official behaviour, in all the circumstances of particular cases, and to interpret them scientifically without preconceptions' (Julius Stone). How adequately does this statement portray the function of Realist jurisprudence?

University of London LLB Examination
(for External Students) Jurisprudence and Legal Theory June 1984 Q7

Jurisprudence: The Philosophy of Law

Skeleton Solution

There are two 'schools'— American Realism — 'the facts of human behaviour' — emphasis on courts — Scandinavian Realism — reject concept of normativity — 'cause and effect' — more theoretical — less research.

Suggested Solution

This is a narrow question, calling for an analysis of the function which the Realist writers considered their work to be fulfilling; for, while it is possible to criticise what they said, and even to criticise the function which they chose to attempt to fulfil, what the function was — and whether the quotation given adequately portrays it — is a factual question. There were, of course, two 'schools' of Realist jurisprudence, termed American Realism and Scandinavian Realism respectively. I will look at each in turn, analysing the quotation to see if it is an appropriate statement of the 'function' of the school.

First, then, American Realism. As the name implies, Realists see themselves as explaining the position as it really is. In terms of explaining the legal experience, this involved stripping away the myths — principally those surrounding the central importance of legal rules — and setting out the reality.

Clearly, the American Realists wanted to look at 'the facts of human behaviour', and in particular at the behaviour of judges. Llewellyn expressly limits himself in some of his work to the appellate courts, in fact. This limitation was attacked by Frank, who thought that it was unrealistic to see the law from the viewpoint of the appellate courts when real legal experience, in fact, occurs in the first instance courts. The emphasis on the courts can be seen from the definition of law in terms of predictions of judicial decisions in particular cases. The 'offshoot' of American Realism, judicial behaviouralism, studies of how judges behave, also follows from this emphasis. Having observed, the Realists saw it as their function to interpret. Llewellyn wrote much about models of judicial behaviour and explained why — in his view — most legal decisions could be predicted with a fair degree of certainty. Frank, on the other hand, denied that such certainty existed because (at first instance) the centrally important task of fact-finding was inherently uncertain. We can see that though the function — to observe and explain — was the same for both, the conclusions of Llewellyn and Frank often differ. It might well be said that Frank far more than Llewellyn was concerned with 'particular cases', since he concentrated on lower courts and not the more rarefied atmosphere of appellate courts making legal — as against factual — decisions.

The scientific interpretation of the facts as observed by the Realists involved contradicting preconceptions based on the centrality of legal rules as the heavily operative factor in judicial decision making. At times, it seems, this rejection of preconceptions was itself the main function of Realism; indeed it might be said that it was the main legacy of the Realist school.

The American Realists did then, in general, see the function of their Realism in very much the same way set out by Stone. By investigating and looking at law in its social context and stripped of preconceived notions about rules, a greater understanding of law could be achieved; this investigation would take the form of studying particularly judicial behaviour.

Does Stone's quotation fit the Scandinavian Realists? They also wish to cut through preconceptions to reveal the true picture — that, after all, is why they are termed 'Realists'. In their case, the preconceptions which they wish to eradicate relate to the concept of normativity, which they reject: there is no such thing as an 'ought', and concepts such as rights and duties cannot be explained in terms of normativity. The Scandinavians do not, however, reject the notion of legal rules ('paper rules') as do the Americans: on the contrary, they clearly see such rules as guides to behaviour.

Much of the Scandinavians' writing is concerned with the attempt to show how legal rules work in the 'real' world of cause and effect other than the fictional realm of normativity. Why do people follow legal rules? It is clear, then, that they see their function as being partly to interpret the facts of human behaviour. Their explanation is in terms of a psychological effect of the rules in making people believe that something will and should happen.

Further, it is clear (still in the terms of the question) that the interpretation is principally of judicial and other behaviour. Alf Ross, for example, thinks that legal rules provide a scheme of interpretation to explain judicial behaviour; both he and Olivecrona explain legal rules as being principally rules about force addressed to officials, although both also see and explain the rules' function in guiding the behaviour of the law-subject.

However, the Scandinavians were not much concerned with observation of behaviour in particular cases. Their work was intensely theoretical and their explanation of the behaviour essentially abstract: they did not encourage research (as the Americans did) nor engage in it themselves.

With the small qualification mentioned in the last paragraph, Stone's statement is an adequate statement of the function of realist jurisprudence and also provides a clue as to why two schools of thought with conclusions as different as those of the Scandinavians and Americans should both share the name 'Realist'.

2) 'The problem we all face is not whether to be realistic but how; not whether to portray law as a fact, rather than fiction, but what counts as a fact, and what therefore is a factual portrayal of it' (D N MacCormick). Discuss.

University of London LLB Examination
(for External Students) Jurisprudence and Legal Theory June 1988 Q5

Skeleton Solution

Basis of American Realist movement – examine reality of legal experience – lacking a technology – Glendon Schubert – judicial behaviouralism – Hunt – 'we are all Realist now' – problem identified in quotation – technology – Scandanavian Realism – rejection of metaphysics – concentration on world of cause and effect – the real world – problem to explain rights/duties etc – psychological explanation – Olivecrona – *Law as Fact* addressees of law – existence as a fact proved by reference to psychological factors – criticisms – Pound – law as fact – social phenomenon – but sociological jurisprudence developed from analytical model of law.

Suggested Solution

Whilst the movement that became known as American Realism sought to concentrate on the reality of the legal experience and move away from a mere logical application of legal rules as the sole method for the prediction of the likely outcome of a dispute, their important corrective to the method of pure analytical jurisprudence has now become conventional wisdom to the extent that Alan Hunt was able to write that whilst Realism is dead 'we are all Realists now'. What he had in mind was that legal scientists do now attempt to take 'the reality of the legal experience' into account; but as MacCormick has identified, the difficulty lies not in whether to look at such reality, but how. Herein MacCormick has isolated the very weakness of the American Realist movement.

Glendon Schubert, an ideological descendent of the American Realist movement, was of the opinion that the American Realists failed to achieve the objective that they set for themselves. He went so far as to say that they lacked both theory and method. That is somewhat of an overstatement. A preferable view would be that they did not fully develop their theory nor did they engage in the very matter that they so strongly advocated, namely a technology for the more accurate prediction of the outcome of the next dispute. As a judicial behaviouralist, Schubert was concerned with the motivations and the attitudes behind judicial decisions. That is exactly the area of interest for the American Realists. The real difficulty is not what to study as such but how to study it. How are jurists to scientifically study the motivations and attitudes that are so important to the Realists?

There have been attempts to deal with this both by American Realists and by those whom I have described as their ideological descendants. The most prolific Realist, Karl Llewellyn, through empirical research in the law reports, identified what he describes as the 'period style of judicial reasoning' by which he examined how a judge comes to a decision, but viewed this in different time periods. He identified that, through time, attitudes changed and that it was possible to outline two polar positions between the 'grand style' in which the judge feels less constrained by rules of precedent and rather adopts what Llewellyn termed 'situation sense' in order to ensure that a reasonable result is attained in a case. The judge would do this by reference to policy and principles. On the other pole, Llewellyn identified the 'formal style' in which a judge considers himself entirely bound by the rules of precedent, taking the view that rules of law decide cases and that policy is a matter for the legislature. As a technology this period style could be used to 'place' a judge in the spectrum between the grand and the formal styles and to use that placement in the prediction process by tailoring a dispute to fall within the area that he will decide in favour of. The difficulty with this as a method is, as Fuller observed, that it is to put consistency at a premium and to view the judicial process as a formalised game of 'snap'. Judges are no more nor less consistent than any other human being and that is quite inconsistent! Indeed Twining has described this period style as 'a relatively simple theoretical model'. It is submitted that as an attempt to answer the question of 'how', the period style is not helpful.

Another attempt to deal with the how question was developed by Loevinger and has become known as jurimetrics. This looks to the role of computers in the prediction process whereby the vast information which is of interest to the Realist is fed into the computer which will then presumably identify a 'pattern'.

Whilst this attempts to undertake in a scientific manner that which is currently dealt with through gossip and rumour – the preferences of judges – it suffers from the same drawback as Llewellyn's model, namely that it assumes a consistency of approach. Such computers will cope with data and identify a pattern. But the pattern that they identify may be of no use because of judicial inconsistency. The difficulty is increased when dealing with an appellate court bench with more than one judge. Then the Realist is interested in group relations among the members of the bench. Such membership may and does change, as do the interrelationships.

The judicial behaviouralists, among whom one could number Schubert and Griffith, seek to examine factors outside 'the law in books' such as the background and environmental conditions of the judge as an explanation for their decisions. Griffith does this with regard to what he sees as anti-Trade Union decisions among the English judiciary and which he explains by reference to the conservative background of the judiciary. This is flawed in that it is not the conservative background of the judiciary that stands behind these decisions but the Conservative ideology of the legislature making the laws which the judiciary are then to enforce, eg sequestration of union assets.

The reality of the legal experience is such as to indicate that judges are not consistent in their approaches and the real problem is, as MacCormick has identified, that no one has yet developed a technology to explain that inconsistency.

The second part of the quotation addresses itself to the issue that concerned the Scandinavian Realists to the extent that it is accurate to so describe them. They were concerned to reject any realm of metaphysics which cannot be verified by empirical proof. Hence, rights and duties would be meaningless and fictional unless they are rooted in actual sense experience. That actual sense experience exists on the psychological level in that the meaning of a normative statement is psychological hence a right exists as a feeling of power and a duty as a feeling of obligation.

Olivecrona looked at the question of the addressees of law in *Law as Fact* in which he identified that if the subject is to have a psychological attitude towards a law then it must at least in the secondary sense be addressed to him. This was a variation from the work of Hans Kelsen which so heavily influenced Olivercrona initially. Alf Ross, who was perhaps the most sophisticated of the Scandinavian Realists, thought that jurisprudence should be rooted in an empirical study of official behaviour and not in norms that ought to be obeyed, but rather in norms likely to be applied by the court. The problem with much of the Scandinavian Realists is that they are not treated seriously, perhaps because much of their thesis is largely guesswork.

Roscoe Pound, as the main advocate for socio legal studies, saw law as a social phenomenon. He was concerned in the making, interpretation and application of laws to take account of law as a social fact. The problem with such an approach is as Hunt has identified, namely that Pound used sociology when it suited him. Harris argues that the socio legal research that seeks to identify law as a fact and to offer a factual portrayal of law engages the same concept of law as analytical jurisprudence. Harris doubts whether anyone has succeeded in identifying a sociological conception of law which transcends or replaces conceptions arrived at in the analytical mode. Hence, while the socio-legal studies attempt to study law in action, their starting point is taken from law in books. There is a merging of the 'fact' and of the 'fiction'.

On such a perspective, indeed, MacCormick is correct. There appears to be little dispute as to whether to portray law as fact. Who would want to portray it as fiction? The difficulty is in identifying what is fact. That difficulty is not resolved by sociological jurisprudence.

5 The Historical School

5.1 Introduction
5.2 Key points
5.3 Analysis of question styles
5.4 Questions

5.1 Introduction
As with Realism, the issue of whether there is a 'school' is pressing. The divergent theories of Maine and von Savigny suggest that 'school' may not be a particularly apt term. Von Savigny and Maine both, however, reacted against the natural law doctrines which espoused unchanging principles and lacked historical perspective. Today, the importance of these writers (most particularly Maine) lies in their influence on anthropological and sociological studies of law.

5.2 Key points

a) *Maine – the 'organic' theory*

   i) The development of legal systems passes through six stages: royal judgments; custom; codes; legal fictions; equity; legislation.

   ii) Static societies move through the first three stages only; progessive societies move through some or all of the latter three.

   iii) Maine's methods have influenced much in modern jurisprudence and sociology.

b) *Von Savigny – the 'mystical' theory*

   i) Law is an expression of the will of the people – it develops from the '*Volksgeist*' (character and spirit of a nation's people).

   ii) Law will thus develop gradually, as reflected in judicial decisions and legislature. Eventually juristic skills will be added and codification will take place.

   iii) Although von Savigny grasped an important point in that a country's values and history do manifest themselves within the law, his concept of 'Volksgeist' was imperfect.

5.3 Analysis of question styles
Questions on the historical school usually treat it as a discrete subject. The student may, however, have to consider the school's influence on the anthropological school and sociological jurisprudence. Most questions call for an analysis or comparison of Maine and von Savigny, although a question on an individual theorist is possible.

5.4 Questions

TYPE ONE

This calls for a critical evaluation of the theory of Maine. There will be some overlap with his contribution to anthropological jurisprudence.

5 The Historical School

'Maine's thesis was always – as he himself recognised – subject to important limitations' (W. Friedmann). Discuss.

University of London LLB Examination
(for External Students) Jurisprudence and Legal Theory June 1986 Q9

Skeleton Solution

Maine investigated law's social and historical context – method followed by sociologists and anthropologists – development of legal systems – considered limited range of societies – *The Cheyenne Way* – significant contribution.

Suggested Solution

Critical reaction to Maine's work falls into two parts – an admission of the great impact he and his scientific method have had on later studies of law from various standpoints, together with a realisation of the shortcomings of his own particular studies and conclusions. In looking at these shortcomings and limitations, we should not ignore the more general impact; nor, of course, should we forget that our criticisms are made with the benefit of hindsight.

It is, I think, fair to put Maine's limitations in perspective by dealing first with the overall effect of his writings. He saw that law could not be understood without an investigation into and understanding of its historical and social context. In his endeavours to produce a theory of how law develops with society through history, he based his ideas on research into the materials at his disposal. This investigative, scientific method has since been followed by many anthropologists and sociologists who have developed legal anthropology and legal sociology, following Maine's emphasis on careful study of records of communities and investigations of surviving primitive communities. Maine might be said to be the father of these two disciplines, particularly the former. Also, comparative law studies such as his now form part of many university law courses.

Having said that, Maine's precise conclusions can be rejected in many respects. His main thesis concerned the development of legal systems. From his knowledge of English and Roman law and from his studies of some primitive Indian peoples, he concluded that law developed in stages. All societies passed through the first three such stages (kingly judgments divinely inspired; customary law in the hands of an aristocratic elite and codes, or written laws) but only progressive (as against static, primitive) societies pass to the further three stages of legal development (by fictions, equity (an alternative body of rules) and finally legislation).

It is not clear how far Maine meant this development sequence to be either rigidly followed in each case or indeed to be universal at all. The range of societies which he considered was very limited. If he had had more material at his disposal, his conclusions would have been very different. For example, it is clear from more modern anthropological studies that primitive societies do have methods of legislation, deliberate law-making processes (see eg Llewellyn and Hoebel's study *The Cheyenne Way*) and many societies do not have the equivalents of fictions and equity in their development. The laws of primitive societies and of societies generally show more variety than Maine allowed for – although it must be remembered that he would probably have been the first to predict that further research would invalidate his detailed views in this way.

Maine also touched upon the development of the content of laws in developed societies; he claimed that the laws of such societies had 'hitherto shown a movement from status to contract'. This movement is one from laws based on a position in family or household – for example, the privileges of a husband and father and the incapacity from a contractual viewpoint of a wife – to laws based on freedom to contract irrespective of status.

It has been claimed that this development has not been continued, but rather that the reverse has occurred. Legal relations are again dictated by status as employees, consumers, tenants, etc – it is said. There is an argument about whether this further movement is in fact a reverse, or an onward development towards a more real freedom of contract; in any case, the claim of a reverse cannot constitute an objection to Maine's theory, since he was simply pointing to the development to that time, 'hitherto' as he put it.

One suggested limitation on Maine's thesis is, therefore, misplaced. More generally, the limitations which I have identified in Maine's work must not be allowed to overshadow the significant and continuing contribution which that work made to the study of jurisprudence.

TYPE TWO

An evaluative comparison of the theories and differing approaches of von Savigny and Maine.

'Maine's theory ... is ... free from the abstract and unreal romanticism which vitiates much of von Savigny's theory about the evaluation of law' (Friedmann). Discuss.

Written by the Editor

Skeleton Solution

'Mystical' – 'organic' – von Savigny – '*Volksgeist*' – custom – juristic skills – decay – criticism of the theory – Maine – six stage development of legal system – scientific empirical techniques – nonetheless flawed.

Suggested Solution

Von Savigny's theory has been described by some writers as 'mystical', whilst Maine's is 'organic'. This points at the differences between their theories; although both reacted against natural law and its lack of historical perspective, their approaches were largely separate. The quotation suggests that Maine's theory is superior to that of von Savigny in that it is free from 'abstract and unreal romanticism'. The two theorists will be examined in turn to ascertain whether this is in fact the case.

Von Savigny saw the development of law as an expression of the will of the nation; it emerged from the 'Volksgeist' (spirit of the people). Thus the concept of a universal natural law was incorrect. He saw the development of law in the following terms:

1 The first stage of law is custom, originating from the values of the people.

2 The second stage is the addition of juristic skills which codify the expression of the '*Volksgeist*'. Eventually law dies away as 'the nation loses its nationality'; that is, its national identity.

It is useful to consider at this point the extent to which von Savigny's theory succumbs to 'abstract and unreal romanticism'. Perhaps a good definition of 'romanticism' is that which is 'remote from experience', or even imaginary. Many have criticised the notion of 'Volksgeist' as being just that – it is simply not true that every 'people' has a corporate spirit or identity. One only has to think of the variety of racial, cultural and political groups in the United

5 The Historical School

Kingdom today to be convinced that '*Volksgeist*' is an unreal concept. Furthermore, there is much technical law which does not really fit into von Savigny's pattern of development. It does seem therefore, that von Savigny's theory was to an extent vitiated by romanticism. Perhaps his real problem was that he took a legitimate idea (that national character does have an influence on the development of law) to fanciful extremes.

Having thus accepted the criticism which Friedmann levels at von Savigny, it is necessary to consider whether Maine's theory avoids the same criticism. Maine shared von Savigny's rejection of natural law, but his approach lacked von Savigny's 'mysticism'. He was greatly influenced by Darwin's *Origin of Species* and studied the historical development of legal systems. He concluded that legal systems followed a six-stage pattern of development: royal judgments; custom; codes; legal fictions; equity; legislation. According to Maine, static societies pass through the first three stages only, whereas progressive societies pass through some or all of the latter three. The fact that Maine adopted scientific empirical techniques to reach his conclusions does go some way to support the view that his theory was free from 'abstract and unreal romanticism'. Indeed his method is now influential in modern sociology and anthropology.

Despite this, Maine's conclusions are not without their critics. Studies such as Malinowski's *Crime and Custom in Savage Society* throw doubt on the sequential development of law espoused by Maine. In all probability the research Maine carried out was inadequate to support his theories. It is thus clear that, despite being free from the defects inherent in von Savigny's theory, Maine's theory was itself flawed.

TYPE THREE

Both of these questions call for an evaluation of the value of the historical school of jurisprudence. The 'quotation question' appears far more complicated, but the student will see that the issues in both solutions are, in fact, broadly similar.

1) Of what value today is the historical approach to jurisprudence?

University of London LLB Examination
(for External Students) Jurisprudence and Legal Theory June 1983 Q4

Skeleton Solution

Laws in their historical context – von Savigny – *Volksgeist* – uniqueness in each society – contrast Maine – Marxism – legal anthropology – sociology – valuable approach.

Suggested Solution

Stated simply, the historical approach to jurisprudence stresses that laws cannot be understood properly unless they are placed in context, specifically their historical context. This insight was shared by two very different scholars of the nineteenth century, von Savigny and Maine, whose viewpoints have the appellation 'historical school' or 'historical approach'. For von Savigny the reason history was so important was that over time a society or law developed from the *Volksgeist* or spirit of the people; unless this process and the importance of the historical and social factors were recognised, the law could not be understood or explained and attempts at reform would fail. The *Volksgeist* theory was one of the uniqueness of law in each society as a result of its own unique history and customs; in this respect it can be contrasted with Maine's exposition of the relevance of history, since he pointed to a developmental sequence in the form of the law (six stages from kingly order to legislation) and in its context (from status of contract) which were common (at least in the former case) to all legal systems.

A brief survey of those views comprising the historical approach is required as an introduction, to precede the general line of my answer to the question. This is that the 'Maine-line' has been influential in several major directions and is still influential today; the '*Volksgeist*' approach is generally rejected although it does have some influence on Marxism, and that the general insight with which we started is an accepted factor in the study and practice of law.

Although few write about historical jurisprudence any more, three 'schools' of jurisprudential thought which are very productive at the present day can be said to be, to different extents, offshoots of the historical approach. First, Marxism. Because Marx was writing at about the same time as Maine, we cannot claim a conscious influence of Maine on Marx, although the influence of Maine and later anthropological and sociological writings on later Marxists is clear. However, Marx and Engels clearly viewed law – to the extent that they considered it at all – in the historical context, and like Maine were much influenced by ideas of evaluation so prevalent in mid nineteenth century thought.

Marxist theory as a whole is historical. Man is emerging through a series of class conflicts, to the ultimate classless state; the law reflects the present situation (the economic 'base' of the relations of production) at each stage. At present, for example, the UK is a capitalist society in which the class conflict is between the owners of the means of production (the bourgeoisie) and the working class. The law is an instrument of the bourgeoisie to oppress the working class, and can only be understood as such; it reflects the present relations of production (eg strict laws of ownership, laws of contract and conveyance to allow for freedom of commerce, etc). The view of law reflecting the particular stage of development of society is one which is very similar to Maine's view; reflections of von Savigny's thought can be seen in the idea of law reflecting the particular economic position of the society. The present day importance of Marxism need not be argued.

Second, Maine is directly responsible for one of the booming fields of jurisprudential study, that of legal anthropology. While Maine's own work *Ancient Law* can be criticised both for lack of research and for over-generalised conclusions, there is no doubt that his innovation in attempting to trace developmental factors relevant to our own law through study of records of old and observations of present primitive societies has been of great value. Studies such as Malinowski's on why Trobriand Islanders followed assessable 'rules' in the absence of visible enforcement mechanisms, Gluckman's on the judicial processes of the Northern Rhodesian Barotse tribe and Llewellyn and Hoebel's on the dispute settlement of the Cheyenne widen our knowledge and perception of social control and dispute settlement. These and wider-based studies on social control generally enable us to question ethnocentric positions on the value of rules, institutions such as courts and police, and coercion: we can learn much about our own legal systems by seeing, for example, that in many primitive societies negotiation and conciliation are more important in settling disputes than is an authoritative decision-taking body.

There are some parallels to be drawn between legal anthropology and the third area in which Maine's views have been influential. This area is the sociological one; like anthropology a discipline in itself outside law, where gradually widening perspectives can tell us much about our legal systems and a proper definition of law. Maine and von Savigny pointed the way to considering not only law as it is laid down in books, but as it relates to the society; this and the growth of sociology outside law have caused a great amount of work and writing on the

5 The Historical School

subject of law and society. The sociological jurisprudence associated with Pound, the earlier sociology of Weber and Durkheim, the work of the realists in America, and modern writers like Selznick, are all examples of this.

Maine, then, has had influence, and his line of thought has had influence, in several directions in which much valuable work is still being undertaken today. Even von Savigny's approach and emphasis on national factors has left its mark, although as a theory it is long since rejected. Indirectly, too, the historical approach has permeated through much writing in analytical jurisprudence; the historical approach ran counter to the imperative theory of Austin and Bentham, since the command-sovereign model sees law-making as the outcome of an individual's will, rather than of a historical process.

Recent positivist theories such as Kelsen's and Hart's are not guilty of this fault: Hart develops his idea of a legal system from a primitive society, and Kelsen's norm chains go back to a first constitution, for example. Both realise the importance of historical factors in law.

Directly and indirectly the historical approach to jurisprudence remains a valuable one.

2) 'Undoubtedly the historical approach contributed an important insight to modern legal thinking by grasping the valuable truth that law is not just an abstract set of rules imposed on society but is an integral part of that society deeply rooted in the social and economic order in which it functions and embodying traditional value – systems which confer meaning and purpose upon the given society' (Lloyd: *The Idea of Law*). Discuss.

University of London LLB Examination
(for External Students) Jurisprudence and Legal Theory June 1985 Q8

Skeleton solution

New insight – von Savigny – Maine – latter pioneered scientific methodology – legal anthropology and sociology – Marxist view of society – historical school was major advance.

Suggested solution

My answer falls naturally into three parts. First I will try to show why it was an insight to see that law was more than an abstract set of rules, by looking briefly at the theories which had prevailed before the historical school. Second will come an explanation of how the historical school (in its disparate forms) grasped and analysed the new contribution, and third will be a discussion of how this 'valuable truth' has been important to modern legal thinking. In a sense, my answer puts the historical school in its own historical context!

Two schools of thought were prevalent up to and at the first half of the nineteenth century when the historical school came to the fore: natural law and the early positivists. Both in their different ways looked at law in terms of an abstract set of rules; for the natural lawyers, human law was controlled by the natural law dictates of reason, so that a large part of that human law was in the form of absolute principles imposed from outside. Human law-givers did have a discretion apart from the rules laid down by natural law, but the concentration was on the imposition of the external, objective (and common to all societies) principles. Positivism in the form propounded by Austin and Bentham also concentrated on the imposition of rules, this time by a sovereign within the society. Laws were not uniform from society to society, but there was no need for laws to be reflective of the society's values; rather, they reflected one person's will.

It was then a breakthrough, a new insight, when historians such as von Savigny and the other German romantics and Maine wrote of law from a different standpoint. Of course, the 'historical school' really consists of two parts, since the work of von Savigny differs from that of Maine in radical respects and it must be said that whilst Savigny focused on the uniqueness of each society (a feature of the insight as presented in the quotation), Maine was more concerned to point to common strands in the development of law in different societies.

Von Savigny's works match the 'valuable truth' as stated in the question almost absolutely. For him, each society's law was an expression of the '*Volksgeist*', or will of the people. In each century, the shared values of the populace were reflected in law at its primitive stage; this law was then honed into perfect shape by judicial skills and if the proper course was followed it would then be codified and preserved before the third stage, that of decay, set in. Hence, law was both an integral part of the society and deeply rooted in its traditional value-systems: indeed, to try to force foreign or external law on the people would not succeed, since it would not fit with the '*Volksgeist*' and would be rejected.

Maine, as I have said, was more concerned with the development of law in different societies. He looked at various societies and formulated a developmental sequence common to all legal systems. 'Static' societies passed through three stages of development and 'progressive' societies through three further stages. The developmental stages, particularly the first three (divine judgment of kings, aristocracy, codes), match a development in society away from kingly authority and on to the age of writing: to this extent law is deeply rooted in the economic and social order in which it functions. Maine, though, emphasises similarity rather than different value systems unique and central to varying societies.

The insight which we are discussing was, therefore, more the work of von Savigny and his followers than of Maine. Maine, though, pioneered the scientific methodology which has been taken up by two of the movements in modern legal thinking which most benefited from the fresh and wider perspective gained from studying not just the rules which make up law, but also the social background. These two movements are legal anthropology and sociology. Maine was, in fact, the first legal anthropologist. An anthropologist must look at law in wide perspective, simply because often the narrower 'landmarks' which he would look for in a developed legal system (courts, statutes, legislature) are missing. Anthropology looks at traditional folk-ways in the context of the particular community to see what lessons can be learnt.

Sociologists obviously are interested in the part played by law in society. From the earliest days of sociology, both sociologists such as Weber and 'sociological jurisprudents' such as Pound attempted to explain law's place in society. Weber, Durkheim and others tried to show how different types of law were to be found in different types of society and Pound tried to point to the way in which law, by balancing interests, tried to accommodate the varying values and choices of different groups in society.

More modern sociologists, heavily influenced by Marxist thought, might reject the first part of the historical insight ('law ... is an integral part of that society') as only partially true. It is the case that law is an integral part of most modern societies, since it is used by those in power in a society to keep them in power at the expense of the majority. However, law is not a necessary part of society: in a Marxist or communist state, law would have withered away. On this sort of ('conflict') viewpoint, the traditional value-system which law embodies is very much a one-sided system which sees the function and purpose of the society totally from the ruling classes' viewpoint.

5 The Historical School

Indeed, the Marxist analysis of history and how the law changes to meet the needs of the dominant class at each stage is very much akin to the 'truth' we are considering, although (as with Maine) the Marxist view is one which looks at similarities between different societies rather than their uniqueness.

6 Critical Legal Studies

6.1 Introduction
6.2 Key points
6.3 Analysis of question styles
6.4 Questions

6.1 Introduction

The Critical Legal Studies movement is a recent development of the Realist movement, especially in the United States, but also in England (for example at the University of Kent at Canterbury, Birkbeck College and the London School of Economics).

6.2 Key points

a) This is on the frontier of legal development.

b) It has still not run its course.

c) It incorporates ideas from American Realism, the social sciences, political studies etc.

d) It is essentially destructive, rather than constructive.

6.3 Analysis of question styles

The Critical Legal Studies movement is so diffuse that the examiner would not expect the student to show detailed knowledge of the individual members of the movement. Rather the examiner would be likely to set a general question inviting an analysis of the movement as a whole, or expect reference to be made to ideas fomented by members of the school as part of a question on other topics such as positivism, American Realism and judicial reasoning.

6.4 Questions

1) 'Although the Critical Legal Studies movement may appear nihilist, it offers scepticism, and scepticism is always a necessary first step towards positive transformation. This is often misunderstood by the movement's opponents.'

   Discuss.

   University of London LLB Examination
   (for External Students) Jurisprudence and Legal Theory June 1992 Q10

Skeleton Solution

Critical Legal Studies movement – Unger – Scandinavian Realism – Alf Ross – scepticism – Hume – excessive scepticism versus mitigated scepticism – discussion of the quotation – scepticism as the basis for all new theories.

Suggested Solution

The Critical Legal Studies movement came to the fore in the 1970s. It is a radical theoretical movement which rejects the distinction between law and politics and the notion that law can be neutral and value free. The movement proposes the integration of law and social theory. The existing social order is not accepted as an immutable state but rather as a state of affairs which represents a compromise of conflicting interests. Law and legal reasoning are seen as elements in the creation of a particular social order. In attempting to demonstrate that existing forms of legal consciousness merely serve certain interests in society, critical legal theorists claim to facilitate greater freedom for the individual.

The rejection by the movement of immutable legal standards has led to the criticism that the movement is nihilistic, that is that it rejects the existence of any values. This is also a criticism which has been levelled at the Scandinavian Realist movement which adopts a liberal approach somewhat similar to the Critical Legal Studies approach. Roberto Unger, a proponent of the Critical Legal Studies movement, says that a regime of rights would be necessary in the 'non-structural structure' which he proposes. Thus he suggests that four broad types of right would be necessary, namely immunity rights, destabilisation rights, market rights and solidarity rights. Unger's acceptance of the necessity for such rights is a movement away from pure nihilism. Alf Ross, a proponent of Scandinavian Realism, argued that the concept of justice is devoid of meaning, merely an emotional expression which does not postulate any material requirement as to the content of law. Thus, he argues, all wars and social conflicts have been fought in the name of some notion of justice. However, he admits that the words 'just' or 'unjust' can be used to indicate conformity or non-conformity to a rule or a set of rules existing at a particular time which suggests that he too moves away from an entirely nihilistic approach.

If it is accepted, therefore, as the quotation for discussion suggests, that the Critical Legal Studies movement is sceptical rather than nihilistic one must question whether scepticism is indeed a worthwhile standpoint as 'a necessary first step towards positive transformation'. David Hume rejected what he called 'excessive scepticism' or 'pyrrhonism'. He argued that such scepticism was an essentially academic pursuit which had no place in the real world. In *Enquiries Concerning the Human Understanding and Concerning the Principles of Morals* Hume argues that no benefit to society can result from such scepticism. If the theory were to be accepted, he argued, all human discourse and action would cease and man would be left in a state of lethargy. Instead, Hume suggested the reality was that even the most trivial event in life would banish such a theory because it is in man's nature to act and reason and believe. The only advantage which scepticism could offer, in Hume's opinion, would be to show the 'whimsical' tendency of mankind, namely that the basis of actions, reasoning and belief cannot always be explained. The excessive scepticism which Hume criticises is basically nihilistic insofar as it is a destructive theory offering no alternative to existing legal thought and values.

Hume also considered the merits of a more mitigated form of scepticism which perhaps flowed from 'pyrrhonism'. Mitigated scepticism might, according to Hume, have the advantage of alerting individuals to the inherent deficiency in their understanding and thereby curb natural dogmatism and intolerance of antagonists. Such mitigated scepticism might serve to demonstrate that human understanding is minute in comparison with the enormous perplexity and confusion which Hume saw as being inherent in human nature. In Hume's view the humility which such limited scepticism would produce would be a characteristic of the just reasoner. In this sense the quotation under discussion identifies what must be viewed as a benefit of scepticism if one accepts that tolerance of opposing viewpoints is an essential prerequisite for constructive discussion. Any philosophical standpoint which denies the immutability of particular values is stultifying. Theorists such as Bentham saw claims to 'absolute' validity as merely a cloak to lend credence to regimes which preserved an unjust status quo. The first step towards setting such absolute values aside, therefore, must result from a sceptical standpoint which questions the claims to validity of a particular order.

In conclusion, therefore, it must be said that by refusing to accept without question the validity of the existing legal order the Critical Legal Studies movement, like Scandinavian Realism, provides a useful starting point for further discussion. It must be said, however, that a limited form of scepticism might fairly be said to be the starting point of every new legal theory, because the basis for offering a replacement for existing legal theory is a criticism of the existing accepted theory. The essential question, therefore, is whether scepticism alone is enough. For my part I see sense in the views put forward by Hume and discussed above, namely that scepticism alone is neither a useful nor a realistic basis for practical discussion since it essentially denies the validity of any of the fruits of discussion. However, as the Critical Legal Studies movement progresses it may develop from the basically sceptical standpoint into a practical and workable theory. The beginnings of this more constructive approach can be seen in Unger's work which acknowledges the necessity for substantive elements such as the broad rights mentioned above.

2) How challenging to jurisprudence are the perspectives of the Critical Legal Studies movement?

University of London LLB Examination
(for External Students) Jurisprudence and Legal Theory June 1993 Q10(a)

General Comment

Candidates are either too dismissive of CLS or are too accepting; make up your own mind about it. A good way is to meet a committed CLS teacher. You will find him – if he is good – exciting and innovative (Duncan Kennedy is a very good example), with a refreshing 'anti-solicitor with 2.4 children and mortgage' attitude. He will make you re-think your ideas about accepting the legal system as it is. But you may also find, after a while, that there is not much of deep intellectual interest in what he says; that in the heat the light becomes dim! There is a lot that is exciting and a lot that just does not stand up to rational analysis. Don't be taken in by nonsense talk; that, for example, 'rational' talk is only a way of 'covering up' 'real' 'contradictions'; 'rational', as you know, does not mean that. In other words, keep a clear head: see the good, see the bad.

Skeleton Solution

History and background – methodology – politics of CLS theorists – Liberalism's contingency and contradiction – philosophical background – positive political programme (Unger) – self-undermining – prioritising of contradictions – contingent nature of human existence – conclusion that not clear what political programme the CLS movement would support.

Suggested Solution

Since the Critical Legal Studies movement is relatively new, its value as a theory of law is still being assessed, but despite its continual development it has given much of interest to

6 Critical Legal Studies

thinking about the law. Indeed, like other sceptical theories it may undermine the coherent world of law which legal academics and practitioners tend to portray.

The Critical Legal Studies movement is a body of like-minded thinkers who claim to attack the virtues that they say are proclaimed by the liberal legal system. This attack is mounted from different points; contract (Unger); property laws (Hay); the Rule of Law (Kennedy and Horwitz); Race and Sex Discrimination Law (Freeman); Employment and the Criminal Law (Kelman) to name but a few of the areas of the application of so-called 'critical' theory.

A word can be added here about the idea of a 'critical' theory. The idea is often bandied about rather proudly, as though the *Critical* Legal Studies scholars were the first to look at the law critically, while clearly the positivists, led by Bentham most famously and effectively, not only built the intellectual framework for that idea, but also carried it out with plans for legislative reform. No, the idea of a 'critical' theory is that it aims to criticise the idea of 'theorising about the law in the first place'; hence, CLS's understanding of positivism is based on a mistake about what positivism was trying to do. Positivism is not trying to make the law *appear* better than it 'really' is; it is attempting to build a way into the idea of law of criticism from *outside* the law. This is a point which the CLS movement has utterly ignored.

The common themes that run through their work is a view that law and legal reasoning is an illusion (although practically all of them teach in law schools!). They also claim that the practice and reasoning of law is riddled with contradiction. They claim, like Dworkin, that there is no distinction between law and politics although Dworkin, for them, is dangerously liberal. For them, values (both social and legal) come from within the community. Therefore, they say, although very unclearly, that truth and justice are mere social constructs, and as a consequence, law is tainted with a false consciousness which pervades the practitioners, law schools and the other institutions which organise the law.

A second area of value is the methodology that is applied by CLS theorists. Much of this represents a kind of mixture of French 'deconstruction', sceptical jurisprudential theories (especially Marxism and Realism) with the language philosophy of Derrida and the social theory of Habermas, Marcuse and Mannheim. But this shouldn't be taken too seriously. The message is: explore *all* the assumptions that you make and never take any as God-given (but this message has been around since Aristotle; Plato made a fine art of it). The reference to these philosophers really provides a modern basis of this 'assumption seeking' and is called by the CLS 'trashing,' or 'deviation,' to use Unger's term. Note this: it is interesting that the CLS, despite its dismissal of objectivity and truth (inherent in its sceptical claims), *claims that its own claims are true.*

CLS, as its name suggests, is critical. It criticises a liberal view of law as presented by American law schools and American legal practice. It castigates such liberal notions as the rule of law, equality before the law, justice, fairness; in short the values that some might claim underpin the legal system. Like Realism, this attack seeks to liberate the individual's mind in order to expose what is really going on. However, the CLS attack is more radical, more sceptical and more far reaching.

Kelman has denied that CLS is merely Neo-Realism; he asserts that a new departure from the Realist movement is a belief that the indeterminacy of legal rules and argument cannot be overcome, that it is an inherent part of the system. CLS also insists that the liberal legal system is 'committed' to indeterminacy.

Few CLS theorists have formulated positive programmes to fill in the gap left by the deconstruction of liberal law. An exception is Unger who claims that he is seeking to restructure law without a structure so that society can evolve a 'super-liberalism' which will truly reflect the traditional aspirations of liberalism (and so he is presumably a liberal who would join with Rawls, Dworkin and so on, although he rather notably does not). He sees liberalism as consisting of the principles of individual freedom, equal claims to social wealth, interactions between people based on love and mutual respect (how, for goodness' sake, it this general programme different from Dworkin's political philosophy?). He claims that we should return to a tribalist form of society which will curb industrial interests in favour of the communitarian interests of mutual co-operation.

Unger raises more questions than he answers. His programme is subject to the self-undermining that will affect any CLS theorist who puts forward any positive proposals. Unger's programme is, of course, susceptible to criticisms of indeterminacy, arbitrariness and contradiction itself.

The value of CLS thought is reduced by the inability thus far to be a programme for action. However, there is much which is of interest in the CLS movement; its energetic urge to modern jurisprudence to examine its assumptions and the assumptions upon which our modern legal system is based must be healthy.

3) Using the perspectives of the CLS movement, what changes to the content and style of legal education would you suggest?

University of London LLB Examination
(for External Students) Jurisprudence and Legal Theory June 1993 Q10(b)

General Comment

The general gist to this type of answer should be gleaned from the answer to part (a) above. If the candidate is not 'fired up' with CLS, he or she is probably best advised to shy away from this question. But it is a question that could be done extremely well – with relatively little knowledge. Be anarchic! Think of your own law course! Is it satisfactory, in the light of what you think is good about the CLS movement (it is doubtful that you could say anything with any verve or interest to an examiner if there was *nothing* about the CLS movement of which you approved). What about the assumptions that your lecturer makes? Does he smugly assume that Commercial law is the be-all and end-all? That nothing is worth while unless it can be reduced to a bill of sale, or a statement which reduces to rights over chattels? Does he ever say anything critical about, not just particular laws (because positivists would advocate *that*, and CLS does not like positivism), but about the whole process of law altogether? If you disapprove here, you probably have a CLS bent. Use it; you will write something good. Don't be cowered by the view that there is a 'right way' to answer the question. The suggested answer below attempts to be as creative as possible.

Skeleton Solution

Origins of the CLS movement – what CLS says that is of importance – English law schools as compared to the US – 'black-letter law' – case-method – approaching a case 'from a critical perspective' – 'trashing' – overall conclusion that there are advantages seeing the law from a new perspective but with rider that the 'trashing' approach is fundamentally nihilistic if it has nothing to offer in its place.

6 *Critical Legal Studies*

Suggested Solution

The CLS movement began in the US after the great expansion of the universities with the coming of the post-war 'baby boom'. It was also a time of increased economic prosperity, although the stability that this encouraged amongst the middle classes was being eroded through the rise of demands for civil rights by black people and the escalation of the Vietnam war. Young people in universities had a degree of both economic power and a political say for the first time in generations, if ever. It was fun to be in universities then, since there was a strong consensus, fuelled by the economic stability, that studying at a university was an achievement in itself, entirely unrelated to the commercial prospects of the degree. This was admirable but would be regarded as an idea wasteful of resources by many in England and the US today.

CLS grew out of this climate and, in short, brought the attitude of 'independent, critical study' to the law schools. Why did this occur in the US and not in the UK until later (although it is not clear that CLS has ever really caught on here)? One of the reasons is the vast difference between US and UK law schools; the great Realist movement in the US law schools of the late 19th century and beyond has already led to a more questioning approach. Endowed with more funds, too, the law schools could bring about reforms that have barely begun yet to reach the UK; the case law method, properly paid teachers, law taught primarily as a postgraduate degree, properly equipped libraries and so on; the differences are well known.

These factors combined to produce, to mention only the more famous, law teachers of the calibre of Roberto Unger and Duncan Kennedy. They were (and are) Sixties-appointed law professors who 'took on' the profession of law teaching. You can see what they were getting at; there is such an animal, as we all know, called the 'black-letter lawyer'; we should focus on him (he is predominantly male) because he is *precisely* the target of the CLS movement. In fact, if you see the CLS movement as having its origins in this attack, a number of seemingly mysterious points about CLS are solved. It explains its prevalence in law schools (practitioners have nothing to do with it), its being a 'movement' as opposed to a distinctive philosophy and, above all, it explains why it is that there seems to be little depth in many of the things that CLS people claim. Indeed, the idea of Critical Legal Scholarship appears odd; there is nothing especially *scholarly* about what they do.

The 'black letter lawyer' has wreaked havoc on the minds of many lawyers, those who expect that there is an 'answer' somewhere, if only they could find the particular word or phrase buried in a casebook somewhere. You know the kind of lawyer; he is the one who craves the certainty of the law (and is probably must better suited to property law and the Chancery chambers than anywhere else) and *never questions the whole set-up – the legal system – that puts him into the position that he is in*. One reason for the creation of this kind of lawyer is the teaching; the teacher who has a set of notes, slightly updated from year to year and who reads these notes out to a large group of students who dutifully write them down and regurgitate them in an examination. What else would these students – future lawyers – know about the law?

Here is where CLS is exciting (and it is exciting to hear Duncan Kennedy speak). Stop being a 'fusty dusty' fogey of 'a law student'; stop thinking about your 'career-as-a-lawyer'; you are a person who can engage critically, Sixties style. Take that old fogey of a teacher and *trash everything he says*. (There is a nasty side to CLS!). For example, take the case of *Carlill* v *Carbolic Smoke Ball Co* (1893). Don't see it as a case about 'the meaning of offer and acceptance in the law' but as a case where commercial interests in advertising are brought to bear on a woman who has been duped by false claims about a smoke ball; see it in the context of times when advertising was even less controlled than now; see how an unsympathetic analytical approach to that case is a doctrinal one liner of: 'advertisements which are 'mere puffs' are not offers that can ripen into binding contracts'.

Of course, good law teachers always pointed these sorts of facts about cases out to their students (and intelligent students always made note of them); and any barrister of decent intellect is always fully aware of this sort of factor (there are a surprising number of critical barristers about; not enough, but nevertheless a significant number). So we shouldn't be too impressed by grand CLS claims about the degree of 'false consciousness' there is about the legal profession. We ought not, either, to be swayed by claims that the CLS makes about liberalism; their claim that the liberalism inherent in the law is a false liberalism because it masks conflict and contradiction is largely unsupported and, in any case, of not much interest to pursue because the CLS thinkers appear to embrace well-known forms of liberalism: justice *for all*; *freedom* and so on (and their claim that 'modern liberalism' is 'atomistic' and 'selfish' is plainly incorrect, as any reasonable reading of Rawls, Dworkin, Nagel, Scanlon, etc, etc, will reveal).

But in the light of what has been said, reforms to my law school would be listed as follows: the formal 'two lectures followed by tutorial' pattern of teaching would cease and students would be forced to engage in discussion; law would not be taught as a set of rules, but instead as an interlocking set of *open* (ie anything *prima facie* goes) principles of the legal system and particular rules. These principles would themselves be open to continual questioning (for example, the principles of democracy). Here, incidentally, is what Dworkin refers to as being 'an internal global sceptic'. (Dworkin's work, despite the dislike CLS 'officially' has for him, has laid the intellectual groundwork for everything CLS says; but they don't seem to understand that – see Guest, *Ronald Dworkin*, 2nd ed, Chapter 6.)

There would also be studied, within the law school, with the aim of increasing the critical perspectives of the law student, subjects such as the sociology of law-making and the effects of laws, political philosophy, the history of laws (eg such as prohibition, the abolition of the caste system, the growth of constitutional independence in colonial states) and the laws of other systems (comparative law). But the depths of 'scholarship' to which the CLS aspires, in French deconstructionism and waffly pseudo-philosophers, such as Derrida, would simply be dropped; it is worse than useless as it encourages laziness. The obscurity surrounding Derrida and his followers allows support to be drawn for almost any proposition.

This is the best that can be taken from CLS; if it is just to be 'critical' then it provides no vision and no law student can be educated to be *just* cynical; indeed, one of the reasons that CLS manages to get a grip is (and this is a good thing) that it can feed off the natural cynicism of youth, and that, interestingly enough, was one of the causes of its rise: the (in large part, healthy) cynicism of the Sixties generation.

7 Feminist Jurisprudence

7.1 Introduction
7.2 Key points
7.3 Analysis of question styles
7.4 Questions

7.1 Introduction

Feminist jurisprudence is a relatively new topic and it has its most obvious roots in Marxist theories of law and in the Critical Legal Studies movement. It often refers to itself as 'critiquing' male values inherent in the legal system and so it is natural that its adherents are not accepting of what passes for orthodox legal doctrine. The secret to answering questions is to try to adopt a committed role in which you imagine the existing legal structures (or the 'gendered justice system' or 'gendered discourse') from the point of view of the oppressed. Like the CLS movement, there are a wide range of writers to write about and so answers have wide scope. Nevertheless, it is vital to inject your own views about the position of women within legal systems.

7.2 Key points

a) The 'critical' position to be adopted, as for Marxism and CLS. It is important to specify why this position differs from more orthodox positions.

b) The description of the theories of law and justice held by at least two feminist jurists.

c) The attitude adopted by the student towards feminine 'justice' in general, linking that attitude to reading.

7.3 Analysis of question styles

Feminist legal theory is burgeoning but rarely are questions asked which call for a mere description of what authors have said. It is usually a question about the distinctive force of the feminist theoretical position as both the following questions are.

7.4 Questions

1) 'Since all previous jurisprudence has been written by men who have laid down the rules of what is acceptable to write, the idea of a feminist jurisprudence is a contradiction in terms.'

   Do you agree?

   University of London LLB Examination
   (for External Students) Jurisprudence and Legal Theory June 1995 Q6

Jurisprudence: The Philosophy of Law

General Comment

This type of question has started to appear regularly because the concept of feminist jurisprudence is now recognised by academics as a philosophy in its own right. The range of reference materials covering the subject has increased and students must use the most contemporary sources. Whether there is, or is not, a feminist jurisprudence will continue to be debated for years to come. However, the student should not be afraid to express a view either way and justify such a view.

Skeleton Solution

Introduction: broad concepts and historical development – the women's movement and female law students – equal treatment – conclusion: the opening of the debate.

Suggested Solution

If the ideal of a feminist jurisprudence is 'a contradiction in terms' as the question suggests, then a great deal of paper and printers' ink has been expended needlessly in the last 10 years upon what some commentators apparently dismiss as a 'contradiction'.

Those who support the idea of a feminist jurisprudence as a 'contradiction in terms' ignore reality and jurisprudence itself, which cannot but reflect the social context from which it springs. As the twentieth century draws to a close, feminist jurisprudence has evolved as a branch of jurisprudential theory which deals with the reality of women's emergence as active participants in the intellectual, commercial and professional life, primarily of western societies, namely the United States, Canada, Australia and, latterly and belatedly, the United Kingdom.

Not unexpectedly, the feminist jurisprudential mainstream has migrated across the Atlantic in much the same way as the women's movement itself. The mere fact of a 'feminist jurisprudence' reflects a vast new paradigm shift, or new movement, which re-examines and challenges current jurisprudential orthodoxy, which undeniably has been sustained by men. Nonetheless, to say unequivocally that men have somehow 'laid down rules of what is acceptable to write' in jurisprudence is a remarkable irrelevancy.

It is submitted that a body of 'rules of what is acceptable to write' does not exist and that therefore the statement is a nonsense. The statement is, however, interesting in that it is perhaps an indicator of the uncertainty, intellectual confusion, even overt hostility and derision which feminist jurisprudence has attracted until very recently. Nonetheless, feminist jurisprudence has successfully pushed back horizons and extended jurisprudential perspectives. As Katherine Bartlett argues in *Feminist Legal Methods* (1990), 'knowledge is located in a social context and reflects different experiences'. The key therefore lies 'in the effort to extend one's limited perspective'.

It could be extrapolated from this that, prior to the emergence of feminist jurisprudence, jurisprudential perspectives were indeed limited by experiences that were exclusively male. It is doubtful though that such an exclusive male perspective will continue to prevail in jurisprudence into the next century.

Contemporary feminist literature is the products of the women's movement of the late 1960s and early 1970s. Its most vociferous and influential exponent, Simone de Beauvoir (with her seminal work, *The Second Sex* (1949)), was followed by other feminist writers including Betty Friedan, Kate Millet and Germaine Greer.

7 Feminist Jurisprudence

The women's movement coincided with, or perhaps led to, a dramatic increase in the number of women students in law schools in the 1960s and 1970s, particularly in North America – a trend which has been mirrored in the United Kingdom. Interestingly the Council of Legal Education in 1996 turned out more women than men who qualified for the Bar. It is now perhaps safer than ever to claim that far from remaining a curiosity, feminist jurisprudence will almost inevitably take its place as part of the jurisprudential mainstream. (How likely is it that an examination question in the year 2020 will even suggest that feminist jurisprudence is 'a contradiction in terms'?) Twining's recent Hamlyn lecture entitled *Blackstone's Tower: The English Law School* (1994) examines the increase in the number of female law students with no definite conclusion as to its effect on the profession.

Despite the dismissive comment which it still attracts, feminist jurisprudence has become both a cause and a result of consciousness-raising in areas of law that were hitherto neglected, including sex discrimination, domestic violence and sexual harassment, issues which have been brought to the fore largely by the increased number of female law students. When such students qualify as practising lawyers, the litigation they undertake on behalf of women does, it is suggested, influence both scholarship and opinion within jurisprudence.

Feminist jurisprudence existed de facto at least a decade before it was labelled as such. The term 'feminist jurisprudence' was not identified, nor recognised as a separate (or separated) branch of jurisprudence, until legal theorists like Ann Scales first used the term at Harvard in 1978, followed by Catharine MacKinnon in 1983. Both regarded feminist legal theory as a belief that 'society and necessarily legal order is patriarchal'. Feminist jurisprudence, therefore, seeks to undermine and eliminate such patriarchy.

Subsequently, feminists have carried on the enquiry, focussing on the politics of law and on 'the law's role', as Wishik says (1985) 'in perpetuating patriarchal hegemony'. The goal of such analysis is change, or 'revision', as Adrienne Rich puts it in *On Lies, Secrets and Silence: Selected Prose 1966–1978* (1986). Clare Dalton, however, seeks to challenge the structure of legal thought as, in Lloyd's words, 'contingent and in some culturally specific sense "male".' Here, the need for radical rather than ameliorative change is implied, particularly as the assertion under discussion that 'all previous jurisprudence has been written by men' is unarguable (if 'previous' means prior to 1980).

Although it may be a matter of dispute that 'men ... have laid down rules of what is acceptable to write', Scales' criticism ('The Emergence of Feminist Jurisprudence: An Essay' (1986) 95 Yale LJ 1373) that, for example, the US Supreme Court's equal protection approach to sex discrimination 'makes maleness the norm of what is human' is less easily argued. 'It is necessary', she says, 'to reconstruct the legal system which 'usurps women's language in order to further define the world in the male image'. 'Domination', Scales says, 'is the injustice of sexism, not irrationality'. Scales, as Lloyd explains (see *Introduction to Jurisprudence* (6th ed 1994)), looks to a feminist jurisprudence which will focus on domination, disadvantage and disempowerment, rather than one which merely examines differences between men and women.

In a 1985 article ((1984–85) 13 NYU Rev L and Soc Change 325), the liberal feminist Wendy Williams dismissed the concept of 'equal treatment' as being beneficial only to women who 'meet male norms' rather than those who engage in female activities such as childbearing or child rearing. Employment practices which continue to place women at a disadvantage if they pursue a maternal role would only tend to confirm Williams' observation. In *Feminism Unmodified* (1987), MacKinnon pursued much the same argument, asserting that feminists should concentrate on identifying dominance, in which social inequalities arise as the result of the subordination of women by men.

These views, however, have come in for criticism. All women cannot be said to be subordinate to all men. Therefore, what is seen as an overemphasis on male dominance is perhaps misleading. Post-modern feminism obliquely attempts to deal with this objection, denying that there is a single theory of equality that will benefit all women. Equality itself is seen as a product of patriarchy and therefore in need of feminist reconstruction. Post-modern feminism thus contributes usefully to the feminist jurisprudential debate as one of the four schools of feminist theory identified by Cain who classifies them as *post-modern*, *liberal*, *radical* and *cultural* feminism.

The liberal feminist, according to Cain, sees equality as *equality of opportunity*. Radical feminists such as Christine Littleton and MacKinnon vociferously support alternative measures to challenge such equality, while cultural feminists like Carol Gilligan and Robin West view male/female differences in a more positive light, advocating change which supports the underlying values of this difference, like 'caring' and 'connectedness'.

Cultural feminism probably lies at the heart of Lucinda Finley's examination of the relationship between language, power and the law. Even less conspicuous areas of law like tort reveal (in Lloyd's summary of Finley's views) 'the law's cognition of women refracted through the male eye, rather than through women's experiences and definitions' and cites as just one example, the traditional prejudice of assessing damages for non-economic loss, pain, suffering and nervous shock as 'marginal and expendable' (see Lloyd and Freeman, *Introduction to Jurisprudence* (6th ed 1994)).

Matters like these, of course, occupy the personal sphere. Feminist jurisprudence nevertheless insists that they be taken no less seriously than so-called 'public' questions, involving all people, which in the past have been the major concern of jurisprudence – once an exclusively male preserve, but no longer.

However, there can be no limits within jurisprudence on the discussion of legal issues, whether or not such issues relate only to feminist concerns. It is somewhat surprising for Lloyd to ask why certain issues like female genital mutilation, population control, mail order bride practices, and so on are 'outside the terrain of international human rights law' when, clearly, they are not.

In fact, since the most recent commentaries on feminist jurisprudence were published from 1994 onwards, events and subsequent legislation have moved forward dramatically, notably in the tabling of legislation which allows for the prosecution of sexual offences against children by British citizens, even when these offences have been committed abroad. Female genital mutilation is, of course, illegal in western countries. That it is a traditional practice in many other areas of the world is a matter for feminist jurisprudence to address, now and in the future, together with other issues which can be categorised as 'human rights' rather than specifically 'feminist' concerns.

Far from being 'a contradiction in terms', feminist jurisprudence has opened up useful areas of debate from which to re-examine and reassess a wide range of issues, issues which, while not necessarily ignored by jurisprudence 'because all previous jurisprudence has been written by men', have been undeniably neglected. It is in redressing this neglect that feminist jurisprudence has revealed its value.

2) 'The strength of the feminist work so far lies in the critique that has been mounted of the foundations of traditional jurisprudence rather than any suggestions for radical improvement.'

Do you agree?

University of London LLB Examination
(for External Students) Jurisprudence and Legal Theory June 1994 Q6

General Comment

This question is a relatively modern innovation for the jurisprudence course. The subject matter of women's rights is of growing importance, being seen as a rights movement which parallels to some degree the rise of natural law. The answer requires examples from recent commentators who have compared natural rights and women's rights on the basis of principle.

Case law on marital rape and the defence of provocation continue to suggest a building on the foundation of traditional jurisprudence rather than issues of radical improvement, though individual judgments, such as the decision in *R* v *R* (1992), point a clear path towards equal rights rather than separate rights.

Skeleton Solution

Natural rights and women's rights – equal rights versus separate rights – sexual discrimination: rape and the defence of provocation – conclusion: wives with equal rights.

Suggested Solution

While many primitive societies are essentially matriarchal, considerable evidence has suggested that over the centuries women have been treated in an unequal fashion when compared with men. J S Mill questioned the traditional position of women in society in his work *On the Subjection of Women in the Nineteenth Century*. The inferior position of women, where for example in the old marriage service they were obliged to *obey* their husbands, and the rule that a woman's property belonged to her husband, did not begin to change significantly until the Married Women's Property Act 1882 came into force.

By the beginning of the twentieth century, writers such as Engels (*The Origins of the Family*) and Safiotti (*Women and Class Society*) began to influence the historic view of the male capitalist being perceived as the villain, and women and workers being oppressed and exploited. The rise of the suffragette movement and the opening of career and educational opportunities enabled women's rights to appear on the political agenda for the first time.

Dworkin's view (in *Taking Rights Seriously*) establishes that there are principles which underlie laws which the courts will apply and include rights which should be respected because of race, sex, language or religion. He cites the 14th Amendment of the Constitution of the United States to justify his view, stating that all people should be treated as equals.

Around the same time, Rawls (in *A Theory of Justice*) suggested that there are principles of equal rights which go to the heart of equal basic liberties for all. His view was that social and economic inequalities should be arranged in order that they are both of greatest benefit to the least advantaged and 'attached to offices open to all in conditions of fair equality of opportunity'.

Nearly 20 years later, the House of Lords reviewed several appeals dealing specifically with male and female rights. In *C* v *S* (1987), it held that, concerning the request for an abortion, a father has no rights. Commentators have criticised the protection of such rights towards a female because they involve the denial of rights to a father or the unborn male or female child.

The House of Lords in *R* v *R* (1992), held that a husband may be convicted of rape against his wife. The justification is that today's marriages are fundamentally different from those of previous generations. In this context, Dworkin and others acknowledge the principles which indicate that a law may change as society develops, with the principle of equal concern and respect requiring free and continuing consent to exist within marriage, so that the relationship is one between equals.

Iris Young (in *Justice and the Politics of Difference*) postulates a modern thesis for feminist jurisprudence. She observes that the law's insistence on treating like cases alike creates the pretence that important differences in people, such as black, disadvantaged women, or white advantaged men, are not real differences because such laws merely reinforce the unjustified differences in the way in which people are treated.

If morality is to be part of the law (as natural law suggests), there will be differences between men and women which are morally relevant in defences raised such as provocation. In *DPP* v *Camplin* (1978), the action of a 'reasonable man' requirement was interpreted to include not only a man but a boy who was both retarded and sensitive. However, legal argument today is not so thinly applied as to disallow the extension of the 'reasonable man' test to include (for provocation defences concerning domestic abuse) a 'reasonable women' requirement.

The mainstream attitude on women's rights today remains in favour of equal rights based on a principle of equal concern and respect. Whilst Phillips (in *Feminism and Equality*) has adopted the widely accepted view that gender will not preclude equal treatment of either sex, positive discrimination in favour of women is also discussed within the foundations of traditional jurisprudence. Feminist writers such as Germaine Greer and Simone de Beauvoir have achieved, with others, many legislative changes (Sex Discrimination Acts, Equal Opportunities Act) which may be termed a 'radical improvement' for women.

It is perhaps important to note also the work of Alice Walker. She takes a view akin to certain civil rights activists who argue a more radical stance. Walker advocates that women are not the same and that separation is the solution if they so choose. It is submitted that true radical improvement would consist of separate societies, achieved by ending economic, social, domestic and legal dependence, though, to many people, the principle of visiting one another solely to reproduce is questionable.

8 The Anthropological School

8.1 Introduction
8.2 Key points
8.3 Analysis of question styles
8.4 Question

8.1 Introduction

This topic has obvious links with the sociology of law (Chapter 7) and the historical school (Chapter 5) and the student would be sensible to revise these topics in conjunction with each other. Clearly, revision of the anthropological school will have to be selective, since the subject encompasses many writers and viewpoints. The most helpful starting point for the student is to consider whether the study of 'law' in primitive societies throws any light on our own concept(s) of law and the legal system. Such an approach can be combined with a general overview of anthropologists and detailed reference to a few interesting contributors – for instance, Malinowski's study of the Trobriand Islanders.

8.2 Key points

a) *An overview*
   i) Law is merely a small part of anthropology as a whole.
   ii) Anthropology involves looking at other societies and then attempting to use the information gained to enhance our understanding of our own society.

b) *Criticisms*
   i) It is affected by ethnocentrism – in simple terms, studying others by reference to concepts developed in our own society. This has a distorting effect.
   ii) 'Law-centred' studies may be contrasted with wider studies of dispute processes. The latter are more successful at avoiding the distortion produced by ethnocentricity.

c) *The value of anthropology for the law student*
   See the suggested solutions below.

8.3 Analysis of question styles

Anthropology has never been a particularly popular examination topic. When it does appear, the question usually calls for some evaluation of anthropology in the context of modern legal study. A student who has considered this issue, and is prepared to come to a conclusion, will be well placed to answer a question of this nature.

8.4 Question

This is typical of questions posed about anthropology. The student must adopt an evaluative approach.

Jurisprudence: The Philosophy of Law

'Anthropology has little to offer the student of jurisprudence'. Do you agree?

University of London LLB Examination
(for External Students) Jurisprudence and Legal Theory June 1987 Q7

Skeleton Solution

Anthropology – legitimacy of cross cultural comparisons – ethnocentricity – different studies – usefulness – problem of language – micro level understanding – relevance of conclusions of anthropological studies – development of heuristic devices – conclusion – anthropological study of our own society.

Suggested Solution

I would answer this question through an assessment of the legitimacy of cross cultural comparisons and the adequacy of drawing conclusions for our own society from anthropological studies. It is on this premise that I will assess whether anthropological studies do have much to offer the student of jurisprudence.

At a funeral oration for the Athenians who died fighting for Athens, Pericles said, 'Our institutions are not borrowed from those around us; they are our own, the creation of Athenian Statesmen; an example and not a copy'. I would take the view that that quotation has a lot to offer on the legitimacy of the application of 'lessons' from anthropological studies to our own society. I take Pericles to say that a conclusion about cheese will not assist in an understanding of wine. I will however indicate those areas where it is my view that anthropological studies may contribute to a greater understanding of our own society, including the legal system.

One of the main difficulties with anthropological studies is the tendency that they have towards ethnocentricity. This involves the study of others through concepts developed by ourselves. On the other hand it could be said that on the micro level at least phenomena in our society also occur in primitive societies. In primitive society the study of these common phenomena may be more simple since they are less likely to be complicated and obscured by the complexities of an advanced industrial society. This view looks to the study of primitive society as if it were a laboratory for the understanding of our own society. The validity of this approach in itself is highly suspect.

Even if the 'laboratory thesis' is accepted, then the scientist/anthropologist will still have to develop a mechanism for the avoidance of the tendency towards ethnocentrism by which the scientist will largely invalidate his study as he takes law out of its context and arranges his observations according to preconceived yet inapplicable notions. Malinowski attempted to get around this defect in his study *Crime and Custom in Savage Society*. Perhaps the only effective way is through the avoidance of translation! In his study of the Barotse of Northern Rhodesia (now Zambia), Max Gluckman came across the notion of 'the reasonable man' which he observed was employed in the same way as in our courts to arrive at an objective test by which to assess the conduct of the defendant. Bohannon isolated the problem as being one of language, hence the point above about translations. He claimed that Gluckman analysed the Barotse according to the doctrines of the common law which is clearly not applicable to them. Bohannan insists that if there is to be any potential for anthropology to truly understand any tribe then it must use tribal terms and not Western concepts. The solution proposed of developing a computer language is unsatisfactory as it would have to be programmed by someone who has his own notions and certainly more importantly, it would be read and understood by comparison with already existing notions in the original language of the reader.

8 The Anthropological School

I do not think that our advanced industrial society developed tribunals because Laura Nader found that the Zapatec Indians had developed something performing a similar task to what she identified as a tribunal, anymore than I would think that becase the Eskimos resolve disputes through 'song contests', by which the person who uses the best insults wins, would be an appropriate method of dispute resolution in our society. Yet it clearly is adequate for their society.

Some of the approaches adopted in the anthropological studies may be of use in an understanding of our own society but these could well have developed without engaging in anthropological studies.

Although Durkheim tried to make a distinction between mechanical solidarity and organic solidarity-type societies, it has to be observed that Western industrial society has both restitutive and repressive laws and that both of these are expanding. That fact does not necessarily defeat the usefulness of Durkheim's model in helping us to understand the difference between the two types of laws, but the conclusion drawn by Durkheim has been proved wrong.

If the models used in the anthropological method from primitive societies are applied to advanced industrial society then that exercise may well enhance our understanding of our own society through sociological inquiry. It is my view though that the conclusions reached in the anthropological studies are inapplicable to our own society so far as the institution of law is concerned and I take it that that must be the prime area of interest of the jurisprudence student. In *The Law of Primitive Man* Hoebel said that 'the more civilised man becomes, the greater men's need for law – law is but a response to social needs.' He thought that the institution of law was a necessity. He observed that without a sense of community there is no law and that without law there cannot for long be a community. For example, the Andaman Islanders (in the Indian Ocean) have no suprafamilial authority. Social control is exercised by and within the family. However, in our society the individual is independent of both the family and the clan. Such a mechanism as is applied in the Andaman Islands would be wholly inadequate here.

It ought to be said that anthropological studies can show us that conclusions that are relevant to primitive societies are not relevant in our advanced society. Felsteiner's study, *Influences of Social Organisation and Dispute Processing* shows that the form of dispute settlement flows from the social organisation. He distinguished between TCRS ('technologically complex, rich society') and TSPS ('technologically simple, poor society') and observes that cross comparisons between these are of very limited value. Perhaps von Savigny had a point in this regard when he noted that each society develops the law it needs and that, indeed, law is a reflection of the particularities of each society (the *'Volksgeist'*).

Anthropological studies do have certain advantages, not least of which is that it provides us with an understanding of law in societies other than our own. Certain heuristic devices have also been developed through anthropological studies and these may well be useful models for a study of law in our own society. At the micro level anthropological studies have pointed to the working of some aspects of our own society. Gluckman's model of testing not only cases – which undergo a transformation when taken to court – but also looking at rules and praxis (the way people act under the law) does not however explain the purpose of law but is useful as far as it goes.

Rather than focus considerable attention and resources on anthropological studies, it would be preferable to pay greater attention to sociological inquiry into our own society from the point of view of the needs of the jurisprudence student. In particular one would look for an inquiry into the nature of our state; the form and function of law; the source, distribution and location of power in our society and the study of conflict in our society. Admittedly, these are rather parochial issues; however they represent a view that although lessons can be drawn from primitive societies such as that coercive law is not always the best dispute resolution technique, these lessons are already drawn and these anthropological studies merely cloak a conclusion in a robe of authority. Our society had already 'invented' tribunals long before Nader told us that they were a good way of resolving certain disputes.

I would conclude that the only really interesting anthropological study would be one carried out by a person from another type of society. His findings would tell us more about our own society than any anthropological study we would carry out on his society. I am therefore drawn to a conclusion that the insights to be gained from anthropological studies are of little advantage to the student of jurisprudence who is interested in studying the law in his own society.

9 Sociological Jurisprudence and the Sociology of Law

9.1 Introduction
9.2 Key points
9.3 Analysis of question styles
9.4 Questions

8.1 Introduction

Although a distinction is often claimed to exist between 'sociological jurisprudence' and 'the sociology of law', the student should revise the two subjects in conjunction. There are obviously significant overlaps – both see law as essentially a social phenomenon and both employ the techniques of social sciences – so that it is convenient to deal with them together.

9.2 Key points

a) *Sociological jurisprudence*

   i) Roscoe Pound was predominantly concerned with law reform, and with law as a social fact. He developed a concept of 'social engineering' whereby the law operates to ensure social cohesion by balancing conflicting interests. Where such interests cannot be accommodated Pound develops the concept of jural postulates. For him these are the means of testing new interests; they are the presuppositions of legal reasoning.

   ii) It will be helpful for the student to have a brief knowledge of the salient points of other sociological jurisprudential writers, eg Ehrlich, Ihering.

b) *The sociology of law*

   i) Max Weber sought to explain the relationship of law and capitalism. He can perhaps best be understood as offering a response to the Marxist attack on capitalism. In particular he criticised Marx for his (as Weber saw it) sole reliance on economic factors as the determinant of the nature of society. Weber also offered a typology of law: legal systems are characterised by either rationality or irrationality. He believed that formal rational legal systems were unique to developed Western society.

   ii) Emile Durkheim also attributed much importance to law in developing an understanding of society in general. For Durkheim there were two types of social cohesion: 'mechanical solidarity' (where there is no division of labour) and 'organic solidarity' (where there is much specialisation of labour). The latter form of cohesion will exist in more advanced societies. The type of law prevalent in society indicates the type of 'solidarity' existing. Law is largely penal where there is mechanical solidarity but more restitutive where there is organic solidarity.

9.3 Analysis of question styles

This is a popular examination topic which can appear in many guises, from a relatively straightforward critique of one particular theorist to a much broader discussion and comparison of theories. Sociology is also used on occasion as a basis for a wider jurisprudential debate (see question Type 3).

9.4 Questions

TYPE ONE

The following questions call for critical analysis of individual theorists. The student may wish to display a knowledge of theorists not named in the question to back up their criticisms.

1) Evaluate critically the following statement concerning Roscoe Pound. 'For him, jurisprudence is not so much a social science but a technology' (Charles Conway).

University of London LLB Examination
(for External Students) Jurisprudence and Legal Theory June 1984 Q8

Skeleton Solution

Sociological jurisprudence – lacked complete theory of law in sociological context – social science techniques – American realists – socio-legal surveys – technology – social engineering – balancing of interests – jural postulates.

Suggested Solution

I think the quotation makes a valid point in an overstated way. It is not true to say that Pound did not see jurisprudence as a social science, but it is true to say that his was a 'sociological jurisprudence' viewpoint which lacked a completed theory of law in its sociological context. Rather, he poses the role of law in society and sees how it plays the role thus ascribed to it: and to do this he uses an engineering analogy. This practically explains why it is accurate to say that he considered jurisprudence to be a 'technology'. It cannot be denied that Pound was intending to apply social science techniques and thought to jurisprudence. His influence as a leader in this field was great. He sets out a 'programme' for the sociological study of law, including the study of the actual social effects of legal institutions, precepts and doctrines; the study of the means of making legal precepts effective in action and the study of juridical method. This emphasis on studying what actually happens was similar to that found with the American realist writers who wrote after Pound; this new emphasis created the impetus for the many – and useful – findings of socio-legal research in recent years.

It is true to say that Pound did not have a complete sociological theory into which law fitted. He was not, therefore, a sociologist. He saw and explained law's position in society, its 'role' or job; his explanation might not find favour with sociologists because it is too simplistic and (more particularly) based on a now unfavourable consensus view of society, with law as one factor in holding that consensus together. Nevertheless, Pound clearly saw law as a 'social science'. The lack of theoretical underpinning does not diminish this fact. I would go further and say that the emphasis on sociological techniques in studying day-to-day law encouraged by Pound and resulting in many recent socio-legal surveys has been of more real and direct value than the considerable theorising that has gone on under the label of 'legal sociology'.

We can say that though Pound does not see jurisprudence through the eyes of a sociologist,

9 Sociological Jurisprudence and the Sociology of Law

he does see it as a social science: he does see that law should be considered with the tools and from the viewpoint of a social scientist. The first part of the quotation must be rejected as inaccurate. Is it correct to say that he sees jurisprudence as a 'technology'?

Certainly the language and analogies that he uses suggest that this is indeed the case. Law is 'social engineering' designed to minimise the 'friction and waste' from the process of balancing the interests which compete in a society. Law then is seen as a 'technology', a means by which society can achieve the balancing of interests required. This is functional jurisprudence; it rests, as I have pointed out, on a consensus model of society which sees law as a cohesive (rather than divisive) force.

Pound devotes much space to this theory of competing interests on their different levels, to the balancing process and to the jural postulates which are to be used in cases of conflict. Much has been written and said about the meaning and force of what he says. Pound has provoked much controversy. What is, however, clear is that Pound's view of law is that it is a tool whereby this balancing process is carried out. The study of law is therefore a 'technology', in the sense of a study of a complex tool and its efficiency in performing a given task.

Contrary to the quotation, Pound saw jurisprudence not as a social science rather than a technology, but as *both* a social science and a technology.

2) Evaluate Weber's analysis of the relationship between law and capitalism.

Written by the Editor

Skeleton Solution

Capitalism – rational legal order – formally rational legal systems – Marxism – economic factors – class instrumentalism – legitimate authority – limitations of theory – England – relevance today.

Suggested Solution

Max Weber sought to understand and explain the distinctive characteristics of modern Western society. In doing so he was the first theorist to develop a comprehensive sociology of law. For him the most important feature of Western society was capitalism. He believed that a rational legal order was crucial to the development of capitalism in Western society. In assessing Weber's exposition it must be remembered that he was writing one hundred years ago, so that his 'modern' Western society was very different to ours. It is thus proposed to analyse his account of law and capitalism in three stages: as a theory in its own right; as a response to the writings of Marx and Engels; and as a theory in relation to Western society today.

Weber divided up the characteristics of a legal system as follows: a legal system characterised by irrationality (ie failure to apply general rules or principles) might be formally irrational or substantively irrational. The former description applies where decisions are made on the basis of tests beyond the control of human reasoning, such as trial by ordeal. The latter description applies where cases are merely decided individually on their own merits. Similarly, rational legal systems may be formally or substantively rational. A legal system is substantively rational when guided by principles other than law itself, such as morals. Only in formally rational legal systems are 'rules expressed by the use of abstract concepts created by legal thought itself and conceived of as constituting a complete system' (Lloyd: *An Introduction to Jurisprudence*). Weber claimed that such legal systems are a characteristic of Western developed society.

Jurisprudence: The Philosophy of Law

It is on the basis of this analysis that Weber rejected the Marxist view. He did not accept that law and the state was determined by economic factors – the relations of production. Instead, economic forces are just one of many factors; the growth of bureaucracy, for example, is highly important. Weber also rejected the Marxist version of 'class instrumentalism'. He spoke of legitimate authority rather than class domination: 'authority strives for acceptance not submission'. Legitimate authority is subdivided into three types: traditional, charismatic and legal-rational. The latter is central to Weber's account of law and its relationship to capitalism. Because there is a system of rationally made laws in developed society which stipulate the circumstances in which power may be exercised, that power is legitimate. Obedience is thus owed to the legal system rather than the person wielding the power. In making these points one might note the similarities between Weber and Hart on obligation to obey the law.

There is no doubting the richness of Weber's writings, both in sociological and jurisprudential terms generally, and in relation to his account of law and the modern capitalist society in particular. Furthermore, much of what he said was an effective response to the writings of Marx and Engels. But his theory is subject to limitations. Weber himself acknowledged problems with the example of England. Although his position has been defended, there is at least ambiguity in his assertion on the one hand that formal rational law assists the development of capitalism and his recognition on the other that capitalism emerged in England during a period of highly irrational law. Another limitation of Weber is that he was writing one hundred years ago: one might question the relevance of his response to 'traditional' Marxism today, for example. Despite these and other criticisms levelled at Weber, his analysis of the relationship between law and capitalism still provides much that is informative and thought-provoking.

TYPE TWO

This sort of question requires the student to consider the distinction between sociological jurisprudence and the sociology of law; the student will of course have to consider the similarities as well.

Examine the difference between sociological jurisprudence and the sociology of law.

University of London LLB Examination
(for External Students) Jurisprudence and Legal Theory June 1983 Q6

Skeleton Solution

Techniques of social science – sociological factors in law – many concerns identical – Pound – Durkheim – distinction – research fields – chronological differences.

Suggested Solution

The growth in literature and thought on the relationship between law and society has been a marked feature of jurisprudence since the latter part of the nineteenth century. On a simplistic level, the 'sociological approach' can be split into two component parts: sociological jurisprudence and the sociology of law (or legal sociology). Both these components share many views and ideas – the importance of harnessing the techniques of social science in the legal area, the importance of sociological factors in law, the rejection of 'formalism' and scepticism about legal rules, and so on – but they are divided by others. It is not, as we shall see, possible to totally distinguish the two; basically, 'sociological jurisprudence' covers studies of how society affects law, and 'sociology of law' studies how law fits into society. The former

9 Sociological Jurisprudence and the Sociology of Law

takes law as an autonomous institution (even a necessary institution) in society, and concentrates on law and the role it plays in society and how that role affects it; the latter sees law as one among social institutions, and questions its role in society, and whether traditional legal rules and concepts adequately explain that. Rather than a distinct break between the two, we should see a spectrum of opinion between the starting points of law and society.

In fact, one of the main ways in which a theory is placed into one or other camp is the label it puts on itself, or at least the label put on its author. So Pound, Ihering, Ehrlich – all jurists – and the American realists, several of whom were judges, of course, are seen as 'sociological jurisprudents', whereas sociologists who turn their attention to law, such as Weber, Durkheim are seen as 'legal sociologists'. This in spite of the fact that many of the concerns are identical. Both Pound and Durkheim, for example, consider the purpose or role law plays in society. Pound sees it as a form of 'social engineering', producing a balance from the interests which the law-making process weighs: judges' decisions balance these interests using 'jural postulates' to attach appropriate weight. Durkheim sees law as part of the cohesive matter of society, with repressive laws forming part of the bond of mechanical, homogenous societies, and restitutive laws part of heteregenous, organic societies. Many other views on the function of law have been expressed, on both sides of the divide.

However, we must not see this identity of interest as denying the reality of the distinction. Even in those views of the function of law in the last paragraph, we can I think see a different emphasis, as Pound looks to see what judges are doing with an eye on the social sanction, and Durkheim clearly using law as a support to his theory of mechanical and organic societies. (In fact, Durkheim is considering what can be seen as a classic sociology of law question: do different types of society have different sorts of law?) The different emphasis can also be seen as one looks at the research fields. The sociological approach as a whole stresses the importance of research as we noted above; not all sociological writing in law is about grand theory. The research on particular matters is divisible into the two strands of thought. On the one hand, there are what may be called 'socio-legal' studies, on areas of the judicial process etc. Attempting to see how the law works in practice – how legal aid, or bail, or sentencing, etc is decided, and whether the practice accords to the theory. This work, as Lloyd points out, is not related to any wider view of society, to any theory on society: rather, it concentrates on the law and legal system. Similar to these are the studies of judicial behaviouralism which follow the impetus of American Realism. On the other hand, some research into individual laws, etc actually tries to explain the social (and economic) context of that law: explaining how laws emerge or have emerged in the past from their backgrounds. Unlike in socio-legal studies, the focus here is on the fact of society which led to a specific piece of legislation.

Apart from labelling theorists in one or other camp, we can also, then, differentiate theories and pieces of research by considering where their main thrust and emphasis lies. Another aspect of the difference between sociological jurisprudence and the sociology of law is chronological: many writers have suggested that sociology of law will – or has – emerged from and after sociological jurisprudence. Hunt's *Sociological Movement in Law* identifies that movement as including the sociological jurisprudence of Pound etc, the American Realist Movement and the historically prior pioneer legal sociologists, Weber and Durkheim; it is followed after the Second World War by 'sociology and law'. Hunt is not impressed by the present output of the new 'school', no one (in his view) having yet produced a general theory in sociology or law to match Weber's. Selznick's developmental model has three stages rather than two; the first is the age of the pioneers, and the grand theories of Pound et al; the second the age of method, where jurists will learn sociological skills and sociologists will assist jurists in

Jurisprudence: The Philosophy of Law

investigation of relevant questions; the third is the era of sociology of law, when questions such as law's function and the meaning of justice and legality will be answered.

In terms of our question, sociological jurisprudence would cover the first and still be involved in the second stage; while the sociologists in that second stage will be doing the sociological research referred to above. The third stage is when present research into sociology of law results in general theories; some do exist today (apart from Weber's): Selznick himself, Parsons and Bredemeier for example, have produced such theories. As this third stage takes over, the importance of the distinction considered in the question will be greatly diminished.

TYPE THREE

The following are more complex 'quotation questions' using sociology as a starting point for a discussion for broader issues. They are useful for the student as they demonstrate how to approach more difficult questions: by thinking first, high marks *can* be achieved.

1) 'Where the lawyer or the legal scholar talks about rights and expectations he does so with normative intentions. He purports to give directives to clients or to legal functionaries and he intends his analysis to form the basis of decisions, ultimately of action. The sociologist, on the other hand, uses the same terms without any directly normative purpose in an attempt to describe, reveal and explain' (Vilhelm Aubert: *Sociology of Law*). Discuss.

University of London LLB Examination
(for External Students) Jurisprudence and Legal Theory June 1985 Q5

Skeleton Solution

Normative statements – rules – committed or detached normative statements – Raz – lawyer – sociologist – Cotterrell – Hart – Ehrlich – common normative vocabulary.

Suggested Solution

Normative statements form a readily discernible part of social intercourse. Such statements, as Aubert correctly points out, are frequently associated with lawyers or legal scholars. Thus, where a lawyer advises that X has a right to inherit under Y's will or that he has a legitimate expectation so to do, such a statement is normative.

It would be a mistake, however, to confine normative statements to lawyers or legal scholars. The key to identifying a normative statement lies in the recognition that such a right or expectation is conferred pursuant to a *rule*. Rights and expectations do not exist 'in vacuo' but are the intended consequence of the enabling rule in question, and it is this intention of the rule that determines its normative character. Thus, in the above example, the rule in question is that the named beneficiary of a duly attested will has a right to inherit under that will.

Normative statements are curtailed by any rule-orientated activity. The most common activity of this type is the playing of games. The chess player who acknowledges that the bishop can only move diagonally across the board does so in recognition of the relevant rule of chess. Equally the footballer who accepts that the ball may only be handled under certain specified conditions does so for similar reasons. Both are making normative statements.

It is important to distinguish between the types of normative statement. Adopting Joseph Raz's formulation, normative statements may be said to be either 'committed' or 'detached'. 'Committed' normative statements are the most common. The maker of such a statement

9 Sociological Jurisprudence and the Sociology of Law

accepts that the rule in question is 'binding' on him. The rule may be binding in one of two ways. Firstly, it may be binding as a standard of conduct to which he must adhere. Thus the participant in a sport accepts that he is bound by the rules of the particular game he plays. Secondly, it may be binding as a standard to be applied in evaluating the conduct of those participating in the rule-based activity in question. The rule states that a footballer may not handle the ball is the same rule that the referee must apply in determining whether a free kick or a penalty should be awarded.

In a legal context, rules of law prescribe standards of conduct just as rules of a game do. Those subject to the law accept that legal rules are binding upon them in the conduct of their daily lives. Those same legal rules are binding upon the judiciary in the resolution of disputes and therefore form the basis of judicial adjudication.

The maker of a 'detached' normative statement, by contrast, does not accept that the rule in question is binding upon him. His statement describes in normative language a rule-governed activity from the point of view of those who accept the rules in question without himself sharing that view. Thus, a non vegetarian may say of vegetarians that the eating of meat is forbidden, whereas in the mouth of a vegetarian such a statement would be 'committed'. Both statements are normative – the difference lies in the intention of the maker of the statement.

A solicitor advising a client does so from the 'detached' point of view. Returning to the example used above, a solicitor who advises his client that the latter has a 'right' to inherit under Y's will is stating the application of the relevant legal rule without, of course, being subject to that rule himself. As Aubert correctly points out, such a statement may well also form a basis for action: in this case, an application by the client to be declared a beneficiary under Y's will. In this context Aubert's analysis accords closely with Raz's general theory of practical reasoning. It is a central tenet of Raz's theory that rules may be viewed as reasons for action. Thus, if there is a rule that 0 then that rule is a reason for doing 0. Perhaps the clearest example of rules, forming the basis of actions, or more especially of decisions, is that of a barrister making submissions in court. The barrister describes in normative language the rules of law applicable to the case before the court, with the aspiration that the judge will use those rules as the basis of his decision.

The legal scholar also talks about rights and experiences from the detached point of view. The textbook writer, for example, is concerned to state the law applicable in a given country as at the date of publication. His written statements are truly detached in that his task is purely descriptive without moral or other commitment to the rules of law which form the subject of his book. Indeed, he may violently disagree with those rules particularly if they are of a legal system to whose political régime he objects. His task is simply to state the law as it is.

Where Aubert's analysis may be subjected to criticism lies in his ascription to the legal scholar of the same normative intention as the lawyer. The lawyer intends his statements to form the basis of action or decision but the same cannot be said of the legal scholar (though he no doubt intends his analysis to be instructive). Take the example of the 'novel' point. The legal scholar who subjects a recent judicial authority to sophisticated analysis may reveal that the rule embodied in the precedent has a previously unsuspected application. Such a statement would still be normative as it describes the intended consequence of the rule but the legal scholar's intentions in making the statement would differ from those of a barrister making the same point in court. The latter would intend the statement to form the basis of judicial adjudication whereas the legal scholar may wish to highlight the absurdity of the rule or just make a clever point.

This example of the legal scholar illustrates the confusion in Aubert's analysis. A rule is normative in character if its intent is to form the basis of decision or action. Statements *about* rules, whether detached or committed, are normative in so far as they recognise this intended consequence of rules. But the 'intention' of the makers of such statements may vary and will not necessarily accord with the intention of the rules themselves.

That said, Aubert provides a useful insight into the lawyer's viewpoint and a ready basis of comparison with that of the sociologist. At a general level normative statements made by lawyers contain an implicit recognition of the law's claim to supremacy. Whilst a lawyer or indeed a legal scholar may disagree with a particular legal rule, he has no doubt concerning its intended effect. The law's primary concern is the governance of those under its sovereignty through the medium of rules, and lawyers (and to a lesser extent legal scholars) form an integral part of the machinery of government.

Not so the sociologist. He is, of course, concerned with the art of governance through the medium of rules but only to the extent that it is relevant to his broader enquiry viz, the nature of society. The sociologist's enquiry will therefore encompass the use of normative statements but it is not central to his purpose.

At this point it becomes pertinent to demarcate the respective fields of enquiry of the lawyer or legal scholar and the sociologist. Contrary to Aubert's claim, both are involved in a descriptive enterprise but the difference is that the lawyer's enquiry terminates at a comprehensive description of law. For the sociologist, a description of law from the lawyer's point of view may afford a starting point for further investigation of social phenomena.

The lawyer's point of view is particularly evidenced in the work of Eugen Ehrlich. Ehrlich identified the lawyer's primary concern as the resolution of legal disputes by the courts. His claim was that this constituted too insular a view of the social phenomenon of law. In the first place, Ehrlich argued, the resolution of legal disputes was often effected without recourse to the established legal institutions. Secondly, it was not true to suggest (as lawyers did) that the rules which governed the institutionalised dispute-settlement procedure were necessarily the same rules that regulated people's daily lives. In short, Ehrlich's view was that 'law' was a normative system embracing not only the courts but much wider vistas of social life.

In this context Ehrlich draws a distinction between 'norms for decision' and the 'living law'. The former may be categorised as lawyers' law, whereas the 'living law' consists of those norms governing conduct which lie wholly outside the ambit of the courts. The latter are regarded as 'binding' by those subject to them, just as norms for decisions are.

Empirical research has borne out Ehrlich's distinction. In the field of industrial relations shop floor practices are often regarded as rigid rules even though no legal sanction is attached. For example, the withdrawal of time allotted to the workforce by management for washing up has prompted industrial action even though it could not seriously be argued that such a withdrawal was illegal.

Ehrlich's point therefore is a good one. In the diverse range of human activity, lawyer's law plays but a minor role. Disputes arise every day in the governance of human affairs but recourse is rarely had to the official dispute settlement machinery. The reasons why this should be so are as varied as the activities in question. This field of enquiry is properly the sociologist's domain. As Aubert points out, the sociologist is concerned to explain *why* the law plays the part it does in human affairs. For this reason 'law', however it may be defined, provides a platform for further investigation.

9 Sociological Jurisprudence and the Sociology of Law

The lawyer or legal scholar on the other hand, is not concerned primarily with the reasons why law plays the special role that it does in human affairs. He is merely concerned to know what that rule is. Thus, while the lawyer and sociologist may share a common normative vocabulary, they do so for different reasons.

2) '... the sociological jurists have taught us to see that even in developed communities law exists on more than one level and that to penetrate its mechanisms it is not sufficient to confine our attention exclusively to the sophisticated documentation of legal rules.' (Lloyd). Explain whether or not you consider that it is sufficient to confine attention exclusively to the documentation of legal rules.

University of London LLB Examination
(for External Students) Jurisprudence and Legal Theory June 1986 Q3

Skeleton Solution

Academic law – legal sources – law in practice – practical life of legal rule – sociology – Devlin – Hart – Von Savigny and Maine – judge's role.

Suggested Solution

I agree with the sociological jurists that to penetrate the 'mechanisms' of law, to understand law fully at all levels, it is necessary to look beyond legal rules at other factors and influences. However, there are other perfectly legitimate aims in connection with law for which an examination going beyond the rules is not necessary or only partially necessary and I will deal with these first.

I refer in particular to the requirements of those studying and teaching law and writing articles and textbooks on academic law subjects. Here, the primary concern is with the developed legal rules as revealed in the authoritative sources (the 'sophisticated documentation' referred to in the quotation), the statutes, cases and legal writings. The student may look at deeper issues in his jurisprudential studies or for his own benefit; they are not strictly relevant to his prime task of getting to grips with the subjects.

The same is mainly true of those involved in the law in practice, whether as litigants, as practitioners or as authors of practitioners' textbooks or articles. However, in this case a partial examination of issues beyond the rules will be necessary: what does the rule mean in practice? For instance, the legal rule might be that an exclusion clause in a particular situation must be 'reasonable' – but what constitutes reasonableness in that situation? Or again, the Bail Act may allow magistrates to keep a defendant in custody on certain grounds at their discretion – but how will that discretion be exercised in practice at this court? The practitioner and the litigant must be concerned with the practical life of the legal rule, rather than with its academic letter.

Once one ceases to think of law in academic or practical terms and starts to think in jurisprudential terms of understanding law, it becomes clear that in this context to 'penetrate its mechanisms', to understand the phenomenon of law fully, it is necessary to look beyond the documented rules to wider questions. The nature of these wider questions can be gleaned by reading the chapter headings of the major jurisprudential textbooks.

The sociological jurists referred to in the quotation would have principally been thinking of sociology and its concerns relating to law; how law cannot be explained correctly save in its overall context in society. Not just the part played by societal factors in law but also the wider investigation of the part played by the law in societies generally is relevant here.

Jurisprudence: The Philosophy of Law

We should not, however, stop with the sociologist, because to gain a complete picture of law much more is needed. An examination of its relationship with morality will raise the argument between Devlin and Hart concerning the extent to which a society should use law to enforce a community morality and the debate between natural lawyers and positivists. A consideration of how law relates to rights and justice will lead onto a study of political philosophy and how it relates to law; the works of historicists such as Savigny and Maine will remind us that law cannot properly be understood in a given society save in the light of that society's history. The work of any 'school' of legal philosophers will spark off some new idea or consideration without which law's full complexity cannot be realised.

Thus far, I have taken the question to refer to confining one's attention exclusively to the legal rules as set out in the 'sophisticated documentation' of developed societies. Read another way, the question could be asking whether attention should be focused solely on *preparing that documentation*, and a valuable point can be made from looking at it in this light.

Although there are some contexts in which it is sufficient to look solely at the 'documentation of legal rules', both a judge and a jurisprudent from their different viewpoints must not limit themselves in that way, but should look to other levels, aspects and potentialities of the law.

10 Marxism

10.1 Introduction
10.2 Key points
10.3 Analysis of question styles
10.4 Questions

10.1 Introduction

With recent developments in the Soviet Union and Eastern Europe, resulting in the overthrow of the regimes claiming a communist ideology based upon Marxist-Leninist doctrine, Marxism has become a topic in flux. Questions were set in both 1995 and 1996, so this is a topic which is very much under the examiner's gaze.

10.2 Key points

a) *Base and superstructure*

   According to Marxist theory, society's base is formed by the relations of production. The state, law and all other social institutions form part of the superstructure built on to the base and reflect that base.

b) *Class instrumentalism*

   In Marxist theory the law is the tool of the ruling class. Since the state and other social institutions depend upon the relations of production, the law will, in a capitalist society, reflect the fact that the means of productions are controlled by a small ruling class. The law both legitimises this situation and oppresses the working classes.

c) *Marxism in reality*

   Marxist theory on the post capitalist society is often crudely described in terms of state and law 'withering away'. In fact, a more sophisticated version of this theory allows for a post-revolutionary period where the bourgeois state is replaced by proletariat power. This state will remain until communism is achieved, at which stage the state and law will disintegrate. Students should consider, however, whether this reflects reality; and whether the so-called Marxist societies were really Marxist at all, or merely very crude approximations.

10.3 Analysis of question styles

Marxism is a popular examination topic. Questions are broadly divided into two main types: questions calling for an analysis of some aspect of Marxist legal theory or questions relating to the value of Marxist thought today.

Jurisprudence: The Philosophy of Law

10.4 Questions

TYPE ONE

The following are all questions on aspects of Marxist legal theory.

1) Is law a tool of the ruling classes?

University of London LLB Examination
(for External Students) Jurisprudence and Legal Theory June 1987 Q8

Skeleton Solution

Marxism – class conflict – historical materialism – law as a tool of the dominant class – law withering away in the classless society – class instrumentalism – Collins – reformism versus revolution – sophistication of capitalist response – Weber – legitimacy – separation of state and civil society – Hegel.

Suggested Solution

Marxists view the history of the world as the history of class conflict. Through their historical materialism they explain history in terms of the conflict between the class that controls the means of production and the class that works the means of production. Marx's exposition of his historical materialism was in itself then contingent on class social practice. This historical materialism saw through its dialectic that the progression of societies is towards the classless society where class conflict would be irrelevant. Thus the bourgeois revolution, eg the French Revolution of 1789, saw the overthrow of the feudal régime and its replacement with the capitalist class. The Bolshevik revolution of October 1917 replaced the bourgeois Kerensky régime with the dictatorship of the proletariat which would work towards the classless society. In such a classless society there would be no need for law as a means of social control; there would rather be reliance on communist morality as a means of behavioural guidance in the communist or classless society. Thus law, as an instrument of class oppression, would disappear with the demise of capitalism.

It is clear that such an analysis holds that the organisation of society is determined by the class structure. The base of economic relations, that is, who controls the means of production, is the key to social organisation. The state and all the institutions of the state – including the law – are seen as reflecting this economic determinate. This view is known as 'class instrumentalism' and it believes that law is the tool of the ruling class. Thus law is used to both legitimise and to oppress the working class in a capitalist society. The laws of theft and of ownership in land are there to protect the interests of the ruling class at the expense of those who work the means of production. They have the effect of legitimating those who already 'have' property by making it an 'offence' to interfere with their enjoyment of their property.

Hugh Collins, in *Marxism and the Law*, has observed that from a Marxist perspective 'practices with regard to law can form only a segment of a revolutionary programme; to attribute greater significance to law would be to succumb to the fetishism of law. Nevertheless, because law serves important functions in modern society it must figure in any theory of revolutionary practice'. The class instrumentalism of early Marxists then would hold that the working class ought to grab the legislature for their own ends. This is because if it were true to say that the law is the tool of the dominant class as a means of class oppression designed to preserve the mode of production or the economic base of the society from attack, then the class instrumentalists argued that the obvious course of action was to seize the legislature and turn it against the capitalists. The programme was to use law to redress the capitalists' control of the means of production. This view is now seen as naive.

The dilemma presented to the Marxist was whether to support legislative measures that had the effect of ameliorating the lot of the working class that they claimed to represent: for example the laws that set up the welfare state. The dilemma was that the welfare state has the effect of undermining efforts to raise class consciousness and building working class solidarity by ameliorating the worst excesses of capitalism. This thus delays (and some would add, prevents) a revolutionary situation. Although according to Marxist dialectical materialism the working class revolution is inevitable (the task of the Marxist being to bring that date forward), welfare legislation obscures the structure of class domination that is based on the relations of production. Thus reformism is seen as self-defeating.

However there is a school of Marxist thought that sees even the use of the legal form as necessarily supporting the ruling class in a capital society. This school would adopt resistance to institutionalised class domination because consensual participation is seen as a betrayal of class as it implies the according of legitimacy to the legal system. This school we shall label the revolutionary movement. Its re-emergence can be seen in the widespread street revolts of 1968, the aim of which was to encourage general violation of the criminal law in order to force the state into using naked force and thus revealing itself to be a tool of the dominant class.

In reality, however, it may be difficult to reconcile the society which existed in Russia after 1924 (the emergence of Stalin) with the ideals of the Marxists. Far from the law withering away it continued to be an instrument of oppression. The NKVD, the GPU and the KGB ruthlessly suppressed any attempt to question what was happening; and most of the old Marxists perished in the show trials of the 1930s. Gorbachev, who himself studied law at Moscow University, and Yeltsin, who rescued Gorbachev from the attempted coup of 1991, would both acknowledge that Marxism had become the pretext for a totalitarian regime.

The interesting question now is what future if any can Marxism have? There are after all still Marxist regimes in China and Cuba. Was Marxism simply an intellectual theory which failed in reality because of the weakness of human nature? Or could a Marxist society someday exist in some ideal world where human nature was not so venial? Plato and Aristotle both raised some of these questions 2,000 years ago. The French Communards attempted to implement them in Paris in 1870, but no attempt to put them into practice has ever been completely successful.

Thus, from a Marxist perspective, law is the tool of the dominant class; but in reality those Marxist societies which have existed have not succeeded in abolishing law.

2) 'Marx and Engels believed that their general account of the state received abundant confirmation from the structure of laws under capitalism. Laws are taken to express or reflect economic relations.' (Duncan). Discuss.

University of London LLB Examination
(for External Students) Jurisprudence and Legal Theory June 1983 Q10

Skeleton Solution

Law as part of class oppression – superstructure – relations of production – economic base – law and state determined by economic conditions – feudal times – capitalist societies – Marxist model too simple.

Jurisprudence: The Philosophy of Law

Suggested Solution

In considering Marxism from a jurisprudential point of view, one is naturally concerned to see what Marx and his later followers have to say about the legal systems and legal theory: this problem, for example, asks about the support given by capitalist law structure to their theory of the state. A major problem arises from this approach; neither Marx nor Engels really concentrated on the law at all or analysed it in any depth. Law was just one part of class oppression, which is not necessary in the communist classless society which will eventually evolve; therefore it did not call for close study. For this reason, the answer to this question is not strictly confined to the words of Marx and Engels, but takes advantage of later Marxist views of the position of law. These views are consistent with the main tenets of Marx's and Engel's writings.

In order to see whether or not legal structure confirms their account of the state, we have to start by identifying what the account is. The Marxist view of law, first of all as part of the superstructure of society reflecting economic relations, and second as an instrument of class oppression, will then be discussed to see if that view, in relation to capitalist society, supports the account of the state. Finally, we will briefly consider whether or not the view of law is acceptable.

First, then, Marx and Engel's view on the state. The state is seen as an instrument of domination and oppression in a time of inequality. In the clan societies of primitive man there was no inequality and injustice, and no state; that only developed when selfishness and greed warped the communist state, to enforce the inequality. Through the various stages of historical development outlined by Marx, the state retains the role of being used by the dominant class to subjugate the subservient class; it will remain until the dictatorship of the proletariat (the stage immediately following the revolution against the capitalist bourgeoisie). At that time, once the state now in the hands of the proletariat has eradicated inequality and oppression by eliminating the relics of the bourgeois state, it will wither away, leaving a communist, classless society.

One general point about this development must be mentioned before we can turn to the position of the law in its capitalist manifestation. The whole development comes about as a result of materialistic considerations, specifically as a result of changes in the relationships of productions. These relationships are what can be called the economic *base*; all social institutions including those conferring political authority and including the law are *superstructural*, determined by that economic base. The institutions of the abstract 'state' are part of the superstructure: judiciary, bureaucracy, etc.

There is an identification of law and state in this way, and other ways: both are institutions of the superstructure, determined by – expressing or reflecting – economic conditions. The structure of laws in a capitalist society can well be seen (in part at least) as reflecting the present relations of production. In feudal times, production was agricultural and stability of land ownership essential. Once capitalism took over land becomes an asset to be exploited to make profits, and so does other property. Feudal tenures disappear, and are replaced by more flexible property laws, developing laws of contract, companies (to reflect a change in ownership of means of production, from landed gentry to businessmen; and to reflect an increasing tendency for combination amongst the owners of those means) and commerce, and a legal system capable of enforcing those laws. Further, the old relationship of master-servant in a feudal context is replaced by the contractual (and therefore more flexible) employer-employee relationship of today.

For Marx and Engels, this new legal structure in capitalist societies confirms the view that they hold about the institutions of the state reflecting the relations of production. Later Marxist theory, particularly Lenin, has emphasised that this reflection takes place in an indirect way: law reflects the relations of production because it is an instrument of the dominant class, used to oppress the subservient proletariat. Earlier versions suggesting a more direct reflection failed to be convincing, and are now rejected in favour of his more complex account, which remains faithful to Marx. The dominant class control the law making process (as well as the other institutions of the society), and use it to pass laws to maintain themselves in that dominant position. By this view, even laws appearing to be remote from the relations of production – for example, crimes of violence and family laws – can be accounted for as laws by which the ruling class attempt to preserve the stability of the society and the status quo. That there are problems with accounting for all laws in this way is a criticism to which we return in a moment.

Thus far, we have seen that Marx and Engels saw the state as an instrument of class oppression, the institutions of which were part of the superstructure of the society reflecting the economic base. The structure of law under capitalism falls into the same pattern, thereby confirming the account of the state: the law is seen as one of the institutions which reflects the material base and relations of production because it is used by the dominant bourgeois class as an instrument by which the subservient class is oppressed.

Duncan's statement quoted in the question can be accepted, then, as a true indication of Marx's and Engels' thoughts on this topic. Now we are in a position to consider whether or not their thoughts were correct: does the structure of law in a capitalist society reflect economic relations? Does it confirm the general account of the state as an instrument of class oppression? In an examination answer it is not possible to attempt a complete answer to these questions, but we can consider the major points.

On the first question whether law is a reflection of economic relations (ie the relations of production, the 'base' from which the 'superstructure' including law develops), analysis will suggest that at the least, the situation is more complex than the simple model suggests. Law has an important part to play, not only in the superstructure, but also in the base, in defining the relations of production and in upholding them. The relations of production in capitalism are those between owners of the means of production and their workers. Ownership is a legal concept, and moreover one that requires legal machinery to uphold and enforce (punishments for theft, evictions, etc); owners frequently now rely on legal forms of combination (companies, partnerships); their relations to their workers are governed by contract and statute and so on. Law is now an integral part of the base.

That complication does not prevent the questions being relevant: we must still see if the law is an instrument of class oppression whose structure therefore reflects the relations of production, and especially the dominance of the owners. This is an empirical question, to which no certain answer can be given. Marxists can give a good explanation in these terms of commercial law, contract, property law and the court system, and even (as we have seen) of other laws upholding the status quo. There are other parts of the modern day UK capitalist legal structure which might be thought to defy analysis in this way: how does the welfare state oppress the proletariat? How does the Employment Protection legislation reflect the dominance of the ruling class? How do compulsory clauses in business contracts (Sale of Goods Acts) and other consumer protection fit in? Marxists can try to account for these laws in various ways. The legal system might be said to be one of relative autonomy, in which pressure groups can pass some laws, as long as the dominant class do not find them an interference with their profit making; or perhaps these laws are minor concessions wrung out of the bourgeoisie class as a first stage on the road to revolution. Perhaps, even, they are a sop to the proletariat which will help to prevent development of a class consciousness.

3) 'The ideas of the ruling class are in every epoch the ruling ideas: ie the class which is the ruling *material* force of society is at the same time its ruling *intellectual force*.' (Marx and Engels)

Does this help us to understand law?

University of London LLB Examination
(for External Students) Jurisprudence and Legal Theory 1990 Q7

Skeleton Solution

Is and ought – Marxist view of ideology – base and superstructure – Althusser – Hay – the complex view of ideology (Summers) – Content of ruling ideology – Thompson's defence of the 'Rule of Law' – critique of Marxist ideological theory.

Suggested Solution

The statement reflects a central tenet of Marxist thought about the structure of society, and more particularly the role of ideology. This view has important implications for how we understand law, but its claim that law is merely ideology may be said to be inaccurate and extreme. These two allegations can be assessed when one lays out the main elements of Marxist ideological theory.

Essentially Marx and Engels claimed that 'is' determined 'ought'. That the 'material conditions' of people's lives, which consisted of the conditions under which they worked (the 'relations of production') and the economic resources of society (the 'forces of production') both constructed and determined the ideas that persisted within society. These economically determined ideas include law. Not only do Marxists claim that ideas and consciousness result from the economic structure of society, they also assert that the ideas within society reflect the ideas and dominance of the 'ruling class'. This class (frequently termed 'capitalists') controls the economic structure of society and as a result are able to present their ideology to the rest of society as the 'dominant ideology'.

Crucial to Marx was a distinction between the 'economic base' and the 'superstructure' of society. The former consisted in the relations of production and the forces of production. Over and above this was the superstructure (which included religion, politics, law and morality) which was merely a product of the economic base. The ideology of capitalism, Marx claimed, became the dominant ideology because capitalists controlled the economic base. Law is reduced to a mere creation of the ruling class whose function is to serve the capitalistic interests of that class. The process by which the ideas of this class become transmitted to the rest of the population and why they should accept it was not fully explained by Marx and Engels. One must, therefore, turn to other Marxist theorists in search of an answer.

Althusser claimed that the intellectual force of the ruling class became dominant by utilising the superstructural institutions such as family, church, media and law. Law was in his term an 'ideological state apparatus'. Althusser claims that it is because the ruling class have the greatest economic power within society that it can use, inter alia, law to force its ideas on the rest of society. Hay presents a similar analysis, claiming that the ability of the ruling class to successfully enforce an increasing number of criminal offences without an accompanied increase in enforcement mechanisms was due to use of legal ideology. This ideology presented law as

10 Marxism

both terrifying and merciful, more importantly it claimed that law was neutral and the product of people's (the 'proletariat's') own minds.

Hill, Abercrombie and Turner doubt the efficiency of this transmission of ideology. They claim that the ideology is not completely accepted and often not at all. How can Marxists account for civil disobedience and criticism of the law if they wish to present the proletariat as blinded into obedience by ideology? No attempt is made to isolate the reasons why people obey laws; sometimes they might refute the ideology but obey for prudent reasons. Summers presents a more sophisticated explanation of the workings of legal ideology. For him, the superstructure consists of a pluralism of different ideologies which reflects the complexity of the power structure of society. However, one class tends to dominate; it can use its power to make its own ideology dominant. The law is both ideology and tool for securing this dominant position. We may feel that this paints a truer picture of law by including its instrumental aspect.

Despite these criticisms, Marxist theory has increased our understanding of the law by providing a possible explanation of the nature of law within Western society. Marx claimed that all ideology was the result of 'praxis' – what people experienced in their everyday lives was reflected in their ideas. This being so, Marx claimed that the economic structure of capitalist society saw people as individuals in a conflict with each other as to who could produce and exchange the greatest amount. This is reflected in the ruling ideology of law as a neutral mediator of individual interests; this view has much in common with that of Hobbes. Marx denounced this view as false consciousness. In order to achieve revolution, the workers had to see themselves in the world as they really were (an aim of both Realist and critical legal studies theorising). It was felt that this could be achieved by piercing through the dominant ideology and seeing workers (ie the proletariat) as a class (not isolated individuals) in relation to the material conditions of production.

Marxist analysis of the ideology of law has been criticised as crude economic instrumentalism, as such it distorts the true and important functions of the law by terming these aspects illusory ideology. An example of such criticism is EP Thompson's defence of the rule of law as an 'unqualified good'. He claims that legal ideology does not always justify dominance. Often it protects the weak and restrains the social elite. Modern examples can be said to be maternity (and now paternity) rights in the employment law field as well as the recent mushrooming in the review of the exercise of public power by the courts. The Marxist response that such functions of law are bribes and concessions to 'buy-off' the working class must be supported by empirical evidence otherwise they fall victim to a charge of conspiratorial paranoia.

Marx and Engels were unclear as to just how much the superstructure was determined by the base. If all the ideas within a given society were the products of its material conditions (as Marx and Engels often seem to claim) this would undermine their own theories of revolution and social change. Engels acknowledged as much, asking 'Why do we fight for the political dictatorship of the proletariat if political power is economically impotent?'

As a result of an unwillingness to have their own theories dismissed as merely economic constructs, Marx and Engels seem sometimes to claim that the superstructure *also* affected the economic base! Therefore, ideology and law could also be a determinative factor upon the economic relations within society. For example, the inheritance laws in England were seen by Engels as not only the result of economic causes but also of tradition.

Horwitz has expanded this complex (and on the face of it contradictory) view of ideology by looking at how the law, as one particular ideological mechanism within the superstructure, was systematically used by the American judiciary to facilitate and legitimate industrial

Jurisprudence: The Philosophy of Law

capitalism. Thus it was an independent institution. It could effect tangible economic change and a recognition of this better fits our everyday experience of the law. Indeed it avoids not taking the law at 'face-value' (to use a Dworkinian term) by not seeing in law illusion.

4) 'Because Marxism has approached law tangentially, treating it as one aspect of a variety of political and social arrangements concerned with the manipulation of power and the consolidation of modes of production of wealth, there has been no commitment towards an identification of the unique qualities of legal institutions.' (Collins). Discuss the Marxist approach to law and explain why this led Marxist jurists to have no commitment towards an identification of the unique qualities of legal institutions.

University of London LLB Examination
(for External Students) Jurisprudence and Legal Theory June 1986 Q8

Skeleton Solution

Materialism – economic relationships – evolution of society – base and superstructure – oppression of the masses – post-revolution period – Soviet Russia – explanation of law is secondary – one of a cluster of institutions – legal fetishism – Pashukanis.

Suggested Solution

Marxism's explanation of history and the evolution of societies is firmly based on materialism; the theory that economic factors and relationships are the determinant forces in that evolution. In this essay, I will show how law and legal institutions are considered in the light of general Marxist theory and how that theory contains powerful disincentives against a commitment such as that mentioned in the question.

Marxism is a materialist theory. The primary focus rests on the economic and corresponding power relationships in society; the evolution of society from one stage of development (eg feudalism) to the next (eg capitalism) occurs as a consequence of economic factors causing one class to rise and wrest the ascendancy in that society from the previous ruling class.

Marxists see societies as containing a 'base', consisting of the relations of production, and a 'superstructure', the institutions of a community which are determined by the base. These institutions include the structures of political authority, the ideologies and the laws of that community. These institutions are, as I say, 'determined' by the base. Thus in capitalist society, the relations of production are between the bourgeoisie (the owners of the means of production) and the working classes; the institutions in the superstructure, including the law, are instruments by which the control of the working classes by the bourgeoisie is effected.

This explanation of the position of law is not, of course, generally accepted. For example, it is said that law operates also in the base in defining modes of ownership and the (contractual) relationship between employers and employed. Be that as it may, it is clear that Marxists do view law very much as suggested in the Collins' quotation in the question; as concerned with the manipulation of power by the bourgeoisie for their own ends and for the consolidation of the present means of production – in the famous Marxist phrase, for the continued 'oppression of the masses'.

Further, it is also clear that Marxists do approach law 'tangentially' from a study of the wider notions of society and social control. This point is emphasised when one looks at the treatment of law in the post-revolution period after the working class has (as Marx predicted) risen and defeated the bourgeoisie. At this time, the bourgeois state, and with it bourgeois law, are

10 Marxism

'smashed'. The ensuing state, during the dictatorship of the proletariat, gradually withers away, and law with it, as the last vestiges of capitalism are removed.

Again, this view has been severely doubted, particularly in the light of the experience of 'Marxist' countries such as Soviet Russia, where it is clear that law has far from 'withered away'. However, one should remember that to an extent the suggestion that law would wither away was a 'definitional' one; law, as identified and associated with the unjust and oppressive class-divided state, would no longer be needed when class divisions had been removed. There would, though, be an administration of things and according to later Marxist writers some economic planning.

Enough, though, has been said to show that the Marxist explanation of law follows from and is secondary to the materialist, economic factor determined, explanation of society as a whole. As such, it is hardly surprising that within Marxist writings, and in particular those of Marxist jurists, there has been no commitment towards the identification of the unique qualities of legal institutions. The whole thrust of materialist Marxist thought is towards seeing law not as unique but rather as one amongst a cluster of institutions forming part of the superstructure and by which the controlling bourgeoisie continued their dominance.

Collins points out that a Marxist developing a general theory of law would be considered to have fallen foul of the 'fetishism of law'. Legal fetishism consists in the belief that legal systems are an essential feature of social order and civilisation, according to Collins. Such a belief underlies most social and political theories outside the Marxist tradition and all current general theories of law. The Marxist rejects it and, therefore, does not look for a general theory of law, which would involve studying law's unique features. The one major exception to this, Pashukanis, did not find favour: his works were rejected and he disappeared.

A study of the Marxist's attitude to law, then, explains why there is the lack of the commitment pointed to by Collins in the quotation set out in the question.

TYPE TWO

Marx has been described as 'a product of his time'. The following questions deal with the status of Marxism today – how accurately did it predict the evolution of society, and does it offer any lasting value?

1) Can Marxist theories of law survive the collapse of Marxism as a political system?

University of London LLB Examination
(for External Students) Jurisprudence and Legal Theory June 1993 Q7

General Comment

Candidates almost invariably do badly on this sort of question, which crops up in different guises very frequently. Why? Candidates suppose that Marxism equals communism and communism equals pre-1989 East European political systems. The mistakes here are fast and furious, the main one being the failure to distinguish between how the world actually is and the ideal system of justice that is pre-supposed by the Marxist theory of law. The East European communist states were not even a poor shadow of anything envisaged by Marx or Lenin; they were mean-spirited, overbureaucratic and dictatorial. Really try to be as sympathetic with Marxist theory. Marx and his followers make an extremely valuable point: that just because things seem intuitively OK, just because our law, our institutions, our legal system, the power structure of society all appear to point in a fairly rational direction, does not at all mean that everything is right. It is an obvious point, but extremely powerful.

Skeleton Solution

What Marxism is in its original conception – analysis of modern capitalism – post-industrial capitalism – the welfare state – class instrumentalist view of the role of law – superstructure as a reflection of the relations of production – reassessment by Marxists of Marxism – Milliband and Hunt – conflict theory – Marxist explanations – Marxist analysis without Marxist conclusions – query how much Marx would accept – ideology a product of class factors – relative autonomy of the state – separation of state from civil society – conclusion that Marxism still relevant.

Suggested Solution

Marx's argument was that every movement is a product of its own time. The question is whether the same can legitimately be said of the way Marxism is used to describe modern forms of government.

In his analysis of capitalism in crisis Marx identified certain important issues and offered an explanation of them in terms of a conflict theory; thus he said that 'the history of all hitherto society has been the history of class struggle'. He developed what he believed to be a science of historical materialism that offered an explanation for everything in scientific and economic terms. This seemed a very attractive idea in terms of the objectivity that science appears to have. How valid is it now? The response could be addressed in Marxist terms by looking at changes in society in economic terms and observing that our society has changed from the rather naked exploitative capitalism of the mid nineteenth century through the growth of the welfare state, working class participation in the forms of government through the growth of electoral franchise and, more recently, the advent of the much vaunted 'Thatcherite' enterprise culture.

It may be that now the distinction between the working class and the ownership capitalist class has become blurred. Workers now own shares; if not in the recently privatised concerns then in their own workplace. A more significant distinction in Britain and the newly 'democratised' East European states, today seems to be between those who have a job and those who do not; between the working class and the non-working class.

The explanation offered in original Marxism that the state and law are parts of a superstructure that is reflective of the economic base – the relations of production – concerned itself to show that the superstructure served those who controlled, by means of ownership, the means of production. This 'class instrumentalism' is rather crude and more recent studies such as those of Ralph Milliband have sought to give a more modern interpretation of Marxism by showing that the relationship resembles something more like a partnership rather than a position where one causally determines the other. What Milliband is trying to do in essence is to show that Marxism can explain modern phenomena and is not restricted in time to the last century.

Another modern Marxist, Alan Hunt, has sought to explain modern events in the post-industrial society in terms of economic factors and of conflict theory. This is a clear attempt to show that Marxism is relevant and can enter the current debate rather than address itself only to rather obscure and historical points. The argument used by modern Marxists is that unless they can offer such an explanation then their theory will lapse into obscurity and they will be excluded from the current political debate. To take an example of a modern application, in criminology, Taylor, Walton and Young, as Marxists, have developed an approach to criminology that does not just call on the rather simplistic Marxist explanation of crime, but seeks to explain crime in more complex terms, whilst remaining faithful to the essence of Marxism as they see it: namely the importance of economic factors and the conflict model of society.

Could we accept Marxist analysis without Marxist conclusions? That is to say that Marx identified important factors at work in society and that his explanation of naked capitalism in the mid-nineteenth century is essentially accurate. If that is the case then Marxism has only a value in terms of the historical development of ideas whose time has since passed. The student of jurisprudence need not, then, be concerned with Marxism. Marx would reject such an approach for he was attempting to provide a general theory of social relations. Marx saw ideology as a product of economic factors governing society. He argued that those who control the means of production also control mental production and that truth would not be truth until applied. Such would then see the discrediting of Marxism in economic terms as an ideology or false consciousness designed to mystify the exploited class and to legitimate the position of the dominant class as those who control the means of production.

Hence, whilst it is probably accurate to argue that original Marxism as an analysis of naked capitalism is dated and not therefore of much relevance to the modern student, it is rather the analysis of the modern post-industrial capitalist state that remains of considerable importance. Here Marxists, rather than Marx, speak of the relative autonomy of the state, the explanation of which can be found in Poulantza's *Political Power and Social Classes*. There it is pointed out that the state that is also the welfare state, and the state that provides for laws on consumer protection that appear to be in the interests of the working class, are nevertheless the state of the ruling class.

The Marxist explanation of the separation of state from civil society which observes that those who govern are not those who control the means of production points out that in the capitalist mode of production there is no need for those who own the means of production to rule. Just so long as their rights in capital are protected the state can otherwise be relatively autonomous. This can be summed up in the phrase of Sigman that the capitalist class 'rules but does not govern'.

It should be clear from this discussion that Marxism survives the collapse of governments professing a 'Marxist' outlook. The reason suggested is that Marxism provides an insight into the injustices of particular structures in society rather than a blueprint for how to run those societies. Look at the world about us; things we take for granted, like advertising, or property rights, *need* not be there. We need to be aware of the fact that their presence, whether presented as an adequate, just, rational, or whatever, ideology, does not guarantee their justice and their freedom from an insidious manipulation of those having power in society from those who do not.

2) Is a 'rule of law' state, such as that envisaged by President Gorbachev in the Soviet Union, compatible with the thinking of Marxism?

University of London LLB Examination
(for External Students) Jurisprudence and Legal Theory June 1991 Q8

Jurisprudence: The Philosophy of Law

Skeleton Solution

Traditional Marxist views of compatibility – Gorbachev's plans – meanings of the 'rule of law' state – Marxist views of the rule of law – Marxist dilemma over rule of law gains – other Marxist views claiming compatibility and Soviet practice – Collins' solution and the 'relative' autonomy' view of the rule of law state – Skocpol's challenge – dangers of incorrect practice.

Suggested Solution

On a prima facie reading the rule of law state would not appear to be compatible with Marxist jurisprudence. Marx and Engels talked of the 'abolition', or 'withering away' of law and the state once the transition had been made from capitalist to communist society. However, the relationship between the rule of law and Marxist jurisprudence was not clearly elaborated by them. Consequently later adherents to the Marxist tradition have had to formulate what should be the correct response to questions of compatibility between the two.

Whilst still claiming to be loyal to Marxist philosophy, Gorbachev indicated he was in favour of establishing a rule of law state in the Soviet Union. His lack of clarity as to what he meant by this notion emphasises the open-endedness of this concept. Before Marxists can have a view as to the correct practice towards the rule of law they must have an adequate picture of what this notion actually entails.

That the rule of law is far from a clear concept has been stated by de Smith and Brazier:

'The concept is one of open texture; it lends itself to an extremely wide range of interpretations.'

Dicey and Rousseau held it to mean the equal application of law to all, be they citizens, companies, public officials or government bodies. They saw the law as having *no specific content*, all that was certain was its *form*; it applied equally and universally. Others have claimed (eg Fuller) that the rule of law also means that the law should have certain minimum standards as a specific content. These have been procedural, such as clarity, predictability and fair hearings. Finally, another influential meaning has been stated to be that the rule of law is concerned with the requirement that all public powers must be based upon the authority of the law.

Gorbachev's rule of law state, subsequently accepted by Boris Yeltsin, appears to be a combination of all these factors. The complex structure of the rule of law has not prevented traditional Marxists from criticising it because they claim that the notion presupposes a kind of 'fetishism of law'. By this they mean that the law occupies a hegemonic and pervasive position within society, instead of withering away, as predicted. From this dominant position the rule of law is seen as both reflecting and securing the domination by the ruling class over the oppressed proletariat.

The rule of law is seen as part of the economically determined superstructure of the state. Within this superstructure, Althusser sees law as one of the 'ideological state apparatuses' which distorts the reality of the experiences of those who work in civil society. These experiences are alienation from other workers and from what workers actually produce. Thus the proletariat is under an illusion of being free to offer their labour and of having influence over the terms and conditions of their employment. These beliefs are conditioned by the economic dominance of the ruling class. This false consciousness is maintained by the ideological institutions of the ruling class, one of which is law. The proletariat is therefore blinded to the true economic and social relations that constitute civil society.

10 Marxism

Thus, the traditional Marxist view of the rule of law sees it as an instrumental and economically determined weapon. Contemporary Marxists have had to face the dilemma facing Yeltsin, namely, what the response should be to the gains in the arena of political rights and liberty which the rule of law seems to offer? The rule of law state envisages political rights, such as assembly and free speech, and liberties, such as freedom from arbitrary arrest and detention. These rights and liberties flow from the already mentioned complex notion of the rule of law. For example, arbitrary arrest and detention are not compatible with a rule of law state if we see the notion as entailing legitimacy. This would mean that public officials must act on the basis of powers given to them by law. Likewise, the rule of law is often said to be embodied in the practice of 'treating like cases alike'. Given this, to allow officials to arbitrarily arrest citizens at their unlimited discretion would directly violate the rule of law.

Thus, the rule of law often seems to bring gains for the proletariat. The dilemma is compounded by Marxist forecasts of a society that would ultimately be free of oppression. If the rule of law is incompatible with Marxist thought, Marxists must endure the prevalence of oppression and the violation of human rights, rather than advocate use of the rule of law in order to ameliorate such a situation.

However, a significant body of Marxist opinion claims the two notions are compatible. Some have seen the law as an instrument *to bring about* the transformation of society to its communist end. This belief can be said to be the basis of the Soviet Union's practice of giving central place to the notion of 'socialist legality'. In practice this entailed an absolute duty to obey socialist laws. The 1961 Party Programme is an explicit example of the perceived necessity of law to achieve socialism (hence each citizen was under a duty to know the full breadth of socialist laws). Renner studied the historical functions of property laws and formulated a thesis that, although the forms of law did not change over time, their *functions* changed over historical periods in response to changes in the economic base. Following from this, it could be claimed that a *communist economic structure* could produce a system of communist property laws.

Despite these views Marxists generally feel unease about the rule of law. Pashukanis voiced this in his theory that only one kind of law existed; that of 'bourgeois law'. For him there could never be 'proletariat law' – the two notions were clearly incompatible.

Collins has supported the non-compatibility view and terms the Marxist's dilemma the 'radicals dilemma'. He advocates a pragmatic approach that Marxists should always act in order to raise the class consciousness of the proletariat in order to effect revolutionary change. This is the ultimate aim of all Marxist action, he claims. When faced with the gains promised by the rule of law state, Marxists should only be in support when it will secure liberties and freedoms which will raise class consciousness.

Therefore, Marxists should generally favour the rule of law when it advocates the right to hold political meetings. Through this mechanism Marxist thought can be disseminated. On the other hand, Marxists should be sceptical about the right to a fair trial because of its less direct effect on raising class consciousness. In such circumstances Marxists should not advocate the rule of law.

The rejection of the rule of law in such circumstances is of paramount importance, according to Collins. He claims that law is a subtle, ideological instrument. As a result of the nature of relations within Capitalist society, the law rarely needs to coerce the proletariat. It can appear as neutral as between classes but it is only 'relatively autonomous'. It is not a direct instrument of the ruling class because it does not need to be, but it remains under the control of the ruling class.

Jurisprudence: The Philosophy of Law

Marxist support of the rule of law will only continue the false picture of the law as neutral, fair and just. Collins urges, further, that Marxists should attack the *political* apparatus, instead of the legal. Attacks upon the rule of law will be converted by it and represented as attacks upon values such as justice. This in turn has the effect of reinforcing the image and hegemonic position of the rule of law.

The 'relative autonomy' view of law has been challenged by Skocpol, who claims that the rule of law state can develop its own independent logic, depending on the degree of dominance enjoyed by the ruling class. In periods when such dominance is challenged, then the state will be less under the control of the ruling class. It may then develop in an autonomous manner in order to control the political and social instability.

Collins, however, issues a warning to those Marxists who see the two notions as compatible. He stresses that the costs of incorrect practice vis-à-vis the rule of law will be the further delay of the transformation of society to its communist end. For Marxists the 'radicals dilemma' is not purely theoretical.

3) How critical of the ideal of the rule of law is the Marxist approach?

University of London LLB Examination
(for External Students) Jurisprudence and Legal Theory June 1994 Q4

General Comment

This is a hard question and the answer requires a reasoned understanding of what Marx left for us as a philosophy, with specific reference to the rule of law and where it operates to continue and reinforce class divisions in society. It also requires an examination of Marxist theories of law because there is no separate treatise on law. Therefore, the question of how critical the ideal of the rule of law is must be judged against the overall Marxist approach.

Skeleton Solution

Marxist theories of law – no separate treatise on law – law and ideology – conclusion.

Suggested Solution

Marxism is in essence a political and social ideology because Karl Marx considered the economic system to be the base for all systems in society, including a legal system. Both Marx and Engels based their philosophies on the insights of Hegel, who saw civilisation as having a defined place in the progress of freedom based on the concept of the dialectic. The Hegelian dialectic is a theory where progress is a result of a clash of theses and antitheses which result in a compromise named 'synthesis'. Through the process of such conflict, a society will progress towards the truth.

Law is not defined in Marx's writings as a specific treatise, although law is considered as a manifestation of 'ideology' which is a central element of Marxist theory. History, to Marx, was a record of conflict of class against class, with the law 'taking sides', where society is divided into base and superstructure. Here, the base is the actual relationship between people who are involved in 'production' which is seen as the economic structure of society. The exploiter of such economic relationships is described as the dominant class.

10 Marxism

A superstructure is made up of:

a) a reflection of these relationships in legal and political forms;

b) the dominant class view of the world; and

c) the development of awareness of social conflict which allows a critique of (a) and (b).

To Marxists, law represents a mirror of inequalities in society which are often obscured by the ruling classes' presentation of it as impartial and detached. Marx suggests that a judge, whilst believing he is working with objective categories, is merely working with categories which are the product of economic forces so that law becomes a false consciousness.

Engels analysed the tension between material forces and ideology in a letter to Conrad Schmidt by suggesting that law can exert itself on the base by:

1. having a crystallising effect which maintains traditions, customs and religious concepts. Such an effect is restrictive on the achievement of awareness of class struggles and, as such, holds up the inevitable process of history;

2. the more antagonistic forces there are in society, the more the law seeks to achieve a compromise of conflicting interests; and

3. the demystification of law has a critical effect on raising class consciousness necessary for revolution.

Thus, Marx and Engels see law as having a relative degree of autonomy, seeing it as an ideological cloak which hides the truth about social conflict through compromise or conservatism and an aspect of state control. Therefore, the Marxist perspective of law is dependent on the Marxist concept of the state which determines how critical the ideal of the rule of law is to Marxism.

Marx identifies the state as an intermediary in the foundation of all communal institutions, which gives them a political form. He considers that there is an illusion of the law being based on will, ie a will cut off from its real basis of free will. The state is viewed by Marxists as no more than an aspect of superstructure which does not exist before the emergence of the classes – the state's consequential growth mirrors the burgeoning of a class system.

To Marxists, the state is 'the executive committee' of the bourgeoisie within capitalism which rules on its own behalf, utilising the legal apparatus, with the threat of coercive action against those who seek to overturn the existing order.

Marxists have prophesied that the state, being affected by change and decay, will wither away when a triumphant revolution replaces 'the government of persons by the administration of things'. If classes disappear, post-revolution, there is no need for a legal apparatus in which to express class rule, so that poverty and exploitation, seen as the root causes of crime, will vanish within the new, classless society. People will develop into 'group creatures' having no need for codes and rules so that the need for an institutionalised law vanishes.

Vyshinsky, and other Soviet jurists, found such a doctrine difficult to accept, relying on the view that the construction of a socialist society would make it necessary to consolidate law and the State. Vyshinsky considered it as essential to retain law as an administrative law as a means of regulating social relationships. However, Pashukanis held that 'all law is bourgeois law', denouncing Soviet law as a relic of the former bourgeois state. To counter such a view, Vyshinsky defined law as the totality of rules of conduct which express the will of the ruling class being laid down in a legislative manner. This, together with the rules and practices of communal life, would be sanctioned by the power of the state.

Excesses within the legal systems fashioned from Marxist theory occurred in political situations where the rule of law and the rights of the accused were banished as 'remnants of bourgeois dominance'. The result saw a denial of human dignity and the growth of legal theories which merely justified the state's political practices. The collapse of some Marxist regimes in recent years illustrates what is widely held to be an essentially flawed theory of law.

11 Utilitarianism

11.1 Introduction
11.2 Key points
11.3 Analysis of question styles
11.4 Questions

11.1 Introduction

Utilitarianism is famously known in terms of the 'greatest happiness principle', the idea first mooted by Jeremy Bentham and his immediate mentors (in particular, James Mill). The idea is simple and appealing: governments should act, by legislation, to produce, amongst all other choices open to them, a state of affairs where the maximum happiness could be enjoyed by the greatest number of people. The appeal lies in the idea that *everyone* is to count; you do not discount some people because of some contempt for them or the way they live. But it is most important to realise that utilitarianism has come a long way since Bentham's principle. The main difference between Benthamic (or, as it is sometimes called, 'hedonistic') utilitarianism and modern doctrines of utilitarianism is that the idea of pleasure, or happiness, both highly subjective terms, are replaced by the idea of 'welfare' as measured by the satisfaction of declared wants. Modern utilitarianism thus is seen to be much more closely linked to economic analysis – it is only a short step to equate *welfare* with *wealth* (they are not the same; just try comparing penniless Tiny Tim, who was happy, with rich Ebenezer Scrooge, who was unhappy, in Dickens's *A Christmas Carol*). The advantage of the modern approach, besides being more realistic (how do you judge whether a person is made *happier* by some policy?), is that it nods in the direction of endorsing the value of personal autonomy by making a person's declaration conclusive of what is good for him.

A student preparing for an examination must be aware of the following points: the difference between 'rule' and 'act' utilitarianism (only rule utilitarianism – the view that the right act is the one that is in accordance with the rule that, if followed, will be productive of the most happiness – makes any sense of the law because the law consists of injunctions to rule following); the difference between 'pleasure' and 'happiness'; the weak position of minorities in utilitarian calculations; the problem of the 'incommensurability of values' (how do you interpersonally measure people's pleasures or 'happinesses'?); and the problem of rights (eg Dworkin's argument that rights based arguments 'trump' arguments of policy).

Utilitarianism is an excellent subject to write an examination answer on because it is a topic full of examples and you can wax lyrical about them with pretty much a free hand! Make sure, however, you thoroughly grasp what utilitarianism is about; it is no use just writing what you *hope* will sound good to an examiner because understanding the basic idea has some difficulties. Once these are grasped, then the essay will write itself. One good way to find examples is to notice just how frequently politicians use utilitarian arguments sometimes to justify otherwise rather shady arguments; note, too, the relationship between the economic analysis of law and utilitarianism. The latter is particularly important given the question because there is a large group of people, known as the 'law and economics' school, who would think that this sort of reasoning (basically cost-benefit analysis) is entirely appropriate for law.

Jurisprudence: The Philosophy of Law

11.2 Key points

This is used by many theorists as a starting point for advancing their own theories of justice. In broad terms utilitarianists regard as just that which maximises 'welfare' or happiness. The student might wish to consider the theories of Bentham and Mill in particular.

11.3 Analysis of question styles

Some questions in Chapters 11 and 12 are relevant for this chapter. 'Rights' is a popular examination topic, both in general questions and, frequently, in questions directed specifically towards Hohfeld's analysis. In particular, the idea of rights as 'trumps' views rights as essentially antagonistic to utilitarianism. Further, since utilitarianism is a theory of *justice*, anything which you can bring in from the Hart/Devlin debate is going to have *some* relevance.

11.4 Questions

This is used by many theorists as a starting point for advancing their own theories of justice. In broad terms utilitarianists regard as just that which maximises 'welfare' or happiness. The student might wish to consider the theories of Bentham and Mill in particular.

TYPE ONE

This is a general question about the nature and varieties of utilitarianism.

'Good legislation is the art of conducting man to the maximum happiness and to the minimum of misery, if we may apply this mathematical expression to the good and evil of life.' (Beccaria). Discuss.

University of London LLB Examination
(for External Students) Jurisprudence and Legal Theory June 1984 Q5

Skeleton Solution

Utility – felicific calculus – mathematical expression – how to measure happiness – moral criteria – economic and social hardship – Mill – Dworkin – average utility not total utility – Rawls – modifications of utilitarianism.

Suggested Solution

Beccaria's statement is an application of the principle of utility, measured in terms of people's happiness and misery, to the process of legislation. I shall look at that application in more detail and then look at various criticisms which may be levelled at this particular aspect of utilitarian theory. Next I will consider if any modification of that theory can help to avoid these criticisms. Even if such modifications are possible, we must next consider whether there are better views regarding legislation: is the utilitarian view the best available one?

The statement brings out three essential points regarding a utilitarian explanation of the role of legislation. First, the explanation is rooted in what Bentham – regarded as the 'father' of utilitarianism, but himself heavily influenced by Beccaria – called the 'felicific calculus': that the rightness of public and private acts is to be evaluated on a basis of maximisation of pleasure and minimisation of pain; in short (and inaccurately) 'the greatest happiness of the greatest number'.

Second, the evaluation of legislation is turned by utilitarianism into a scientific exercise, a matter of calculating mathematically the happiness and misery caused. The decision of what is 'good' and what is 'evil' turns on the 'mathematical expression', the measurement of the felicific calculus.

Third, the effect of utility will be that private and public interests will coincide. The public interest decision of what legislation to enact is decided on a measure of individuals' happiness and so, inevitably, that decision will maximise individual happiness. Good legislation is seen, in Beccaria's words, as 'the art of conducting man to the maximum happiness and to the minimum misery'.

Thus stated, the utilitarian position on the role of legislation presents itself as a beguilingly simple method for use by legislators. Is this picture correct? Unfortunately not. There are many criticisms of the utilitarian view which are specifically relevant to the question of legislation. For a start, how are legislators to go about measuring people's happiness and misery? How does a sighted man's pleasure at seeing beautiful countryside or good paintings measure against a blind man's distress in not being able to do so? There are innumerable such problems: stating the felicific calculus is one thing, putting it into practice another – much more difficult – one. On the legislative scale, can legislators know what the consequences of (say) a new Bill controlling police powers will be even if they – the legislators – concentrate on the (more) objective measure of people's well-being (as against their happiness/misery)?

Even if the calculus was practicable, is it right? Should some pleasures be more important than others; to use an extreme example, should the happiness of a psychopath who murders ten innocent people be of equal value to the misery of the mourning victims? Or the pleasure of looking at the Mona Lisa be compared to that of reading a pornographic magazine? In short, hasn't legislation any role in promoting certain values – or at least, in not promoting certain activities such as violence even if (on balance) they increase happiness? Shouldn't moral criteria play a part in the calculation?

Further, let us assume that a majority had strong wishes which involved legislating that a minority be their slaves. Shouldn't the majority be constrained? And yet, the utilitarian can simply ask for the best balance of happiness, and if it favours slavery then that is the correct solution. Another unsatisfactory consequence is that happiness might be maximised by measures intended to increase the population greatly because the majority of people are more happy than sad; yet such an increase may lead to great economic and social hardship.

These and other attacks on the unmodified version of utility set out in Beccaria's statement have led to thinkers who follow a utilitarian line adopting modifications. John Stuart Mill, with Bentham the main exponent of utilitarianism, did allow for some pleasures to count for more than others: human beings have a capacity for pleasures more elevated than animal appetites and wish to gratify the former rather than the latter. This might be so (but do people prefer Beethoven to Dallas?), but in its turn it leads to further problems (which pleasures are the elevated ones?) without solving the central problem: that of the measurement of happiness. Various alternatives to happiness have been suggested, but all seem to share this problem. Dworkin has recently suggested that a democratic system with the constraint of rights (limiting decisions likely to have been taken as a result of external, others-regarding, preferences) is the best approximation to a measure of utility which is available. If so, it must be admitted to be an imperfect one.

Another modification of the theory is intended to 'cure' the over-population example: this is the use of *average* utility rather than *total* utility, so that the number of people involved becomes a central question. Legislation to encourage child bearing, for example, would be judged not on whether each new child would increase marginally total happiness but rather whether the average happiness of all, including the new child, would be enhanced.

Even with this modification, the felicific calculus is still attacked by modern theorists who claim that in its concern for the effect of legislative decisions on the mass of people, it ignores the separateness of individuals, which is a main tenet of views as disparate as those of Rawls and Nozick. Dworkin argues that democratically-taken utilitarian decisions must be constrained by allowing for 'rights' of individuals to 'trump' the wishes of the majority. All three of the theorists just mentioned, and, of course, many others, present detailed alternatives to the felicific calculus as the basic measure of 'good legislation'.

Rawls, for example, sets out his two principles of justice derived from a 'social contract' position. Far from adopting a utilitarian position, he argues that once liberty has been maximised economic and social well-being must be so arranged that the position of the least well off class is as advantageous as possible. Nozick, on the other hand, rejects the notion that the state may legislate beyond a 'minimal state' position.

Although it is not possible here to analyse and compare these alternatives with the position of utilitarianism as expressed in Beccaria's statement, enough has been said to show that utilitarianism requires major modifications before the statement can be accepted as accurately representing the proper role of legislation. Such modifications do not deflect all of the serious, perhaps fatal, objections to the utilitarian view. I would reject the utilitarian path because of these objections and look to other theories to provide a better answer to the question of what constitutes 'good legislation'.

TYPE TWO

This is a question about the relationship between the utilitarian considerations and rights-based arguments.

Can utilitarianism account for the idea of people having rights?

> University of London LLB Examination
> (for External Students) Jurisprudence and Legal Theory June 1992 Q8

Skeleton Solution

Utilitarianism – Hume, Bentham – rights theories – Dworkin – HLA Hart – utilitarianism and rights – the meaning of 'right'.

Suggested Solution

Utilitarianism is a theory of justice which postulates, broadly, that justice may be defined as the greatest good for the greatest number in society. Such a theory would allow the interests of the individual to be sacrificed if this would produce a 'net gain' for society generally. To some extent the political system of majority rule could be said to reflect this notion of the achievement of the greatest good for the greatest number, although utilitarian theorists tended to deal in more abstract terminology.

Utility was a key element of David Hume's theory of justice. In *Enquiries Concerning the Human Understanding and Concerning the Principles of Morals* Hume described the ultimate end and justification of all laws as the achievement of the good of mankind as a whole. Bentham developed the principle of utility in more detail and attributed central importance to it in his *Theory of Legislation*. For Bentham the principle of utility was an objective arithmetical formula for the evaluation of law avoiding the pitfalls of subjective theories based on natural law or morals which Bentham saw as mere vehicles used to justify a corrupt status quo. The principle of utility purported to allow the analysis of human actions in terms of pleasures and pains which could notionally be weighed in a balance. The goal of utility was to maximise the welfare of society generally. John Stuart Mill followed in the wake of Bentham in asserting that utility alone could arbitrate between apparently equally plausible but competing notions of justice.

In modern times the principle of utility has been overtaken by the notion of the existence of basic human rights. To generalise, the essential attribute of basic human rights may be said to be their inalienability. If the notion of basic inalienable human rights is accepted, therefore, it is difficult to understand how a principle of utility can survive given that it might require individuals to give up certain rights if to do so would result in a greater happiness for society as a whole. Rawls claimed that utilitarianism failed to attach sufficient importance to the separateness of individuals. Utilitarianism has also been criticised for attaching no worth to individuals except as the source of experience of pain and pleasure, and for failing to appreciate that while it may be logical for an individual to order his life on the basis of the principle of utility, this principle does not necessarily translate to the ordering of society as a whole.

One of the principle modern rights theorists and a critic of utilitarianism is Ronald Dworkin who in his book *Taking Rights Seriously* describes a right as an anti-utilitarian concept. According to Dworkin a right cannot be denied to an individual even if to do so would be in the general interest. For Dworkin it is foundational to political morality that individuals should be treated with equal concern and respect. However, Dworkin asserts that there is no general right to liberty, only to specific liberties such as freedom of speech, freedom of association and freedom of contract. Dworkin's theory allows for state intervention in the exercise of some liberties in order to advance overall social welfare. Thus an individual's freedom to contract might be restricted in the interest of society as a whole by virtue of laws prescribing maximum daily working hours. However, Dworkin asserts that liberties, which rank as moral rights, such as freedom of speech, cannot be overriden if they conflict with the common good. In order to distinguish an inalienable right from a liberty liable to restriction one must, according to Dworkin, ascertain whether the right in question is likely to be restricted by what he calls the 'corrupting element' in utilitarian analysis. This corrupting element is described as the tendency to include in an assessment of the aggregate general welfare not only the personal preferences of individuals for their own good but also their preferences, known as external preferences, with regard to others. This, in Dworkin's opinion, results in an unacceptable form of 'double counting' of votes which fails to treat individuals with equal concern and respect. Rights which would be restricted on such an analysis are, in Dworkin's opinion, inalienable.

In his essay 'Between Utility and Rights' Hart criticises Dworkin's theory and points out that the so-called external preferences might in fact tip the balance in favour of a particular right, such as the right to sexual freedom for homosexuals. Hart points out that it is not the exercise of ascertaining the maximum aggregate good through the wishes of the majority that is at fault but the wishes of the majority themselves. This echoes Bentham's defence of utilitarianism against the accusation that it was corrupted by subjectivism, in which he claimed that the principle of utility itself was not necessarily faulty merely because it was applied in a faulty manner. Hart maintains that the mere fact that a minority group is out-voted on a particular matter is not to say that that group is thereby being considered as not worthy of equal concern and respect.

Dworkin himself admits a limited role for the principle of utility in relation to the balancing of those liberties which are not inalienable, which suggests that utilitarianism and rights are not totally irreconcilable. The question whether utilitarianism accounts for the idea of people having rights may also be viewed in the context of the general meaning of 'rights'. If one ascribes to the absolutist view that there are certain inalienable rights which never change in content, then utilitarianism cannot account for the existence of such rights since from time to time the wishes of the majority might result in an impairment of the content of such rights. However, if one adopts a relativist standpoint, namely that there are inalienable rights but their content may change from time to time in accordance with the views and dictates of society, then the principle of utility continues to have a role in the ascertainment of the wishes of society as to the content of such rights. Thus an absolutist might say that several years ago utilitarianism denied the inalienable right of sexual freedom to homosexuals in England, whereas a relativist would say that such a right has only evolved in recent years in accordance with the changing views of society, and that the principle of utilitarianism has now given it recognition. Thus, the principle of utility should not be rejected solely on the grounds that it fails to protect certain rights, viewed in an absolutist sense. Even in relation to such absolute rights it may be asserted that the principle of utility, as part and parcel of the notion of majority rule, has contributed to the advancement of certain rights in accordance with the views of society generally.

TYPE THREE

This is a question which tests specifically the candidate's views as to how utilitarian reasoning might be applied to *legal* reasoning. Such questions *may* be answered by reference to Posner's theory of judicial wealth-maximisation.

What is utilitarianism? Is it a good guide to judicial decision-making?

University of London LLB Examination
(for External Students) Jurisprudence and Legal Theory June 1993 Q9

General Comment

The question can be answered in many ways, and it is not necessary to go into the economic analysis of law to provide an excellent answer. Nevertheless it is one very fruitful way of doing so as the answer below takes this line.

Skeleton Solution

Bentham's doctrine and act and rule-utilitarianism - general problems with utilitarianism: its inability to identify the dignity of individuals and its wrong assumption that values are commensurable - the connection with economics: the Pareto criterion of measuring welfare and the Kaldor-Hicks criterion - application of economic analysis to law - conclusion that individual dignity, in the form of rights, cannot be measured or protected in money terms.

Suggested Solution

Jeremy Bentham proclaimed that political acts (eg those of the officials in a legal system) should be morally adjudged according to whether they produced consequences for the maximum

11 Utilitarianism

happiness (or pleasure) for the maximum number of people; a political action, say, of legislative enactment, was therefore right if there were no alternative action which would produce even better consequences. The important things was that everybody's potential happiness had to be assessed and added together and seen as a consequential state of affairs. The idea did not allow room for the 'act that is right *in itself*' or the idea that an act could be judged independently of the consequences it produced (assuming, of course, that a clear distinction could be drawn between a description of 'the act' and 'the consequences').

Later utilitarians, predominantly legal thinkers, refined this 'act' utilitarianism to what became known as 'rule' utilitarianism, which said that an act was utilitarianly right if it supported, or was in accordance with, a rule which, if followed in general, would bring about the greatest happiness of the greatest number. This idea was developed to meet the criticism of utilitarianism that it could not account for the way we think that it would be wrong to overturn rights that people have acquired through the application of rules such as those in legal systems, or in useful social institutions such as the institution of promise-keeping, just because it would be 'useful' to do so. Rule utilitarianism thus purported to say that people have rights, to have their valid contracts enforced, for example, because, in the long run, having contracts in society is more conducive to happiness than not having, *even although in the short term* greater utility would be achieved. It is easy to see, however, that rule-utilitarianism is not the slightest bit different from act-utilitarianism; it just says that you do some acts with the long term in mind! That is the only extra explanation it gives about the nature of those acts which consist of conforming to a rule. The rule utilitarians therefore come nowhere near explaining our strong moral belief that certain acts are right *in themselves* and that situations should *never* arise in which human beings might be treated as *means* to ends rather than as ends in themselves.

This idea that individuals don't have their own inherent rights to be treated as 'ends in themselves', as having their own individual dignity is matched by another equally unsavoury idea of utilitarianism, that all happiness and pleasure (or 'welfare' as modern utilitarians describe it) is inter-measurable. Think about it; if the injunction is to go for the greatest happiness of the greatest number, you have to make calculations such as the following: if we raise interest rates, that will make a further one per cent unemployed and that creates a certain amount of unhappiness; on the other hand, it will increase the amount of interest that those with savings receive and will make them happy and it will keep inflation down which will ensure more overseas investment here which in the long run will get the economy going and that will make people happy. This seems very practical, but it amounts to saying that the unhappiness of those about to be thrown on to the dole queue can be 'traded off' against those who will gain from higher interest payments. Is this really *possible* - apart from whether it is just? Take two people, one of whom likes to drink two pints of beer each evening, another of whom prefers to make leather sandals each evening. Can we measure in any way the relative worth of these activities, such that we could trade them off?

Here is where the connection with economics comes in. We can imagine the drinker and the sandal maker to strike a bargain in money terms. If only one of the two activities could be carried out, the person who was prepared to pay the most money for the activity would be the one who would value it most and thus the greatest happiness of the greatest number (in this case, two) would be served by allowing the person who values it most, *in money terms*, to do it. Simply put, because money is a fungible, the commensurability of value, when converted into money terms, seems perfectly feasible, indeed, practically sensible. (Although, note that to ensure a fair system, both participants in this mini-market would have start off with roughly equal amounts of money in order to make the assumption that the value of each activity is properly measured.)

The law and economics movement seizes on this idea and says that people's legal rights are best determined by reference to a hypothetical market. If in this ideal world, the two litigants would have bargained, *in money terms* again, for a particular outcome, but it is only the real world that is preventing them from doing so, perhaps because of transaction costs, the courts should impose the ideal solution. This would have the advantage of either bypassing a number of expenses that would otherwise have to be met, or by coming closer to a solution that could not otherwise have been reached. In other words, the law and economics movement would have judges making a cost-benefit analysis of legal decision-making. Give Mrs McLoughlin damages only if giving them to her will first deter in future people like Mr O'Brian doing what he did and so prevent hospital costs, and second, not require a disproportionately high increase in traffic insurance premiums.

But the problem with this approach is that it can give no sense to Mrs McLoughlin *having a right* to damages, whatever the rule utilitarians say. Why? Because whether she is paid damages or not is entirely dependent upon the current economic climate; sometimes people in her position will be paid damages, other times not. That sense of her being injured through someone else's negligence *and that being in itself* the reason for her receiving compensation is notably missing. I conclude, therefore, that utilitarianism in its modern 'economics and law' form is wholly inadequate for dealing with problems arising in legal reasoning; legal systems are about fairness, justice and people's rights and not just about increasing the gross domestic product.

PART C
JUSTICE

12 Justice and the Legal Enforcement of Morality

12.1 Introduction

12.2 Key points

12.3 Analysis of question styles

12.4 Questions

12.1 Introduction

This is a large and diverse topic, which calls for a knowledge of many different theorists and theories. It is also closely linked with the jurisprudence of 'rights' (see Chapter 12). The student's response to theories of justice is bound to be partly subjective, as theories of justice are closely allied to particular political standpoints.

12.2 Key points

a) *Rawls*

His theory is of 'justice as fairness'. Justice is based on the principles which individuals in the 'original position' would choose. By his 'original position' he means a hypothetical situation where individuals would be ignorant of the likelihood of them occupying any particular social or economic position in society.

b) *Nozick*

His theory of justice rests on the tenet that the individual is inviolable. Any state besides a minimal state is unjust: for example, the Welfare State is unjust because it violates the right to property.

c) *Dworkin*

His theory of justice rests on the principle that the state should treat everyone with equal concern and respect. Redistribution can be justified but there is a host of specific rights which act as 'trumps'.

d) *Hart-Devlin debate*

Devlin argues for a conservative approach which says that English society consists of a broad consensus on moral matters. If the juryman is 'really disgusted' by, say, homosexual acts, then that makes that conduct a candidate for prohibition by the criminal law. Hart says that this kind of approach introduces bigotry in the law and that a lot of misery would be unnecessarily created by thinking that morality was merely a matter of consensus and not carefully considered conviction. The liberal approach is better, he says, because that treats as fundamental the principle that people should be in control of *their own* lives where what they do does not restrict the freedom of anyone else.

Jurisprudence: The Philosophy of Law

12.3 Analysis of question styles

The question of what is justice, and its accompanying question about the proper role of the criminal law and punishment, can be answered in many ways. Usually, the question will be directed towards some quotation by Rawls or Nozick or Dworkin and, while the answer will have to draw upon what those writers actually said, it is always possible to take in ideas from other writers, for example, on rights and utilitarianism, and to give free comment. The Hart-Devlin debate is a little more specific since the debate there was directly connected to criticism and endorsement of the Wolfenden Report on the legality of homosexual acts in private, but even here the connection with rights (a person's right to self-autonomy) and utilitarianism (the greatest happiness might require suppression of 'disgusting' activities) could be discussed.

The important point to remember is that questions on justice are about *justice*, not Nozick, Rawls, Devlin, etc. You must understand their theories but, as is usual in Jurisprudence, that understanding is a pre-condition for talking about what is just, and why. For example, Nozick has a fairly icy view of human nature and human society (see Hart, 'Between Utility and Rights'); nevertheless, his theory is elegant and seems very consistent. From the logical – but not the moral – point of view it is fairly well unassailable. But there is great room for comment about it from the moral point of view. Even the often maligned doctrine of utilitarianism has the following over Nozick's theory of rights: it takes into account the importance we attach to the idea of community – every person's happiness counts – whereas Nozick paints a bleak world where the only people who are likely to be happy are those who have, in the end, historical 'entitlements'.

To repeat that point, while questions on justice often relate to specific writers their general import is to get you to criticise and/or endorse the different theories and cross-refer to others.

12.4 Questions

TYPE ONE

One type of question calls for a critical analysis of Nozick's theory of justice. The student must be prepared to refer to other theories of justice, and to come to a firm conclusion.

'Nozick's principal argument against distributionist theories of justice rests on their failure, as he sees it, to cohere with his idea of individual liberty.' (Lloyd: *An Introduction to Jurisprudence*). Discuss. How attractive do you find Nozick's theory?

Written by the Editor

Skeleton Solution

Rights – based theory – distributionist theory – need – equality – welfare state – individual rights – minimal state – taxation – subjectively unappealing.

Suggested Solution

Robert Nozick's *Anarchy, State and Utopia* stimulated much debate when it was published in the mid-1970s. Among the issues dealt with by Nozick was a rights based theory of justice, which held that any scheme of patterned distribution was unjust. In these days of the welfare state such views may seem shocking or out of step. It has, however, been pointed out that modified versions of some of what Nozick has said are not too far removed from the policies associated with 80s 'Thatcherism'. It is proposed to examine Nozick's argument against distributionist theories before considering which theory is the most appealing.

12 Justice and the Legal Enforcement of Morality

A distributionist theory is one that advocates a patterned distribution of the benefits and burdens or 'goods' in society. Distribution is usually based on need, such need being determined on principles of equality. Distributionist theories are thus goal based: distribution is just because it achieves a certain goal (eg equality). The welfare state is clearly justified by distributive theories of justice. Money is taken from the richer members of society through taxation to benefit the needy. This is justified by the goal of equality: all individuals should have at least a minimum standard of living (it should be noted that distributionist theories do not require total equality).

Nozick utterly rejects this model of justice. For him the individual is inviolable. Man has certain rights, including the right to liberty and the right to acquire property. Such rights may only be violated with the consent of the individual. It follows from these propositions that any state beyond a minimal state is unjust. Nozick accepts that a state is necessary to protect the individual against violence and theft, and to enforce contracts. But beyond that, state intervention is unacceptable as it violates individual rights.

Thus Nozick sees distributionist theories as unjust. He views taxation, for instance, as no more than forced labour. For him the distribution of property in society is based on historical entitlement: provided property is acquired by just acquisition, legitimate transfer or rectification of past injustice, it cannot justly be taken away. According to Nozick, 'if each person's holdings are just then the total set of holdings is just'.

Although Nozick's theory is stimulating and thought-provoking it has been subjected to criticism. One might question, for example, the basis on which he arrives at his list of rights. But for many, Nozick's theory appears inherently unjust in its rejection of equality as a starting point or as a goal to be achieved. I share this view; I find distributionist theories far more appealing.

TYPE TWO

This question calls for consideration of Rawls' theory of justice. Although much has been written by, and about, Rawls, Rawls has not been a popular examination topic in recent years. Students should note that the aspect of Rawls' theory discussed below is not the only important or interesting issue.

What do you understand by Rawls' concept of the 'original position'?

Written by the Editor

Skeleton Solution

Justice as fairness – original position – veil of ignorance – unanimity – social contract theory – rejection of utility – 'maximin' principle – principles of liberty and equality – criticisms – value.

Suggested Solution

The concept of 'original position' is crucial to Rawls' theory of justice. For him the ideal is 'justice as fairness' – a society organised on principles resulting from the original position. Although there are many strands to Rawls' theory, the 'original position' is one of the most central, and also one of the most criticised.

Rawls imagines a (hypothetical) situation in which a group of individuals set out to agree the principles on which society is to be organised. These individuals operate behind the 'veil of ignorance': although they are aware of the existence of different sexes, races, levels of intelligence, wealth, social status etc, they are ignorant of the characteristics they themselves possess. Thus it is not possible for an individual behind the veil of ignorance to know the probability of being at any particular economic or social level in society. Since all in the original position are equal there will be unanimous decisions as to what principles should inform society.

Rawls' theory is thus a social contract theory, although his contract is hypothetical. He attempts to justify the application of his principles on the ground that any rational person entering the original position would choose the same principles. Thus his theory goes beyond other social contract theories in that it attempts to show why the 'contract' binds those who are not a party to it. Starting with his original position Rawls believes he can deduce the principles which the individuals in that position would choose. For example, they would reject average utility as a principle upon which to organise society because of the risk of being in the lowest echelons of society. He believes that the parties in the original position would choose principles which would offer the highest possible total of basic goods such as rights, powers, health etc. They would then opt for the 'maximin' principle; in other words, principles which ensure that even the very worst situation an individual might end up in is the best of the available alternatives. Thus a person in the original position will choose the following two principles:

1) 'Each person is to have an equal right to the most extensive total system of equal basic liberties compatible with a similar system of liberty for all.'

2) 'Social and economic inequalities are to be arranged so that they are both:

   a) to the greatest benefit of the least advantaged, consistent with the just savings principle; and

   b) attached to offices and positions open to all under conditions of fair equality of opportunity.'

The first principle has priority over the second, as Rawls believes that no person in the original position would wish to risk his or her liberty once the veil of ignorance is lifted.

There have been many criticisms of Rawls' theory but it is proposed only to consider those relating to the concept of original position outlined above. Fisk argues that the individual cannot be abstracted from his or her material circumstances in the manner assumed by Rawls' original position, and so Rawls' theory is riddled with ideological assumptions. A more general criticism is that the original position is too artificial a device to have much meaning. It is also hard to see the justification for Rawls' assertions about which principles people in the original position will choose. Are all people risk averse? Why would people necessarily prefer liberty to equality? Perhaps Rawls' theory of justice only works for one type of character. The concept of original position is important to Rawls' theory and valid criticisms of it can only damage his theory of justice as a whole. Despite this it should be remembered that Rawls' writings are rich and stimulating and have provoked much valuable debate.

TYPE THREE

The legal enforcement of morality

This is a narrower issue, focusing on what is conveniently known as the 'Hart-Devlin debate'. The main issues are as follows:

12 Justice and the Legal Enforcement of Morality

i) Should there be a realm of private immorality which is not the concern of the law?

ii) The 'harm principle'.

iii) The concept of shared morality.

The two questions below are good examples of the popular examination topic of the legal enforcement of morality. Although the first question calls for a fairly straightforward evaluation of the debate about punishing immorality practised in private, it is made more interesting by the use of a quotation. Students should ensure that they are capable of dealing with such questions: they should be able to demonstrate their understanding of the quotation and its relevance to the issues raised by the question, rather than simply ignoring it and trotting out a prepared answer on a topic. The second question is interesting because it calls for an examination of the practicalities involved with the legal enforcement of morality – students should consider such issues when revising.

'Let a man therefore be ever so abandoned in his principles, or vicious in his practice, provided he keeps his wickedness to himself, and does not offend against the rules of public decency, he is out of reach of human laws.' (Blackstone). Discuss.

University of London LLB Examination
(for External students) Jurisprudence and Legal Theory 1983 Q1

Skeleton Solution

Realm of private immorality – 'Hart-Devlin' debate – should immorality be punished? – Stephen J – pro-punishment view – shared morality issue – Devlin – less extreme pro-punishment view – standards of the reasonable man – J S Mill's 'harm principle' – Wolfenden Committee – Hart – paternalism – matter of personal choice.

Suggested Solution

Should the law punish wickedness practised in private, or is there a realm of private immorality which the law should not concern itself with? This vexed question is at the centre of a long standing debate, now known as the 'Hart-Devlin' debate. Blackstone's statement shows him to be on Hart's side, feeling that such wickedness should not be punished. By wickedness, I refer to vicious *conduct*, not abandoned principles; the law does not generally attempt to control people's thoughts or wishes and could not be expected to (although the Devlin side might suggest that quashing the wickedness could have beneficial effects on the wicked thoughts). The reference to the 'rules of public decency' appears ambiguous; I take Blackstone to mean those rules protecting individuals from seeing or being directly exposed to the wickedness.

We are asking then, if wickedness is practised in private without directly affecting those not practising it, should the law punish such wickedness: should the law enforce the general sense of morality that deems the conduct wicked? (Examples of the sort of conduct involved include homosexual acts, prostitution, sodomy, adultery: primarily we are talking about sexual morality.) The onus of justifying punishment must rest on those who wish to punish; first, therefore, we will look at the famous exponents of the pro-punishment view, Stephen J and Lord Devlin, to see if punishment can be justified.

Stephen held an extreme version of pro-punishment view; he thought society should uphold its moral code as an end in itself, and should to that end persecute the grosser forms of vice. There are several problems with this basic point of view; for a start, where is the 'moral code' that is being enforced? It can't, ex hypothesi, be that of everyone in the society: is it just that of the majority, and if so isn't there a danger of its consisting of the prejudices of the majority? As always with such questions of morality, the impossibility of showing any objective moral standards to be correct weakens the argument. Further, wouldn't most modern-day codes allow moral autonomy to others, to decide for themselves: Devlin suggests that even those practising immorality in private admit it to be evil, but this is surely not true of homosexuality and frequently wouldn't be true of prostitution, adultery etc. Finally, is the law the right medium by which to preserve a moral code: isn't argument and discussion the way to do it, with legal coercion not only failing to do justice to people's motives in many cases, but also being more likely to strengthen the will of those opposing the code?

Devlin's is a less extreme pro-punishment argument, although he has at times been represented as holding the more extreme view. The moderate position is that private wickedness may be punished because it harms society. Devlin asks three questions in turn: (i) *Has society the right to pass judgment on morals?* Yes, he answers, because society is a community of common thought and ideas, and if those bonds are relaxed the members drift apart. (ii) *To what extent should society use law to enforce its moral judgments?* Since private vice harms society in both tangible and intangible ways, because those involved are less useful to society in other ways, and because weakening any part of the morality weakens the whole, society – to preserve its integrity – must always reserve itself the right to punish this private vice. (iii) *In what circumstances should the state exercise its power?* The moral judgments of society are the standards of the reasonable man: the state should exercise its power to enforce those standards when the reasonable man feels disgust, when the vice is so abominable that its mere presence is an offence.

There are many arguments that tell even against this moderate version. For a start, again, we must question whether or not there is a shared morality in the community: modern political theory rather suggests that instead there is a toleration of different moralities: this is liberalism. In any case, the way Devlin identifies the morality and decides when to enforce it in a way that moves from 'integrity of society' as a justification for punishment, to 'disgust' as a measure of when that integrity is threatened is just moral populism of the worst sort. Devlin says he wishes personal freedom to be upheld: what sort of freedom is it that allows you only to do what your neighbours don't strongly disapprove of? And finally on Devlin would a failure to preserve the shared morality (would enforcement by law preserve it anyway?) actually harm society: couldn't it improve it? Is a more liberal or permissive society better or worse than a morally repressive one?

Since the onus is on the Devlin side, most of the argument on the 'anti-punishment' side has been critical, making the sort of points made in the last paragraph. Hart, especially, has not fully explained his views. In the 19th Century, J S Mill asserted that society only had the right to interfere with individuals' liberty if their actions harmed others directly. Enforcing a view of morality against them if other people were only contingently affected could not be justified: the society's view of morality might be wrong. Only if other people's interests were prejudiced, should a welfare calculation on the activity be considered. This view was known as the 'harm principle', and it was followed in essence by two influential reports.

In 1957, the Wolfenden Committee followed it, saying there was a sphere of private morality which was not the law's concern. Neither homosexual acts (between consenting adults) nor prostitution should be illegal if they were private; only if they directly affected those not involved (for example soliciting on the streets) should they be punished. The Sexual Offences

12 Justice and the Legal Enforcement of Morality

Act 1967 on homosexual offences followed this advice. The Williams Report on *Obscenity and Film Censorship* (1979) took a similar line, recommending that public displays of pornographic material should be curtailed, but that pornographic material itself should not be banned.

Devlin didn't accept the harm principle because it did not include protection for society as a whole (as against individuals); even the leading 'anti-punishment' exponent of recent times, Professor Hart, has not totally accepted it. He justifies the rule denying consent as a defence to crimes of serious violence as paternalism, rather than enforcing a moral view against such consent. Society is justified in making an offence conduct which it considers would be bad for or harmful for him (as against would be right for). Obviously this will be limited to physical (and psychological!) harm, and examples of it might include drug abuse, the definition of obscenity ('tendency to deprave and corrupt' – psychological harm), seat belts, crash helmets, and many laws protecting minors and people who are mentally deficient. Hart strongly criticises Devlin's arguments, particularly on the lines that there is no freedom if disgust of others is the test of what society would prescribe. He does, however, agree that there is a 'shared morality' in societies, and that such a shared morality is essential.

With a concession on paternalism, and agreeing that a shared morality as essential, is there really a difference between Hart and Devlin? The answer is, yes. Hart does not discuss paternalism in enough depth for us to be certain what is included, but one might use the example given above; presumably, however, adultery, homosexual acts, prostitution are not. 'Moral paternalism' is only relevant properly to minors and others of not full capacity; apart from that, only 'physical paternalism' is at all acceptable in a society which values freedom (since 'moral paternalism' would surely be as much an erosion of freedom as a 'disgust' criterion?). On this basis, perhaps the present definition of pornography is not acceptable, although, of course, use of pornography is not a crime.

Paternalism does then leave an area of private morality, and Hart's shared morality, unlike Devlin's, does not encroach on this. For Devlin, all moral views are included; for Hart, only those principles (against violence etc) necessary for any society to exist 'shared' by all societies, rather than by all members of one society (cf his 'minimum content of natural law'). The area of private, sexual morality or immorality is, for Hart, not the law's concern. As long as it is in private and so does not offend the rules of public decency by being in public, it should not be punished even if other members of society are thereby disgusted or offended.

The 'punishment or not' question in the end then depends on whether the stated values of society in Devlin's sense are more important to it than the freedom of values and ideas expressed by Hart.

13 What Are Rights?

13.1 Introduction
13.2 Key points
13.3 Analysis of question styles
13.4 Questions

13.1 Introduction

The discussion of rights can broadly be divided into two: the normative (which overlaps with Chapter 11) and the analytical. The value of the analytical approach to rights lies in the clarification of words used in legal relations so that the solution of legal problems is both easier and more certain. Since the normative jurisprudence of rights relates so closely to theories of justice, one's political standpoint will be of much greater importance here.

13.2 Key points

a) *The normative jurisprudence of rights (see also Chapter 11)*

   i) The libertarian view, such as that of Nozick, is that man's rights (such as the right to property) are inviolable.

   ii) The liberal view espoused by Dworkin starts from the premise of equal concern and respect for individuals. This is a fundamental right and there are also other rights which are protected to preserve that fundamental right. For Dworkin, these rights are 'trumps'.

b) *The analytical jurisprudence of rights*

   i) Hohfeld's scheme of jural relations is the starting point for any analysis of rights. He saw that the word 'right' can encompass the concept of right, of privilege, of power, and of immunity. He attempted to clarify legal relations in terms of jural opposites and correlatives of rights, privileges, powers and immunities.

   ii) The value of Hohfeld's analysis to the lawyer should be considered. If his analysis were to be really useful should law not be discussed in terms of his jural relations?

   iii) The 'will' theory (Hart) versus the 'interest' theory (MacCormick) is an interesting debate. For Hart, rights are legally protected choices; for MacCormick rights protect certain interests. As with the normative jurisprudence of rights, a political perspective is important to this debate.

13.3 Analysis of question styles

Some questions in Chapter 11 are relevant for this chapter. 'Rights' is a popular examination topic, both in general questions and, frequently, in questions directed specifically towards Hohfeld's analysis. If the student is familiar with Hohfeld's scheme of jural relations and criticisms of that scheme, it should be easy to score high marks.

13 What Are Rights?

13.4 Questions

TYPE ONE

These are good examples of questions on the normative jurisprudence of rights. Dworkin's 'Rights as Trumps' thesis is clearly relevant.

1) Under what circumstances, if any, can rights be justifiably overridden?

University of London LLB Examination
(for External Students) Jurisprudence and Legal Theory June 1988 Q3

Skeleton Solution

Nature of rights – statements about claims, powers and immunities – not absolute – Orwellian principle on protection of rights – require limitation on rights – Dworkin – proviso – wishes of majority subject to certain rights of minority – otherwise rights of minority subject to majority – eg slavery – but majority can override minority – allocation of resources – distinguish due process right from substantive right – right to due process not normally overridable – but emergency – Article 15 European Convention on Human Rights 1950 – war or national emergency – threaten life of nation – eg Northern Ireland – Greece – Cyprus – European jurisprudence on these matters – non use of rights to destroy rights – Article 17 – *Federal German Communist Party Case* (1957) – right of association – also – *Glimmerveen & Hagenbeck* v *The Netherlands* – freedom of speech – racism – contrary to Convention – limitation on rights justified.

Suggested Solution

The question presupposes the existence of rights and implies the desirability of the protection of rights. In order to address the question fully it would be necessary to examine whether this contention is unchallenged.

From a Marxist perspective individual rights are incompatible with socialism in that social change is not effected by moralising about rights. Marx spoke of the distinction between the rights of the citizen being those political rights exercised in common with others and which therefore involve participation in the community from the rights of man which he thought were private rights exercised in isolation from others and therefore allowed for withdrawal from the community.

The new left also reject rights as such, as these are not required in a classless society. Campbell in *The Left and Rights* identifies the reasons for such rejection as legalism; coerciveness; individualism and moralism. By legalism is meant that rights subject human behaviour to the governance of rules; by coerciveness that rights protect the interests of capital; by individualism that rights protect the self interested atomised individuals and by moralism the point is made that they are essentially utopian and therefore irrelevant to reality. Yet even under socialism there is a requirement for rules to facilitate social interactions and that in so doing certain rights will be enunciated. Under socialism then the right to work is more important than the freedom of labour. So that everyone has the right to do some work because it is only through work that the individual can fully realise his potential as a person. This means that it will be the socialist state that will determine what work people will do. Under the freedom of labour which is the prevalent philosophy under liberal capitalism the individual chooses his profession and whether to work at all. Under socialism and the right to work in some instances it will not be possible to satisfy everyone's preference for the type of work they wish to engage in. Hence the prior decision about political preferences will determine much of the discussion on the protection of 'rights' and the circumstances under which they can be justifiably overridden. I will base the rest of my discussion on this topic on the premise of a liberal capitalist conception of rights.

The views of Ronald Dworkin are particularly illuminating in this regard and it is proposed therefore to deal with these in depth. Dworkin refers to the political neutrality of the state in that the state will treat everyone with equal concern and respect. He speaks of auction equality on the desert island where decisions are taken on the basis of a majoritarian democratic process on the basis of utility but subject to the proviso that the basic rights of the minority not be infringed. Every majority decision infringes the rights of the minority; however the rights that Dworkin is referring to are those which a liberal holds as fundamental human rights. Thus, in order to avoid the excesses of utilitarianism, Dworkin speaks of 'protected interests'. Although there is no list of these provided it is submitted that those rights that are non derogable in the European Convention on Human Rights and Fundamental Freedoms 1950 probably express the more important of these and would therefore include the right to life, to freedom from torture or other inhuman or degrading punishment, and the right not to be subject to retrospective criminal legislation. The protected interests of Dworkin possibly go even further than this list.

In order, then, to answer the question, a distinction would have to be made on the type of rights that one is prepared to override. Not all rights are overridable with legitimate justification. I have in mind the ones mentioned above as non derogable. However the European Convention provides that in certain circumstances other rights and freedoms may be justifiably overridden. It lists two other categories of rights. Firstly, those that are subject to limitation or restriction and secondly, those that are derogable in times of war or other public emergency threatening the life of the nation, however such derogation is legitimate to the extent strictly required by the exigencies of the situation. The jurisprudence of the Council of Europe allows a certain margin of appreciation to the state concerned in the determination of how far this goes: see *Ireland* v *The United Kingdom* (1978) concerning conditions at prisons in Northern Ireland. Dworkin would view the restrictions on rights in line with the derogation clause of Article 15 of the European Convention as a restriction on policy grounds, whereas we would regard other restrictions (such as that contained in Article 17 which provides that rights contained in the Convention cannot be pleaded in order to defeat the exercise or enjoyment of rights by others) as existing on grounds of principle.

Thus Dworkin's rights thesis sees rights as trumps placing individual rights over considerations of general welfare and that these rights ought not be interfered with unless one is faced with the type of situation covered by either Article 15 or 17 of the European Convention. The problem is that such a view is not devoid of political considerations, whatever Dworkin may say about the political neutrality of the state in this matter.

Any discussion on rights is inevitably going to make political assumptions. It is on these political assumptions that most criticism is made. What is clear from Dworkin is that rights are anterior to law, not *vice versa*..

When rights can justifiably be overridden depends then firstly on political assumptions about the nature of rights; secondly on the type of rights, whether substantive or procedural, and thirdly on the circumstances one is minded to allow for such restriction. The difficulty with this question is that it seeks a response to the third question without addressing the first and second questions.

13 What Are Rights?

2) When may rights be trumped?

University of London LLB Examination
(for External Students) Jurisprudence and Legal Theory 1990 Q4

Skeleton Solution

Kantian influence – Kantian ethics – liberal interpretation – liberal dilemma – Millian solution – Hart v Devlin; what is 'harm'? – Dworkinian rights theory – utilitarianism – economic analysis of the law – differences between liberal theories – Rawls v Nozick.

Suggested Solution

Modern jurisprudence has been much influenced by the work of Kant. His theories can be said to be the basis of much 'rights-talk', which can loosely be termed liberal jurisprudence. This is advocated by such diverse theorists as Dworkin, Hart, Nozick and Rawls. Kant believed that each person had the capacity to make his/her own decisions about what was good in life. Each individual should be allowed to form their own conception of the good, to make their own choices, plans and decisions. Society must show respect for each person's ability to make these decisions, as well as the responsibility they had for those decisions. Society should not treat persons as means to an end. It should value each person as an end in themselves; not as an instrument to achieve certain goals.

Rights can be seen as the liberal's attempt to achieve this Kantian ideal. Although there is much disagreement between liberals, all basically agree that society should provide a framework within which the individual can exercise his/her moral capacity. Rights are part of this framework because they protect the individual's plans and decisions from being overridden by other individuals and groups within society.

However, there are problems. Sometimes two legitimate rights will conflict and then a choice will have to be made. One can claim that this is an instance of rights being 'trumped'. John Stuart Mill recognised this problem within liberalism; in *On Liberty* he felt that individual rights should only be trumped when their exercise would harm or interfere with the rights of others. Beyond this there should be no trumping of people's rights, as this would reduce the quantum of utility in society. This is because there is always a danger that truth would be prevented from coming to light in the process of trumping.

Another problem, which is emphasised in the debate between Hart and Devlin, is the considerable differences as to the meaning of harm. Devlin argues that society must trump the individual's rights to prevent the decay of society's moral foundations. For him, the right to sexual freedom between two consenting male adults in private must be restricted even though no physical harm is caused to others. This is because of the harm done to the *morality* of society. Devlin, therefore, feels that it is legitimate for rights to be trumped on this occasion.

What about when individual rights clash with collective rights? Liberals have struggled to explain how they can advocate the importance of rights and yet at the same time accept that they are not absolute. Dworkin has claimed, in an attempted solution to this dilemma, that in order to take rights seriously one must recognise that rights have normative force. Therefore, they must be supported by judges, it being only politicians who can override rights. This seems descriptively accurate and Dworkin has been accused of placing undue emphasis upon what judges *say* they are doing. Even the traditionally conservative British judiciary are gradually admitting the policy element in their decisions (*Home Office v Dorset Yacht* (1970)).

Jurisprudence: The Philosophy of Law

Utilitarianism provides a simpler answer by stating that the way to keep faith with Kant (ie treating people equally) is to accept the principle that we are all concerned to maximise our own happiness. In such a situation no one person's happiness is more important than another's. Therefore, to uphold one individual's rights against the collective interest is to treat people unequally. Utilitarians claim that rights should be trumped when to do so would maximise utility, or conversely, when the exercise of individual rights would reduce utility. Another consequentialist theory; economic analysis of the law has a similar monist (the advocation of one supreme value) approach. This theory asserts that rights should be trumped when to do so would maximise efficiency.

Consequentialist theories face severe criticism, mainly over the immoral and unjust consequences that would be justified if their views were followed. A utilitarian would countenance the activities of a sadist against an unwilling victim if the sadist derived greater happiness than the reduction in happiness of the victim. Similarly, an economic analyst would countenance the forced taking of a book that belonged to A if the taker B valued the book at £3, whereas A only valued it at £1.

At the same time as trying to reject these consequentialist theories, liberals have failed to agree on the conditions under which rights may be trumped. An example can be seen in the differences between the two liberal theorists: Rawls and Nozick. Rawls claims that rights can be trumped in order to give effect to the collective interests of society. An individual's right to his/her income can be trumped in order to redistribute it to the less well off members of society. He claims that we would agree to this if we were in the hypothetical situation he calls the 'original position'. In such a situation each individual is ignorant of his/her socio-economic position within society and his/her talents. Each realises that they could end up as one of the least well off members of society. We will agree to redistribution because of a rational fear of ending up at the bottom of the social pile. Since we would have agreed to this redistribution of wealth, the trumping of rights to income and the wealth generated by individual talent by such mechanisms as income tax is *fair*, according to Rawls.

Nozick (also a Kantian liberal theorist) claims to be taking rights seriously. He asserts that to redistribute wealth (eg by taxation) is theft because it trumps people's legitimate claims to what belongs to them. For him fairness is to be found in the mixing of a person's labour with an object. After such a mixing the individual has a property right in what he/she has produced. Redistribution is the worst kind of theft, since it denies that a person has rights in themselves; their talents and labour. Nozick criticises Rawl's theory as permitting individual talents and qualities to be seen as common assets available to all. Nozick states that rights can never be legitimately trumped, unless by the owner's consent.

Various theorists present different responses to the question when can rights be trumped? In so doing they also go some way to explaining *why* rights are trumped. The diversity of theories highlights how it is possible to have an almost infinite number of interpretations of the Kantian ideal, with the liberal's concern with rights professes to give effect.

TYPE TWO

A selection of questions calling for a critical evaluation of Hohfeld's thesis, and (often) an evaluation of his contribution to legal or juristic thinking.

1) Assess the contribution of Wesley Hohfeld to our understanding of law.

University of London LLB Examination
(for External Students) Jurisprudence and Legal Theory June 1987 Q4

13 What Are Rights?

Skeleton Solution

Hohfeld's aims – his scheme of correlatives and opposites – assessment – not widely used – even though can assist in avoiding confusion – takes no account of a concept of law – no account of process of according legal character to conceptions – narrow and restrictive interpretation of rights – important though seldom acknowledged contributions.

Suggested Solution

Hohfeld has made a considerable, though hardly acknowledged, contribution to our understanding of law. In his work, *Fundamental Legal Conceptions As Applied In Judicial Reasoning*, Hohfeld stated that the aim of his theory was to clarify different kinds of legal relations and the different uses to which certain words that are employed in legal reasoning are made. He sought to expose the ambiguities and to eliminate the confusion that surrounds these words. That objective can be achieved by the concept of rights; of privilege; of power and of immunity.

For Hohfeld, these words are to be explained in terms of correlatives and opposites, as each of these concepts has both a jural opposite and a jural correlative. These contain eight fundamental conceptions and all legal problems could be stated in their terms. They thus represented a sort of lowest common denominator in terms of which legal problems could be stated. This he did by method of the following:

Jural Opposites – Right/No Right; Privilege/Duty; Power/Disability; Immunity/ Liability.

Jural Correlatives – Right/Duty; Privilege/No Right; Power/Liability; Immunity/ Disability.

The aim of Hohfeld was to provide a model for the correct solution of legal problems and to make that solution easier and more certain. He would advocate that the judge and the legal theorist employ the above scheme in order to ensure greater understanding of these legal concepts.

His contribution has been useful, although the difficulty is that it is not as widely used as he would have advocated. Nonetheless, as Lloyd and Freeman observe, it is the point to which all lawyers return. They perceive the value of his analysis in enabling the reduction of any legal transaction to relative simplicity and precision and in the enabling of the recognition of its universality.

Harris identifies three important advantages to his approach. Firstly that it enables real normative choices to be disentangled from verbal confusions. Secondly that if lawyers and judges were to employ his terminology that was not too far removed from that already employed, then clarity would reign. The third advantage lies in their use. Hohfeld believed that juristic problems concerning the nature of compound concepts could be dissolved.

Although he has been criticised for insisting on correlativity in situations where correlativity is hardly present, eg the criminal law, the implicit answer that Harris finds in his defence of Hohfeld is that all cases involve two parties and, as such, viewing these concepts as correlatives is in that frame quite meaningful. It does however make an explanation of rights in rem impossible. Nonetheless there are important criticisms of Hohfeld's scheme. In that he purports to analyse fundamental legal concepts, he does so without taking account of any concept of law. He fails to provide an explanation of the process by which those conceptions are given their legal character. He further assumes that there is only one concept of duty. It is said that this is because his examples are drawn from civil and private law.

Jurisprudence: The Philosophy of Law

As Cook observes, Hohfeld mistakenly considers all rights as sets of any number of his four elementary rights: namely, claim; privilege; power and immunity. Rights are not sets of these. Their possession entails the possession of other rights or of powers and duties. For example, the concept of ownership includes rights of possession, transfer, sale, hire and use and enjoyment. Thus, ownership creates a set of claims and powers. The concept of ownership can be seen as a set of rights; it does not denote the relationship between the owner and the tangible object.

In spite of these criticisms, viewed in a chronological frame, his contribution has been substantial. There have however, since his work, been further developments and elucidations such as the works of Hart and MacCormick on rights. They benefited from having available to them Hohfeld's analysis.

2) 'If a homely metaphor be permitted, these eight conceptions – rights and duties, privileges and no-rights, powers and liabilities, immunities and disabilities, seem to be what may be called "the lowest common denominator of the law".' (Hohfeld). To what extent may this analysis still be seen as useful?

> University of London LLB Examination
> (for External Students) Jurisprudence and Legal Theory June 1986 Q1

Skeleton Solution

Correlatives – opposites – legal relationships between people – clarity of thought and exposition – isolation of normative choices – explanation of legal concepts – limits – still valuable.

Suggested Solution

A brief explanation of Hohfeld's explication of the eight 'lowest common denominators of law' will be necessary before turning to consider whether that analysis is useful and to look at the word 'still' in the question; a word which (as will appear below) I find puzzling in the present context.

Hohfeld sought to reduce legal quantities to their basic components: the 'building bricks' of law. The eight 'conceptions' set out in the quotation given in the question are those 'building bricks'. They consist of two 'blocks' of four 'bricks', each block in turn comprising two sets of correlatives. For instance, the latter four conceptions (powers and liabilities, immunities and disabilities) can be represented diagrammatically as follows:

```
Power   ━━━━━━━━━━  Liability
             ╲ ╱
             ╱ ╲
Immunity ━━━━━━━━━━  Disability
```

In the diagram, a horizontal line represents a 'correlation' and a diagonal represents an opposite. Hence, if a person has a power, he can by his voluntary act change the legal position of another person: that person is under a correlative liability to have his legal position changed by the exercise of the power. If, on the other hand, a person does not have such a power, he has the opposite of a power, a disability which corresponds to the other person's immunity from having his legal position changed.

The correlatives govern the relationship between just two people: because I have a right (or perhaps more accurately a 'claim right', since Hohfeld gave the name 'right' to rights, privileges, powers and immunities) against another who has a relative duty, that says nothing about my relations to any person. Every other person in the world may have not a duty in that regard, but rather a privilege correlative with my 'no-right'. However, Hohfeld saw that as well as such 'unital' relations (with just one other person), I may have the same relationship in a certain regard with a few people ('paucital' relationships), or with many ('multital relationships').

This, then, is the basic Hohfeldian position. How is it useful? The first advantage that is claimed for it is its clarity of thought and exposition, which could prove particularly useful for a judge. Take, for instance, the position of a trespasser on land, who is told to get off it by a third party (who, let us assume, has permission to be there – a privilege granted by the landowner). The trespasser should not be on the land, but it is not for the third party to tell him so; in trespassing he is in breach of the duty which he owes to the landowner (and no one else) correlative to that landowner's (and no one else's) right that he forbear from entering the land. Hohfeld's analysis allows us to see this clearly.

Further, it allow us – and the judge (we should focus on the position of the judge, since Hohfeld was discussing conceptions 'as applied in judicial reasoning', according to the title of his major work) – to isolate the normative choices facing him. When dealing with the cases resulting from cricket balls causing damage to houses near cricket grounds, for example, the judge is not faced with simply conflicting 'rights' of landowners and sports players; rather, he is faced by the question of whether the privilege of each of the players correlative to the landowner to play cricket should be curtailed where this involves the possibility that a player will breach his duty to the landowner not to invade (or send a flying object to invade) the landowner's property. Such an analysis might assist the judge in seeing the choice he has to make more clearly.

Hohfeld's analysis is not simply useful in relation to understanding individual situations such as the trespassing and cricketing ones discussed above. It will also help to explain legal concepts such as ownership and possession. Take the ownership of land; the landowner's 'rights' consist of a bundle of claim rights, privileges, powers and immunities; the privilege to walk on his land (everyone else in the world having a 'no right' that he not do so), the right not to have anyone to whom he has not given permission walking there (everyone else having a duty not to walk on his land) and so on.

There are limits to the usefulness of this analysis, though I do not think that these limits have increased over time and I am, therefore, puzzled by the use of the word 'still' in the question, which implies that the analysis might be less useful than in the past.

The limits are two-fold. First, it does not cover certain situations. In particular, it has difficulties with criminal law: to whom do I owe my duty not to commit murder or theft? If it is to every potential victim, then why is it generally the case that crimes are prosecuted in the name of the state rather than of the individual victim? Also, Hohfeld has difficulties fitting procedural rights and remedies into his theory. If I breach a contract, the other party can be granted certain remedies against me – which ones, of course, depending on the exact circumstances. Is it accurate to say that my duty is either to perform or (when ordered) to satisfy the appropriate remedies?

Second, reducing complex ideas such as rights and ownership to bilateral relations in terms of the eight 'lowest common denominators' misses the essence, the central meaning, of such concepts. What links the four senses of the word 'right' which Hohfeld identifies; when are they all termed 'rights'? There is an extent to which Hohfeld would have us ignore the wood for the trees.

Viewed with those limitations in mind though, Hohfeld's analysis is a very valuable tool and could be most useful still: it is unfortunate that it is not more used in practice.

3) Examine critically the following statement: 'In any particular legal order we may say that a right or claim in a person of inherence is generally correlative to a duty in the person of incidence; that where it is not so correlative it constitutes a one-sided privilege, since the person of incidence has himself no right or claim successfully to prevent the person of inherence from exercising the privilege.' (BA Wortley: *Jurisprudence*).

University of London LLB Examination
(for External Students) Jurisprudence and Legal Theory June 1985 Q6

Skeleton Solution

Hohfeld – four senses of 'right' – correlatives – opposites – individuals – 'legal atomism' – clarity of thought and exposition – normative choices – complex concepts – criticisms – lack of use of terminology – non-correlative situations – no essence of concept of a right – clear aid.

Suggested Solution

Wortley's statement sets out part of an explanation of the concept of a 'right' in legal reasoning to be found in its most famous form in Hohfeld's essay *Fundamental Legal Conceptions As Applied in Judicial Reasoning*. I will examine the content of this explanation in some detail before rising to look at the advantages and disadvantages of considering a legal right in this sort of way.

Hohfeld identified four senses in which the word 'right' is used in the law; he termed them a right (or claim right), a privilege, a power or an immunity. Wortley's statement concerns the first two only and, beyond making the point that a detailed analysis similar to the one which I am about to look at is to be found in Hohfeld's work concerning the latter two senses of right and their correlatives, liability and disability, I shall not mention powers and immunities again.

Hohfeld explained claim rights and privileges by analysis of their relationships with their 'correlatives', duties and no rights respectively. A person has a claim right where another person is under a corresponding duty; this latter person is the 'person of incidence' because it is he who is under an obligation and the right, in fact, concerns his conduct; it has been pointed out since Hohfeld that claim rights are only possible in respect of the actions of others, putting them under a duty to do or to refrain from doing something. Thus, if I make a contract with you whereby you agree to do X, you are under a duty to do so; similarly, an employer has a right that his employee shall not divulge confidential information since the employee is under a duty to that effect.

If the employee was not under such a duty, he would have another sort of right, a privilege (also called a liberty or freedom or, perhaps more correctly, as Glanville Williams put it, a 'liberty not'), not to forbear from divulging such information. A privilege is, therefore, the opposite of a duty, and the opposite of a claim right is a no right which in turn is the correlative of a privilege. In this correlative relationship, the person of incidence, the person 'on the receiving end' as it were, has no claim to prevent the person having the privilege from exercising it.

The important thing to realise is that the correlative relationships are between individuals. I

13 What Are Rights?

have a right *as against you*, in respect of a certain thing, a contract, say: you have a duty *to me* in respect of that contract. You need not have that duty in respect of anyone else and I may not have that right. Assume that you own a picture and contract to sell it to me; I have a claim right that you transfer it to me and you are under a duty to me to do so. You do not, however, have that duty to Mrs Thatcher; she has no such claim right against you. One conclusion from this is that you are giving something extra if you enter into a separate contract with her to sell to me and hence you have given good consideration for that contract.

We can turn now to some advantages of this type of analysis or, as it has been called, 'legal atomism', in the hope that further features will be revealed by looking at these advantages. The advantages are linked, but we can separate them. First, the use of Hohfeldian concepts by judges would be an aid to clarity of thought and exposition. It would no longer be acceptable to say that a striker has a right to picket and so a right to force people to stop and listen; instead it would be realised (as it has been by English judges) that the 'right to picket' is in fact a liberty or privilege, so that nobody has a right to stop the picketing, but on the other hand, nobody is under a duty to stop and listen.

The second advantage is, as I said, linked. The increased clarity would lead to a clearer view of the normative choices which face a judge. The judge in the picketing case would be able to understand that he was not dealing with two competing rights (right to picket and right to be unmolested) but rather with a privilege (to picket) and a right (to be unmolested). This makes the upholding of the latter right a clearer moral choice.

A third advantage claimed for Hohfeld's conceptual analysis is that complex juristic concepts and problems can be explained and solved. The classic example is the concept of property rights, rights in rem. How these are to be analysed is a long-standing puzzle. Hohfield's answer is that property ownership consists of a bundle of the different types of rights, including claim rights that others do not walk on the land and the privilege (as against everybody else) of walking on the land oneself. Such relations, where there is a myriad of identical relations with different people, Hohfeld described as 'multital'; relations with just a few people he termed 'paucital', and those with just two parties 'unital'.

There are, though, criticisms of Hohfeld's scheme. First and most obvious is that some of the terminology is not commonly used in the precise way Hohfeld suggested and in particular the term 'no right' is an invention. I do not set much store by mere terminology criticisms, but it is true that while the explanation of rights and privileges set out in the statement is (generally) conceptually clear, it has not 'caught on' and been accepted and used by judges and other lawyers.

There are clearly areas where Hohfeld's explanations are not complete. For example, some situations seem to be non-correlative; I am under a duty not to commit murder, for example, but it is far from clear to whom I owe the duty or (in other words) who is the person with the claim right. Also, it is not a settled question what Hohfeld, thought about the relationship between primary, secondary and tertiary (or adjectural, procedural) rights. So, if I have an employment contract, my employer cannot specifically enforce it against me; does it make sense to say he has a right or claim that I work (the 'primary' right under the contract) when the right cannot be enforced? Would it not be more realistic and correct to concentrate on the secondary rights, the remedies, and so to say that he has a right to expect my performance of the contract or to damages, in lieu, at my option? Would Hohfeld take this latter (Hamegian, American Realist) view or is it going too far? To put this point in other words, the relevance of remedies (or the absence of them) to Hohfeld's view is not clear.

That point could be settled, I think. A more fundamental criticism is that in analysing the concept of a right, Hohfeld makes – and the explanation in the statement makes – no attempt to get at the essence of the concept, its central meaning. Knowing that there are four types of right takes us no closer to understanding what is for many the central question: what is a right? What links the four senses of the word analysed by Hohfeld?

For me, this misses the point. Hohfeld was not concerned, and nor was Wortley in his quoted statement, with abstract philosophy about rights. They were concerned with the practical world, of judges deciding cases – hence the title to Hohfeld's essay, emphasising *As Applied in Judicial Reasoning*. Within the perhaps limited sphere of practicality, the Wortley-Hohfeld analysis is a clear aid to the judge and to other jurists in the careful solving of practical (as well as some theoretical) legal problems. The failure of many jurists to take and use Hohfeldian analysis is a lamentable commentary on the failure of successive students of jurisprudence to realise the practical relevance of their studies.

TYPE THREE

This is a more general question on rights which, being more difficult, will call for some thought. Since the question is potentially broad, the student must select material to be used carefully.

'A world with claim-rights is one in which all persons, as actual or potential claimants, are dignified objects of respect ... No amount of love or compassion, or obedience to higher authority, or noblesse oblige, can substitute for those values.' (Feinberg).

Assess the importance of rights in contemporary legal and political philosophy.

University of London LLB Examination
(for External Students) Jurisprudence and Legal Theory June 1991 Q4

Skeleton Solution

Kantian ideal – Utilitarianism and economic analysis of the law's rejection of rights – Dworkin's defence – Rawls and justice – Nozick's response – Finnis and natural law rights – problem of harm – Mill's principle.

Suggested Solution

Feinberg's conception of rights envisages that their importance is in ensuring that each individual is treated in accordance with the Kantian ideal. If we take contemporary legal and political philosophy to mean Western liberalism, we can see the importance of rights as the legal expression of that political system. The Kantian ideal that underpins liberalism is that each individual should be treated as being capable of determining their own best ends; their choices should be respected equally. Most fundamentally, each person should be treated with dignity in that they should be treated as ends in themselves and not means to an end. Rights are seen as important in contemporary thinking because they are said to secure the attainment of Kantian politico-legal philosophy.

This view of the fundamental importance of rights is not without challenge or criticism. Liberals themselves disagree as to the importance of rights in achieving the Kantian ideal. Utilitarians, for example, claim that the most effective way of treating people with equal dignity and respecting their differing choices of values and aims, is to recognise their desires. Based upon a belief that all people wish to maximise their happiness (or 'utility'), they claim

13 What Are Rights?

to accord equal respect to each person's preferences which maximise utility. Utilitarians are hostile to rights because they see them as potential obstacles to the maximisation of happiness. They privilege the happiness of some at the expense of others – thus violating the Kantian ethic.

We can understand the utilitarian hostility to rights (Bentham described them as 'nonsense upon stilts') if we examine the following hypothetical situation. If A is pregnant but would like an abortion, let us imagine that to have an abortion would increase her utility. If this is so then a right to life that prevented A having an abortion would reduce her utility – in fact it would prevent her from increasing her utility. The right has the effect of overriding her preferences. Instead, it privileges the preferences of those who are anti-abortion, instead of investigating which policy would maximise utility to the greatest extent.

Similar criticisms are made by those adherents of the economic analysis of the law movement. Like utilitarianism, this theory claims that it best gives effect to Kantian principles of equal respect and choice. The choices it respects, according to its leading exponent, Posner, are those that maximise value. Only those preferences that are backed up by the willingness and ability to pay for them can be respected. He asserts that those who value a preference most, will be willing to pay the most for it. Rights, on the other hand, may be given to those who do not value them, or at least not as much as others. These right-holders will thus be enabled to override the preferences of those who most value their preferences.

Another benefit claimed by Posner, is the avoidance of having to make comparisons between individuals as to whose preferences are to be granted. The principle of wealth maximisation provides an allegedly *neutral* criterion upon which a choice can be made. Judgments as to the moral worth of persons are therefore avoided, each person being treated equally in a society viewed as a market.

Rights are defended against the criticisms and claims of utilitarians and economic analysts. Against the former it is claimed that utilitarians would be unable to prevent many immoral and cruel activities. Maximising utility is not always morally sound. For example, a utilitarian sadist may derive great happiness from carrying out sadistic acts upon a victim. If the sadist's extra utility adds more to the sum total of the population's utility than the victim's disutility subtracts from it, then a utilitarian would countenance the right to perform such acts.

As far as regards the economic analysis of the law, Dworkin has criticised Posner for also being unable to prevent cruelty and exploitation. He highlights this with the example of a book belonging to A but desired by B. A values the book at £1 but B values it more highly at £3. Posner would claim that value would be maximised by A selling the book to B for £2. Both A and B would then be better off because A would have received £1 extra above the value he placed on the book, whereas B would have secured the book at £1 less than he valued it. Dworkin claims, however, that if A refused to sell the book, Posner's theory would advocate a legal rule authorising B to forcibly take the book, as this would maximise the total wealth of society.

Far from being obstacles to the Kantian ideal, those who support rights claim that it is faithful to this ideal because it *protects* citizen's from the circumstances described above. It is claimed that the two consequentialist theories actually violate the Kantian ethic by permitting people to be treated as means to the attainment of other people's ends, as opposed to ends in themselves.

Dworkin has emphasised the importance of rights in stressing that they may only be overriden (trumped) by arguments of principle – these typically involve the normative pull of other rights. From this strong position, he does concede that policy arguments can override rights but only in limited circumstances and judges cannot use policy arguments — that is the prerogative of the legislature. Policy arguments may often be paternalistic. Feinberg would reject overriding rights on this basis. He would claim that to override a person's choice is to privilege the legislature's choice as to the good. He clearly rejects the overriding of rights by reason of 'love', 'compassion' or *'noblesse oblige'*.

Rawls agrees with the view that rights are important as a legal method of securing the Kantian ideal, but he feels that they are pointless unless there is a prior equal distribution of resources amongst citizens. He consequently advocates the overriding of rights where to do so would ameliorate the situation of the less well off in society. To secure the Kantian ideal there must be distributive justice *before* there can be effective rights. Rights are of secondary importance to Rawls, the primary value being justice.

Nozick rejects Rawls' view of rights. Instead, he sees them as primary. They secure a sphere of freedom around each individual, in which persons, property and values are free from the interference of other citizens and government. He describes Rawls' re-distribution of wealth as theft, since it overrides individuals' property rights. More fundamentally, it fails to treat the individual with Kantian dignity because their choices (as manifested by their rights) are sacrificed to the collective interests of society.

In rejecting any resort to higher values as overriding rights, Feinberg underlines the importance of rights over natural law doctrines of fundamental values. Rights are expressions of individual choice as to conceptions of the good in life. These choices cannot be dictated to people by reference to a set of fundamental values. To do so would once again violate the Kantian basis of liberalism. Finnis has attempted to formulate a natural law concept of rights. He envisages that people should be free to make choices, but that these choices will be limited by the aim of choosing the best methods to attain the seven 'basic goods' of life. These are fundamental values, without which human flourishing would be impossible.

In his concern for human flourishing, Finnis reflects the Kantian belief that free individuals are the best people to decide which ways of life will lead to their personal fulfilment. The inherent problem, which Finnis tries to resolve, is that people may exercise their rights, and the freedom that these secure, in order to make choices that are harmful to themselves, or others. We saw this possibility with the utilitarian and economic analysis theories. Given the avowed importance of rights to liberalism, how can restrictions on those rights, when they cause harm, be justified?

Mill's thesis that citizens should have the right to as much freedom as possible, as long as the exercise of their rights does not harm others, provided liberalism with a principled response to this problem. Rights, although important, had limits. Even though Feinberg appears to reject any limits on rights, most liberals agree that the unlimited exercise of rights would destroy the rights and freedom of other members of society.

Essentially, Feinberg is correct in seeing the importance of rights within contemporary politico-legal philosophy as being a mechanism for allowing people to be self-determining agents. Nevertheless, despite this importance, there is much disagreement as to just how important rights are. Some claim they are a hindrance, others that they are not as important as other mechanisms (eg justice). It has also been shown that an over-emphasis of the importance of rights can lead to a situation in which some are prevented from exercising their own rights. Whilst seeing rights as important elements of liberal thought, we must recognise their limitations and the existence of other essential concepts.

PART D

JUDICIAL REASONING

14 Legal Personality

14.1 Introduction
14.2 Key points
14.3 Analysis of question styles
14.4 Questions

14.1 Introduction

The concept of legal personality has been the subject of some jurisprudential debate. The student might wish to consider why certain bodies are treated as having such 'personality' whilst others are not, and also why (if at all) we need such a concept. This is a subject where it is necessary to consider case law and practical situations.

14.2 Key points

a) *The different types of legal personality*

  i) Human beings – this could be a more complex notion than at first appears. What, for example, is the legal status of a foetus?

  ii) Corporations sole, such as the Crown.

  iii) Corporations aggregate; these are treated as persons in law unless the contrary is stated.

b) *The theories of legal personality*

  i) The 'fiction theory' – the treatment of legal persons as persons is merely a fiction.

  ii) Hohfeld's theory – companies must be explained by looking at the capacities, rights, powers and liabilities of the individuals involved.

  iii) The Realist theory – 'artificial' persons have a real personality with a real mind, will and power of action.

  iv) The 'purpose' theory – the law protects certain purposes in addition to human beings.

c) *Evaluation of theories of legal personality*

  i) The 'fiction theory' fails to explain why the concept of legal personality is used at all.

  ii) The Realist theory has, according to Hart, illogical boundaries.

  iii) The 'purpose' theory fails to explain why the purposes protected by law need to be called, and treated as, persons.

  iv) Theorists such as Paton and Hart think that the above theories deal with the wrong issues: to consider the nature of legal personality is unhelpful.

14.3 Analysis of question styles

Legal personality has not been a popular examination topic in recent years. Questions may

Jurisprudence: The Philosophy of Law

concern all types of legal personality or simply corporate personality. The student will need to be conversant with the major theories of legal personality and their flaws.

14.4 Questions

TYPE ONE

This question requires a relatively straightforward analysis of the theories of legal personality. The only difficulty lies in deciding which are the more important theories, and thus how much detail to ascribe to each.

'... we constantly need in modern law the conception of an artificial person ...' (Sir Frederick Pollock). Examine critically the attempts made by English legal theory to provide for this need.

University of London LLB Examination
(for External Students) Jurisprudence and Legal Theory June 1983 Q8

Skeleton Solution

Fiction theory – artificial persons treated as persons – no explanation for idea of 'personality' – Realist theory – artificial person as a real personality – illogical boundaries – corporate veil – purpose theory – attempts are unsuccessful – is the wrong question being considered?

Suggested Solution

Legal theory constantly wrestles with the problem of the nature of an artificial person. This strange animal appears in the notion of 'legal personality'; that a body or group or office is in the eyes of the law a 'person', and is treated in the same way as a natural person – a human being – is treated. It might be thought that this notion requires little explanation: an artificial person is an entity which the law (a legal system) considers 'a person' (ie clothed with some of the rights and duties of a person). This simple view has not been enough for legal theorists, and we must consider those theories giving more complex explanations which appear in the English writings on the subject. (Some views, such as those of Ihering and Kelsen, find no support over here, and are thus not treated). Our criticism will concentrate on the implications of the theories, and whether the English law of 'artificial persons' can be said to be based on them.

First, we will look at the 'fiction theory', supported in England by Coke, Blackstone and especially Salmond. Juristic or artificial persons are only *treated* as if they are persons, under this view. They are *fictitious*, not known as persons apart from the law. The law gives them proprietary rights, grants them legal powers and so on, but they have no personality and no will (except to the extent a will is implied by the law). This is an obviously flexible viewpoint, since it can account for any apparent inconsistency in legal treatment by simply saying that they are only treated as persons 'to that extent'. The doctrine of ultra vires, under which a company cannot do anything not authorised by its memorandum of association, might be thought to support the fiction theory, for example (the law only gives personality to the limit of the memo), and so might the doctrine that a company is separate from its members, epitomised in the leading case of *Salomon* (the law treats the company as a separate unit, even though in fact it is not, especially in the one-man company cases like *Salomon*). Further support for the theory could be claimed from the criminal law, which originally accepted that a company could not commit a criminal offence, which depends on mental intention. The fiction view explains this on the basis of the 'will' of the 'person' only being that given by law, and therefore presumably limited to *lawful* intention. Recent developments show a more pragmatic and sensible approach, with companies subject to more criminal liability (and also subject to liability for the torts of their servants). Also, the cases where the law allows the veil to be turned aside can be explained as limitations on the grant of the fictitious personality.

Acceptable explanations, then, for many aspects of company law (although many of them can be explained acceptably by other theories, see below). However, no explanation is given for why the law uses the idea of 'personality': is there an essential similarity to real persons or not?

Some other theories are similar to and bound up with the fiction theory, notably the concession theory (that legal personality flows from the state) and the symbolist theory of Ihering.

The second main theory is termed 'Realist' and is expanded in English theory by Maitland, Pollock and Dicey. (Closely related is the 'organism' theory, the name of which gives an accurate guide to the contents). This view sees an 'artificial person' as a real personality, having a real mind, will and power of action.

If independent power of action was the only requirement of our definition of 'person' and 'personality', perhaps an artificial person would qualify (but has a company really got a power of action independent of its members and officers?); surely though there is something more. To say a corporation is a real person implies an individuality, and that implies some consciousness, experience, inner unity. Some groups may seem to have such an unity and consciousness – one could talk of such a feeling over the British reaction to the Falklands crisis, for instance – but do all legal personalities fit? Surely a corporation sole (consisting of successive holders of one office) hasn't a 'consciousness', nor a multi-national company, nor even a small company? Perhaps a university might be thought to fit?

In any case, even if the legal personalities could be counted as real persons, a further problem arises. If a two man company is a person in reality, why not a two man partnership? If a one man company, why not a one man business? In everyday life, ordinary people treat them as if they did have real personality, though in law they did not. The 'Realist theory' fails to explain why the legal definition of personality does not match the extended Realist definition.

Returning to some of the aspects of English law already considered, Realist theory can account for ultra vires (the real personality constituted by the company as set up by its documents), albeit rather weakly (isn't it a weakness to have to refer to the legal documents to establish the limits of reality?); but can't successfully accommodate the tearing aside of the corporate veil. If the company is a real entity distinct from its members, surely it should always be viewed as such and not sometimes viewed as a collection of its members? Finally, Realism can account for those instances where criminal law applies to a company: can it account for those when it *doesn't* (if a Board meeting orders an 'execution', the company isn't guilty of murder: why not?).

The third major opinion is the purpose theory developed in England by Barker. Only human beings are persons, but the law protects certain purposes other than those human beings. The creation of artificial persons just gives effect to that purpose (for example, a charitable corporation is created to give effect to various devices by which the law aids the charity). So company property is held not by a person, but for a purpose; the company is 'subjectless property'.

This view has a fundamental flaw. It does not answer the question. It is obviously true that companies and other artificial legal persons are given their status for a purpose (or various purposes). The question remains: why call them 'persons'? What aspect of these entities makes them so akin to real people that the law uses the same name and, to a great extent, applies the same rules?

A purpose view can explain ultra vires (a company is limited to its express purposes, as mentioned in the memo), and even the tearing aside of the veil (the countering weight of other legal purposes), but cannot explain the concept of an artificial person.

The various attempts of English legal theory to provide an adequate concept of artificial persons do not succeed. Paton, in *Jurisprudence*, suggests that the reason for the failure is that the wrong question is being considered. Asking what is the essence of, the connecting factor between, the various different types of legal 'persons', natural and artificial, is the wrong approach, since there is no essential connecting factor except the similarity in treatment meted out by the law.

Perhaps, instead, legal theorists should ask why artificial personality is given by the law, and why and when it *should* be given.

TYPE TWO

This question is more interesting (and perhaps more difficult). It leaves scope for discussion of the Hartian view that theories of legal personality have floundered because theorists have used the wrong approach.

'As to what the nature of corporate personality may be in itself, no positive rule at all is laid down.' (Sir Frederick Pollock). Discuss how far you believe this still to be true.

University of London LLB Examination
(for External Students) Jurisprudence and Legal Theory June 1984 Q10

Skeleton Solution

Realist theory – corporate person has mind, will and independent power of action – consciousness? – 'fiction theory' – how can companies commit crimes? – 'purpose theory' – why 'persons'? – Hart – asking the wrong question – no such rule possible.

Suggested Solution

There have been many attempts to lay down a positive rule to explain the nature of corporate personality. It is my view that none have been totally successful, each attempted explanation illuminating some characteristics of such personality while obscuring or distorting others. I will set out and discuss some of the main theories which have been developed to illustrate my point. I will then consider the application by Professor Hart in his inaugural lecture *Definition and Theory in Jurisprudence* of modern linguistic theory. Hart concludes, in effect, that the search for a positive rule has been misconceived and misleading; and he thinks that a new approach is required.

The first theory we shall look at is the 'Realist' theory, expounded by Gierke, Maitland and others. Under this theory, a corporate person is a real person, with a mind, will and independent power of action. Clearly there is an extent to which a company has a power of action independent of its members, at least when it is a big company and the members are not in control of its management. But surely something further is required to constitute a 'real person' – consciousness, experience, inner unity. Has a corporate personality (even a small company or a traditional organisation such as Marks & Spencer) these characteristics? Even if it has got those characteristics, the Realist view does not explain why a two man company has them but not a two man partnership, a one man company and not a one man business. The specific legal definition of a corporate personality is not sufficiently explained.

A second major attempt to lay down a rule to explain the nature of corporate personality is the 'fiction theory', evolved by Savigny and Salmond. This theory denies that corporate persons are real 'persons' at all: their 'personality' is a fiction, they are not persons at all apart from the legal treatment. The law gives them rights and duties. This is a flexible 'rule'; any apparent inconsistency in treatment can be explained as the law treating the organisations as persons only to a given extent. Support for this view can be taken from the *Salomon* case (1897): the law treats a one man company as a person separate from its owner, even though they are clearly identical. The ultra vires rule is explained by the fact that the law allows 'personality' only to a defined extent, in this case the extent set out in the memorandum.

The problem for the fiction theory is that no explanation is given of why the law imputes a corporate personality: why is the idea of 'personality' used. And if the idea is a fiction, how is it that companies are now held able to intend to commit crimes and torts? There is at least one aspect, then, of the phenomenon that the 'fiction' theories have failed properly to capture.

A third major theory is the 'purpose theory', expounded by Barker. Companies are not persons, but the law protects certain purposes other than human beings. A company's property is held not by a person but for a purpose; similarly the right to bring a court action is given to a corporation for a purpose (the purpose differing, presumably, between the different types of corporation). Again, this view leaves the fundamental question unanswered: why are they called 'persons'? Is there a necessary similarity between corporate and individual personality?

Many other answers have been put forward to the search for a rule to explain the nature of corporate personality. The 'organism' theory, similar to the Realist viewpoints, sees a company as a living organism; the symbolist or bracket theory, allied to the fictional 'school' of thought, is a perhaps self-explanatory view. There are others.

Our conclusion at this point must be that, as in Pollock's time, no positive rule is laid down as to the nature of such personality. Professor Hart has argued persuasively in *Definition and Theory in Jurisprudence* for a viewpoint which can be considered as amounting to a claim that the search for such a 'positive rule' is misguided.

In Hart's view, attempts to understand and explain the concept of corporate personality have floundered because the wrong question is being asked. To put it in perhaps an over-simplistic fashion, the question 'what is corporate personality' can never be answered because, in common with other concepts to be found in different areas of law and different legal systems, there is no physical referent to which the concept relates. The usual form of definition 'per genus et differentiam' is therefore not suitable and a different mode of explanation is required.

This role of explanation involves looking at and explaining in context a typical sentence using the concept. To explain the concept of a 'legal right', for example, one must look at a sentence in the form 'X has a legal right as against B' and explain what the sentence means – which explanation will include the complex details of the legal system, a law passed by one of its law-making organs, the possibility of sanctions if the legal right is not properly fulfilled. A similar explanation of sentences in the form 'Smith and Co Ltd owes wife £10' must be used to explicate the concept of legal personality.

Let us revert to the concluding sentence of the third last paragraph. Is Hart saying that the search for a positive rule is misguided, or is his just an extension (in a rather Hohfeldian direction) of the fiction theory? Hart himself is clear that he is rejecting the theories (even that of Hohfeld, which sees corporate personality as a complex myriad of rights, duties and so on, which seems at first sight to be similar to Hart's own position). We must, I think, agree with him that his answer (in rejecting the theories and the very idea of there being an answer to the question 'what is corporate personality') is a denial of the claim that there is any positive rule to be found as to its nature.

In short, then, not only is Pollock right to say no positive rule is laid down: there is strong support for the view that no such rule is possible.

15 The Judicial Process

A JUDICIAL DISCRETION
15.1 Introduction
15.2 Key points
15.3 Analysis of question styles
15.4 Questions

B LEGAL REASONING
15.5 Introduction
15.6 Key points
15.7 Analysis of question styles
15.8 Questions

C PRECEDENT
15.9 Introduction
15.10 Key points
15.11 Analysis of question styles
15.12 Question

D STATUTORY INTERPRETATION
15.13 Introduction
15.14 Key points
15.15 Analysis of question styles
15.16 Questions

A JUDICIAL DISCRETION

15.1 Introduction

Since the publication of Dworkin's *Law's Empire* this has become a hotly debated topic, as well as a popular examination choice. Students should not only consider judicial discretion from both a descriptive and a prescriptive viewpoint but consider, too, Dworkin's invocation that we *interpret* – that is, *make best sense of* what judges and lawyers do. It is useful to revise this topic in conjunction with Hart's theories. Furthermore a consideration of the Realist approach may provide an interesting point of comparison.

15.2 Key points

a) Dworkin – *Taking Rights Seriously* and more importantly, *Law's Empire*. This is both a descriptive and prescriptive account, which sees law as a 'seamless web'.

Jurisprudence: The Philosophy of Law

b) Criticisms of Dworkin – Hart, internal scepticism etc.

c) Alternative views – what do pragmatists or Realists have to say?

15.3 Analysis of question styles

This has become a popular examination topic. Questions usually call for a careful analysis of Dworkin's theory in the light of conventional theories of judicial discretion and of his more recent critics. The student may find it helpful to refer to decided cases such as *Anns* v *Merton* (1977), *Shaw* v *DPP* (1962), *McLoughlin* v *O'Brian* (1983).

15.4 Questions

TYPE ONE

This is an analysis of Dworkin's so-called 'one right answer' thesis.

'... the skeptical challenge, sensed as the challenge of external skepticism, has a powerful hold on lawyers. They say, of any thesis about the best account of legal practice in some department of the law, "That's your opinion," which is true but to no point. Or they ask, "How do you know?" or "Where does that claim come from?" demanding not a case they can accept or oppose but a thundering knock-down metaphysical demonstration no one can resist who has the wit to understand. And when they see that no argument of that power is in prospect, they grumble that jurisprudence is subjective only. Then, finally, they return to their knitting – making, accepting, resisting, rejecting arguments in the normal way, consulting, revising, deploying convictions pertinent to deciding which of competing accounts of legal practice provides the best justification of that practice. My advice is straightforward: this preliminary dance of skepticism is silly and wasteful; it neither adds to nor subtracts from the business at hand. The only skepticism worth anything is skepticism of the internal kind, and this must be earned by arguments of the same contested character as the arguments it opposes, not claimed in advance by some pretense at hard-hitting empirical metaphysics.' (Ronald Dworkin, *Law's Empire*).

Discuss.

University of London LLB Examination
(for External Students) Jurisprudence and Legal Theory June 1993 Q6

General Comment

Candidates always have difficulty with questions generally on what has become known as 'Dworkin's one right answer thesis'. It is not a question to make a big meal of; nor is it a question to dismiss lightly. Rather, it requires very careful preparation. Don't be frightened by the fact that the question of truth and objectivity is one of the most difficult questions of any discipline – not just philosophy! If you show an examiner that you are dismissive you will get few marks. You must show that you've thought carefully about the matter. It is a topic that displays sloppy logic very easily. For example: 'There is no right answer because people disagree' is just a foolish comment. True, there may be no right answers, but not for that reason, because people disagree all the time about what the right answer is (NB courtrooms!). Or, 'There is no right answer because morality is subjective.' Here by 'subjective' it is usually meant that 'no right answer is possible', so the sentence is as tautological as: 'There is no right answer because morality doesn't have one right answer.' If, on the other hand, by 'subjective' is meant 'people's beliefs differ' then we have the same mistake as before. The moral: *tread very carefully!*

15 The Judicial Process

The way to answer this sort of question is to discuss obvious distinctions such as these just pointed out, after having discussed what the question means. Use Dworkin's arguments, and that means referring to his distinctions between internal and external scepticism, and taste and judgment. Refer to the construction of the best theory underlying legal practice by Hercules, the superhuman judge. Also, difficult perhaps as the idea is, try to grasp his criticism of the idea of 'demonstrability' (see Guest, *Ronald Dworkin*, chapter 6) and explain that. Best of all, though, refer to one or two of the cases that have struck you as either confirming or contradicting what he says. Referring to what goes on in court is always useful in jurisprudence – try to bring the subject alive. After all, it must be an important question whether lawyers and judges in court are disputing about a correct decision or whether they are just 'trading tastes'.

Skeleton Solution

What question means; the arguments *for* subjectivity; the futility of the simple arguments for subjectivity; Dworkin and the consequences for his theory if morality were subjective; morality's being subject to a 'sieve' of rationality; the idea of external and internal scepticism; the difference between 'taste' and 'judgment' – the demonstrability thesis.

Suggested Solution

The question refers to the facts, which seem undeniable, that people who suppose that there is no objectivity to questions involving controversial issues of law and morality, will, in their ordinary lives refer constantly to the 'right' way of doing things, to producing arguments that are 'better' than others and so forth. This seems particularly true of legal argument; after all, what is the business of legal argument – working out what judges should do in relation to putting people in prison, or taking money by way of fine of compensation from them – if it is not about rival accounts of what should be done? If people really thought there was no 'right' or 'wrong' to the matter why would they bother to supply arguments? Why wouldn't they just say: 'this is my opinion' and 'your opinion is as good as mine'?

There are some arguments for this approach; some people would say that is in fact all that people can do, that is, give their opinion. Further, if we accepted, like Fuller and Dworkin, that moral reasoning were an integral part of legal reasoning, we would have to accept that moral reasoning was objective, and that is one idea that many people just cannot accept. Even further, what sense can be given to an argument's being *right* if there is no way at all of *establishing*, ie proving, it to be right?

But these three arguments for the subjectivity of legal reasoning, which are very common, cannot be sufficient in themselves. Take the first one; does the mere fact that something is a person's 'opinion' make it thereby 'subjective'? The answer is a crashing 'no' because even scientists, who *clearly* accept that there is an objectivity to many, if not all, statements of science, use the phrase 'in my opinion' with great frequency. Further, in courtrooms, opinions are frequently expressed about the truth of objective matters; the giving of expert evidence is an obvious example, but (although barristers are not permitted to give evidence of 'their opinion') virtually all arguments on questions of law are without doubt the result of the 'opinions' of barristers, solicitors, government departments and pupils. Indeed, the usual phrase is: 'let's seek the opinion of a barrister'. Maybe one thing that is being claimed here is that when someone gives an opinion, he is not saying he is right, just that he wants to convince the other so that the other will accept the opinion.

But it cannot be true that if you say that X is your 'opinion', you mean that there is no right or wrong of the matter. Tell that to the flat-earthers: they believe that their opinion that the world is flat is right and we believe that their opinion is wrong. Any barrister, too, will claim that his opinion is the right one (otherwise, we might wonder why he was advancing it: no-one has an interest in a wrong opinion). Further, it cannot be an answer to say that something is put forward as an opinion in order *only* to convince; what is it that 'convinces'? Is it conceivably possible that it is the objective truth for the opinion that has to convince?

The second argument suggested above for the subjectivity of legal reasoning arises from the supposed subjectivity of moral reasoning; if Dworkin is right that morality is part of the law, then, if morality is subjective, so is legal reasoning. Is morality subjective? In some senses it is clearly not; although equally clearly, matters of morality cannot be proved in any way. First, people argue about morality (eg about the rightness and wrongness of abortion), as in law, as if they believed there were right answers ('abortion is a right'; 'abortion is murder'; etc). Second, people assume that arguments about morality should be subject to rational enquiry. They assume, for example, that moral judgments that are illogical ('pacifism is wrong because people like Bertrand Russell are pacifists'); based on false premises ('homosexuals have weak wrists'); assertive ('abortion is just wrong'); or just amount to parroting ('adultery is wrong *because my father said it was*') are all ruled out as sensible, intelligible statements of moral positions. We might accept that abortion, homosexuality, adultery, pacifism etc *are* wrong; but we certainly do not do so for these reasons.

All this shows that there is a difference between assertions of 'taste' and 'judgment'. 'Taste' refers to our subjective states such as when we say that we like vanilla ice-cream; there is no right or wrong of it. Judgment, on the other hand, *is* a matter of right and wrong; it is just that the arguments are controversial and, in a nutshell, very difficult! Dworkin puts the point in another way. He distinguishes between external skepticism, whereby one stands outside some intellectual scheme (eg legal argument) and says that there can be no *truth* there because there is nothing in the *external* world, by virtue of which it could be true; and internal skepticism, where one says, there *could* be truth, but the arguments are just not convincing! Dworkin says the internal sceptic doesn't say anything contrary to there being right answers; only the external sceptic does that and, he says, this is exemplified by the passage in the question, there are few, if any, of them. The CLS movement, despite what they say, are not external sceptics, but (dubious) 'global internal sceptics'; they claim there is no truth for legal reasoning on the grounds that the law is too conflicting and contradictory. 'Being *non*-conflicting and *non*-contradictory' is therefore the CLS criterion for truth in law; and hence their argument of saying that there is no truth in law does not rest upon any external premise such as, in the external world there is nothing by virtue of which 'law is true'!

The final argument is straightforward: there can be no truth unless it can be demonstrated. Look, we can cut the argument very short on this one. The statement 'there can be no truth unless it can be demonstrated' *cannot itself be demonstrated* and yet it is put forward as true. Enough said? Well, if we are being urged to adopt this view of truth for law, which is possible, but not the way proponents of the demonstrability thesis put it, why should we accept it? The usual answer is that it makes for certainty, objectivity and clarity. Well, we've heard those arguments before. They are not arguments about law's truth, but the arguments for legal positivism, which moves us to an entirely different battlefield.

TYPE TWO

This is a question about 'hard cases' which is a common way of looking at Dworkin's thesis. It is crucial to have revised the more traditional theories in addition to Dworkin.

'Since no real judge can be Hercules, Dworkin's picture of judicial integrity is a myth and has no use for real judges.'

Discuss.

University of London LLB Examination
(for External Students) Jurisprudence and Legal Theory June 1995 Q9(a)

General Comment

A relatively easy question which relies on an evaluation of Dworkin's creation. This thought-provoking quote requires a strong defence of the purpose behind the concept of 'Hercules' with an examination of the criticism levelled at Dworkin for creating him in the first place.

Skeleton Solution

What is Hercules about? – Hercules and 'hard cases' – the real value of Hercules – conclusion.

Suggested Solution

To suggest that Dworkin's creation of Hercules in his article 'Hard Cases' is a 'myth' is to misunderstand the very nature of his fascinating and highly practical theory. The quote is in danger of being interpreted with an underestimation of Dworkin's subtlety and intellectual power as our most important contemporary in legal philosophy.

There is a tendency to dismiss Hercules by suggesting that no such judge ever existed. However, this view is too glib. Hercules is a model against which, like any other ideal, legal arguments are to be judged. A good illustration of this can be found with the idea of the ideal market. The commentator would go away from the main point if he were to argue that the ideal market does not exist, because saying such a thing is to recognise the idea of the ideal in any case. The concept of an ideal market illustrates how, in the real world, imperfections exist because of monopolies or other restrictive practices which 'distort' the real market.

Dworkin posits the ideal judge because his theory is about law as an argumentative attitude. He provides a scheme of argument which is sufficiently abstract to draw controversy. However, he does not provide a set of premises from which conclusions may be drawn by the use of syllogisms because Hercules is not that sort of theory. Hercules is intended to point the way to correct legal argument. It is not a method to point towards a right answer, but to raise the question of whether there could be such a right answer. Thus, it is about objectivity and not a criticism of the ideal module of Hercules.

Dworkin establishes his idea by saying:

'If a judge accepts the settled practice of his legal system – if he accepts, that is, the authority provided by its distinct constitutive and regulative rules – then he must according to the doctrine of political responsibility, accept some general political theory that justifies these practices.'

The judge has convictions about his role and his duties which are defined by his judicial oath and by other sources. It would certainly be surprising if he did not. Thus, the judge has an idea about legislative purpose and the principles enshrined in common law.

Hercules has a use for real judges because, to make sense of his position, he must be able to make general statements about what judging entails. It is not enough to declare that he accepts

Jurisprudence: The Philosophy of Law

a set of rules without the need to explain or justify why he accepts them. For real judges, the magnitude of their coercive powers indicates a requirement for some form of justification when such powers are used. It is, therefore, eminently reasonable to suggest that there is a rationale behind the business of judging.

Dworkin says that we can assume that Hercules accepts most of the settled rules of his jurisdiction. Such rules lay down the familiar characteristics of the law. An example is given of the constitutive and regulative rules that grant the legislature powers to legislate, and give judge the powers to adjudicate and to follow previous decisions in addition to settled areas of law such as contract.

Hercules has, however, a real and not merely mythical value because he goes further. He can produce theories underlying all the above rules. 'Democracy' underlies, albeit in different forms, jurisdictions in both the United States and the United Kingdom. In such examples there is the basic justification for judicial coercion which exists in accordance with the requirements created by the legislature, democratically elected.

However, from these beginnings, a justification for common law precedent is based upon fairness where citizens are treated in a consistent fashion. The justification for particular statutory or common law applications comes within more elaborately worked out theories such as a theory of responsibility in criminal law, and so on. From each theory, there are sub-theories. A good example is the defence of duress in criminal law. One theory suggests that duress is a justification for action (ie for self-preservation), whilst another suggests duress is an excuse which absolves the defendant from blame, and is a recognition of human weakness in dire circumstances. An extension of such theories questions what constitutes 'dire' circumstances, such as whether duress can be a defence for murder in the first degree. A further theory then examines the question of a moral difference between degrees of murder and how far the defence can be extended.

Whilst such theories are discussed in law reports and by academics, one's own theories and arguments can also be perfected. Dworkin uses Hercules to illustrate the general form, or scheme, of the types of arguments which are used. Hercules can be thought of as producing all these theories for all areas of law but he will have to justify the particular settled rules with such substantive theories as he has devised.

There is, too, the need to do more. A judge may draw a conclusion about the 'clear' law in a way which is different from merely 'reading off' the law. Such a judge might conclude that he would exceed his judicial powers were he to depart from clear law and extend, for instance, the defence of duress. Lord Kilbrandon, in *Lynch v DPP for Northern Ireland* (1975), expressed such a warning by suggesting that such a decision to so extend the law would step 'outside the proper functions' of the court. It is submitted, therefore, that whilst the purpose of Hercules, as a judge of integrity, is an ideal, it has a very real value for the responsibilities exercised by real judges.

TYPE THREE

This is a question which invites a discussion of Dworkin's distinction between principle and policy.

'Judges neither should be nor are deputy legislators, and the familiar assumption, that when they go beyond political decisions already made by someone elsse they are legislating is misleading. It misses the importance of a fundamental distinction ... between arguments of

15 The Judicial Process

principle on the one hand and arguments of policy on the other.' (Dworkin) Discuss critically Dworkin's theory of adjudication.

Written by the Editor

Skeleton Solution

Taking Rights Seriously – *Law's Empire* – principle and policy distinction – theory of adjudication – rejection of Hart's free discretion – affirmation of principle decisions – nature of principles – one Right Answer Thesis – interpretation – constraint and freedom – rejection of law as pragmatism (policy arguments) – criticisms of theory.

Suggested Solution

In *A Matter of Principle* Dworkin makes a distinction between arguments of principle and those of policy. He argues that judges should only adjudicate on cases that concern principles, whereas politicians should, and indeed, are engaged in questions of the collective interests. These he terms issues of 'policy'. In *Law's Empire* Dworkin places within a wider conception of the nature of law and adjudication. Central to Dworkin's thesis is that what judges *say* they are doing must be taken seriously. He notes how judges deny that they are legislating, on the contrary they talk as if they are making decisions according to what the law requires. Dworkin sees law as a seamless web and strongly rejects Hart's view that there are penumbral areas within which a judge exercises 'free discretion'.

Dworkin claims that a judge is always free and yet constrained when he/she adjudicates. Another claim is that judges can make decisions that are political in content and implication without at the same time law-making. This theory seems most relevant when seen as an attempted explanation of American Supreme Court practice – his wider message is that judges (but more especially Supreme Court judges) can be political without merely expressing subjective judgements.

How does Dworkin support these claims? If we begin with the distinction between policy and principle, we see how in *Law's Empire* Dworkin offers a view of law called 'Law as Integrity'. According to this view, judges should make decisions with integrity. This integrity is displayed by his ideal type of judge (called Hercules) who adjudicates by following principles which run through the political and legal culture. Such principles includes :'due process' and 'equality of resources'. These principles can be political but they may conflict with policy goals. In such instances, a judge must give effect to politico-legal principles.

Earlier in *Taking Rights Seriously* Dworkin explains the nature of principles. He feels that unlike rules, they can be applied or not applied without affecting their existence. A principle is not all or nothing in its application, instead it has weight. A principle does not depend for its existence upon judicial pronouncement; a judge may never have articulated a particular principle but it is not right to say that it does not exist within a legal system. To illustrate the nature of principles, Dworkin uses the case of *Riggs* v *Palmer* (1889) where the judges 'found' and applied an equitable principle that one should not benefit from one's own wrong doings.

When a judge adjudicates he ideally should recognise these principles because they make sense of the enterprise of adjudication he/she is involved in. A judge is forced to recognise these principles because of this reason. As a result a judge cannot simply apply his/her subjective prejudices (as someone like Griffith in *Politics of the Judiciary* would claim) to a case before him/her because she/he is constrained by principles of impartiality and fairness which permeate his/her judicial activity.

In addition, where Hart would claim there is no law covering a particular situation – a gap – Dworkin claims that there lie principles. Sometimes these principles conflict but there can be a right answer. The 'one right answer thesis' is the most controversial aspect of Dworkin's theory of adjudication. His claim is not as absurd as it initially sounds. Like Hercules, a judge, when adjudicating must choose the appropriate principles. He/she is restrained from simply making new law but instead looks *within* the legal system to see what decision would best give effect to the principles which that particular legal and political system claims to embody. His/her choice or decision is therefore a principled one; not one of policy. What makes it right? The answer is somewhat complex but essentially a judge's adjudication is said to be right when he/she has made an *interpretation* of what the best adjudication would be.

Dworkin claims that adjudication is an interpretive exercise, it is like writing a chain novel. The next writer is simultaneously free to carry on the story in an infinite number of ways but at the same time is constrained by the enterprise he/she is engaged in and the preceding text. According to Dworkin, the chain novelist faces two threshold requirements; to find the best textual fit (what particular manner of continuation best fits in with the preceding text?) and secondly, the best justification (what particular continuation best carries out the claims made by the chain novel and the novelists?).

When these two requirements are transferred into the realm of legal adjudication we can see that institutional fit and justification permit a judge to be engaged in political decisions, but at the same time be constrained by principle so that he/she does not legislate. If, as Dworkin claims, the law professes to use coercion because of past political decisions, then a judge's adjudication must justify such use. Dworkin personifies the state as acting coherently according to principle. A judge's function is to try to trace the thread of the state's principled coherence – its 'integrity'. In order to fulfil this function, he/she must engage his/her own interpretative skills and providing this is done genuinely the adjudication that results is said by Dworkin to be the correct one.

A number of criticisms can be made of Dworkin's theory. Firstly, virtually any policy decision can be dressed up as a decision based upon principle, as long as judges talk the language of 'institutional fit' and 'justification'. A second objection was most clearly made by the American Realists; one should avoid excessive interest in what judges *say* they are doing and pay more attention to what they are *actually* doing. Thirdly, the law must perform mundane, everyday functions but Dworkin's method of adjudication is so incredibly complex that no judge could attempt it in practice without sacrificing this mundane function. If a judge did aspire to Dworkin's Herculean ideal there would be of a great cost in legal certainty. Fourthly, what if a judge is under a state of false consciousness and therefore believes that he/she is institutionally constrained, but in reality he/she is expressing his/her own *subjective/political* bias in his/her adjudications? Here a judge may justifiably be accused of not merely applying, but making the law instead.

Finally, it may be claimed that Dworkin's theory is very culture specific; concerned with defending the liberalism of the Supreme Court. This liberalism can be seen in the landmark cases of *Roe* v *Wade* (1973) and *Brown* v *Board of Education* (1954). Dworkin claims that we can trust the judiciary, even when their decisions seem highly charged politically. However, in claiming that political decisions are part of the legitimate judicial adjudication, Dworkin's theory can defend the modern day conservatism of the Supreme Court. It may be said that contemporary Supreme Court decisions are examples of the judicial politico-legal interpretation that Dworkin puts forward as the ideal.

B LEGAL REASONING

15.5 Introduction

This has become a more popular examination topic in recent years. Questions often concern logic – is legal reasoning logical? It is thus necessary to consider what 'logical' means. Some useful cases for illustrating points about legal reasoning might be *Donoghue* v *Stevenson* (1932), *R* v *Allen* (1872), *Fisher* v *Bell* (1961). The student will be able to think of others.

15.6 Key points

a) *Deductive reasoning*

   A logical necessary conclusion is drawn from major and minor premises.

b) *Inductive reasoning*

   Propositions are arrived at after collection and sorting of data.

c) What is the meaning of logical?

15.7 Analysis of question styles

As discussed above, questions have tended to concentrate on 'logic'. Provided the student has considered what is to be understood by 'logic' it should be possible to achieve high marks.

15.8 Questions

The following are recent examples of questions set on legal reasoning.

1) Why are judges bound by legal precedents?

University of London LLB Examination
(for External Students) Jurisprudence and Legal Theory June 1995 Q11

General Comment

This is a very wide-ranging question. The student should take great care with it. Detailed books on the subject have already been written, so the main solution is to select points which attract comments when judges do not feel bound by legal precedent. Explain why judges apply precedents, and how they interpret the ratio decidendi of a particular case.

Skeleton Solution

Introduction – what is precedent? – the doctrine of stare decisis – ratio decidendi – conclusion.

Suggested Solution

The judge has two tasks:

1. to resolve the dispute before him;
2. to reach his decision by reference to some impartial rule of law.

A main aspect of formal justice is that all cases should be treated alike where there is a repetition of earlier practices which follow earlier patterns. Most legal systems have developed a system of precedent, including the use of past decisions as a guide to present decisions.

Jurisprudence: The Philosophy of Law

In England, precedents of an appropriate authority not only guide decisions in later cases but they bind the judges in those later cases. The doctrine of stare decisis has developed whereby a judge in an inferior court may obey the decision of a higher court on the same point. The main argument for stare decisis is certainty, which is valued in our legal system because it allows people to arrange their affairs in accordance with the law, by not breaking it, or by taking advantage of it. If judges depart from previous decisions at will such arrangements are upset. Also, individual earlier cases would become, in effect, retrospective laws which change the old law and apply a new law in the present case to be decided.

Cardozo J, in *Great Northern Railway Co v Sunburst Oil* (1932) suggests that in order to avoid this problem, the court could adopt prospective overruling. The present case would then be treated in accordance with the old law, whilst a new law would be announced for future cases. Although retrospective argument is avoided, could it be so arranged (by applying the new law to future arrangements only) to avoid affecting settled arrangements? It would seem to be unfair to the losing litigant because he would have persuaded the judge to accept his legal submission, but would still lose the case. It is submitted that the question posed is whether certainty and the development of the law go together.

The doctrine of stare decisis has been criticised for its rigidity and inflexibility. In practice, however, judges do have a wide measure of flexibility and movement where devices can be used to avoid a particular precedent. The authority of a particular law report is weighed up, with more weight becoming attached to those reports thought to be of a higher quality than others. The judge then decides which parts of an earlier case will actually bind him. He will distinguish the 'ratio decidendi' of the earlier case from the 'obiter dicta' which will not bind him, hence the measure of flexibility.

A traditional definition of the ratio decidendi is that it is the rule of law enunciated by the judge to the extent that it is necessary for the decision of the case. Therefore, the question is what part of the judgment is relevant: see *Donoghue v Stevenson* (1932) per Lord Atkin who developed the neighbour principle, as compared with the narrower principle concerning manufacturers' liability first pleaded in the lower court.

Some judges are said to decide the case before them rather than stating the law. Certainly the House of Lords, which no longer binds itself with earlier decisions, attempts the latter course, although often a policy of law rather than the law itself can emerge. Wallbaugh puts forward a reversal test against this traditional view. He suggests that if the reverse of the proposition leads to a different decision in the case, that is the ratio decidendi. Such a distinction, highlighted in *Donoghue v Stevenson*, suggests, however, that Wallbaugh's reversal test will tell us what is *not* the ratio whilst failing to assist us with what it is.

Lord Devlin's approach says that the ratio is the reason for the decision which the judge wishes to be the source of precedent. Therefore, would it be incorrect to say that a case is a precedent, and, as such is binding in a way the judge never intended?

Goodhart sees the ratio as the decision based on the facts which are treated as 'material' by the judge, putting less emphasis on the judge's statements of law. He sees the judge as viewing certain facts, explicity and implicitly, as 'material' where his decision on those facts becomes binding as the ratio.

Stone, however, maintains that there is not a unique ratio of a case, but a choice of rationes available to later judges to make a choice from. The two possible rationes are the descriptive and the prescriptive, whereby a descriptive ratio is ascertainable from the decision once given,

15 The Judicial Process

but the prescriptive ratio is how a subsequent court treats the earlier decision: see *Evans* v *Triplex Safety Glass Co Ltd* (1936) where a windscreen smashed causing injury. The court, bound by *Donoghue* v *Stevenson*, held that the ratio of the earlier case was that a duty of care arose only when there was no possibility of interference with the product between the time it left the manufacturer and the time the loss was caused. In the later case, the court held that there was such a possibility and the plaintiff did not recover.

Dias goes further by saying that the ratio should be viewed in a continuing time framework, as the interpretation of the case given by later judges.

Whilst such views give an understanding of the central feature of why judges are bound by legal precedents, it is nevertheless important to identify how cases are treated in later cases to discover for what they are taken as authority. Montrose argues that the ratio is essentially one of a terminological nature, reasserting the common law tradition by suggesting:

1. the rule of law is to be found in the actual opinion of the judge which forms the basis of his decision;

2. there is the rule of law for which the case is binding authority;

3. any reason which ultimately brings about the decision – which essentially relates to the reasons for the ratio.

It is submitted that Montrose takes the argument little further.

It is worth noting de Smith's view from *Nissan* v *Attorney-General* (1970) where it is possible that the case will have no ascertainable ratio at all. However, today the doctrine of stare decisis appears fixed and settled – in practice it is a flexible weapon in the hands of a judge. What occurs is the establishment of a core area of fixed law surrounded by a fringe area where the judges distinguish, approve or follow cases whilst steadily developing the law.

2) What are the differences, if any, between describing the law, saying what the law ought to be, and interpreting the law? You should illustrate your answer with examples, referring to the point, if any, of each activity?

University of London LLB Examination
(for External Students) Jurisprudence and Legal Theory 1992 Q2

Skeleton Solution

Parameters of answer: point of each activity in brief – differentiation often difficult – why difficult – when differentiation possible – examples – conclusion: inter-relationship of three functions.

Suggested Solution

When one uses the term 'the law' as opposed to 'law' it is generally recognised that what is meant is the content of rules which regulate conduct within society rather than the more abstract notions of 'law' as propounded by the various legal theorists. In relation to 'the law' then the possible point of each of the three functions described in the question can be summarised briefly: (1) Every individual should have the means of knowing what conduct is required of him or her by law, therefore it should be possible to describe the law; (2) the law must deal with conduct in a somewhat generalised form at the outset, therefore it may be necessary to interpret the law in order to decide whether a particular type of conduct falls within the general parameters set by that law; (3) it may be thought that the law ought to deal with a particular type of situation, therefore one might have an opinion as to what the law ought to be in order to achieve this.

The differences between the three functions are not, in practice, always clearly definable. Take, for example, the situation of two advocates arguing a point of law before a judge. Each advocate would doubtless argue that the version of the law which they propose to be applicable is the correct description of the law as it is. Plainly this cannot be true in both cases. Therefore, in order to 'describe' the law a certain amount of interpretation must be taking place otherwise there would be no difference of opinion between the two parties. The judge in making his decision must decide between the two versions of the law proposed and, indeed, on the basis of argument before him, may come to a conclusion which is a hybrid of the two versions put to him. In so-called 'hard cases', where the law is perhaps very unclear on the factual situation facing him, the judge may interpret the law in a manner which leads to accusations of 'judicial law-making' and he therefore might be described as having ruled not on what the law is but on what the law ought to be.

The prerequisite to any clear differentiation between the three functions is a clearly defined content of 'the law' at any given moment. In the common law system, based as it is upon laws derived from evolutionary case law, from statute and applied by an independent judiciary, it is not always easy to state with clarity the precise content of the law on a particular issue. This is often the case with controversial aspects of law, for example the law relating to rape which until very recently was thought to exclude the possibility of rape within marriage. It took merely the pronounciation of the House of Lords in a single case to completely overturn this notion and to require the consideration of whether there had been actual rather than implied consent in cases where a wife alleged that her husband had raped her. It is almost impossible to say in such cases whether the law has been merely described as encompassing a situation which it had always applied to, or whether it had been interpreted in a progressive manner. Once it is accepted that the functions of describing and progressively interpreting the law may become blurred, the function of saying what the law ought to be becomes, in turn, difficult to define.

In less controversial matters the nature and purpose of the three functions can, however, be more easily defined. For example, one might undertake to describe the law for a number of reasons in addition to that already mentioned above. The law may be described for reasons of academic interest, for example in order to compare the law on a particular issue in different jurisdictions or in textbooks. Descriptions may be general, referring only to the core statutes and applicable case law, or particular, dealing with the specific types of conduct which are allowed or disallowed by a particular law. The more particular the description, the more it is likely to border on interpretation. Further, the law may be described in the context of law reform studies, as a basis from which to evaluate whether it is achieving any particular aim for which it was intended.

Saying what the law ought to be is a purposive exercise, in other words one is saying that the law ought to be X in order to achieve Y. This is a function undertaken by law reform groups, academics and practitioners alike. To take a fairly uncontroversial example, in the sense that there is little argument about what the law actually is on the matter, the European Convention on Human Rights and Fundamental Freedoms is not incorporated into English law. The lack of incorporation means that individuals cannot directly invoke the provisions of the Convention in the English courts, as could be done, for example, in relation to many provisions of the EEC Treaty. One school of thought would argue that because the United Kingdom has agreed to be bound by the provisions of the Convention it ought to be incorporated as part of the

15 The Judicial Process

internal law of England. The purpose of this would be to have a written bill of rights for the individual. The contrary argument is that there is no need for a written internal bill of rights and that the law therefore ought not to be changed.

To expand upon the example of interpretation of the law, mentioned in the first paragraph, it is useful to consider the rules of statutory interpretation. As every law student knows, the courts are often said to apply particular rules such as the 'golden rule' and the 'mischief rule' when interpreting the meaning of a statute. In applying such rules the court does not purport to change the meaning of a statutory provision, rather it is attempting to define the parameters of the provision by determining whether the case at hand falls within its scope as originally intended by Parliament. Thus they are interpreting the law so as to apply the general proposition to the particular situation at hand. In the case of rules which have not yet been the subject of judicial interpretation, academics or practitioners may undertake a similar exercise for the purposes of comment.

In conclusion it should be noted that there is an inter-relationship between the three functions which are the subject matter of the question. Detailed description of the law will deal with specific interpretations of the law which have been made. Saying what the law ought to be depends on a particular view of what the law is, which in turn depends upon description and interpretation. Interpretation, even statutory interpretation, may be coloured by the particular purpose which Parliament had in mind when a statute was promulgated – in other words Parliament's view at that time as to what the law ought to be. Nevertheless, each function, however difficult to differentiate from another, may rightly be described as an essential feature of the law's development and day-to-day application.

3) What, in your view, does *interpretation* of the law involve? Does it bear any analogy with intepretation in other fields, such as the interpretation of literature, or art?

University of London LLB Examination
(for External Students) Jurisprudence and Legal Theory June 1993 Q8

General Comment

This is a difficult question although, for a person who has interests in fields other than law, such as literature or music, it is possible to write very interesting answers. It requires a close look at Dworkin's theory of interpretation and then some views of your own; it is best to contrast the idea of interpretation with that of description (NB Hart's *descriptive* sociology of law) and 'normativity', with a look at some cases. Then it is important to explore the analogy; don't be dismissive because legal argument shares many features with interpretation in the arts (both discourses, for example, make extensive use of the idea of interpretation). Explore the strengths and the weaknesses of the analogy. The best way to do this is to pick on (if you have one) your *own* speciality, whether it be music, literature, poetry or painting. Remember, too, in this kind of question, to come to some kind of answer: do *you* think that there is a reasonable analogy to draw?

Skeleton Solution

The meaning of interpretation as opposed to describing and saying how things ought to be – Dworkin's theory of interpretation and how it is supposed to apply to law – an analogy with interpretation in music.

Jurisprudence: The Philosophy of Law

Suggested Solution

The idea of interpretation is one that occurs frequently in the law; the barrister, solicitor, judge and law student have to 'offer an interpretation' of some legal point. What does it actually mean? We could take the famous case of Hart's statute prohibiting 'vehicles' in the park; we could, for example, be asked by a client to say whether his having taken a skateboard through the park was in breach of this statute. We start with a baseline, that of agreement with the provision 'Vehicles are prohibited from the [such and such] park'; after that, however, we have only interpretations as to whether 'vehicle' includes skateboards. There is no 'read off' sense in which we can find the answer to this difficult question, yet barristers spend all the time trying to make their living out of making this sort of interpretation. Put in another way, there is no *descriptive* sense in which we can simply describe what the law says. Further, it does not seem to be correct that, say as barristers, we can merely exhort a judge with the *normative* statement: skateboards either ought or ought not to be covered by the word 'vehicle'. What is it, then, that we do?

Ronald Dworkin claims that interpretation is central to legal argument and that we cannot have a proper account of law until we have a proper account of legal interpretation. He says that interpretation means 'making the best sense' of some activity (like legal practice) in the following way: we try to construct the most coherent account of the practice in terms of what is of moral importance. He imagines a society in which one of the rules is that people doff their hats to their superiors; if they do this unthinkingly, he says that the rules function in that society in a pre-interpretive way. It is only when people start to question the *point* of such rules that the society (perhaps only by its officials) has entered the interpretive phase. People might ask why they do this and come up with some interpretation such as that hat doffing is a mark of deference to people whom they perceive to be superior; others might come up with the idea that hat doffing is a mark of respect to all members of the society. In fact, there may be arguments about which interpretation is the 'better' one; some will argue that members of the society are better than others and that deference is therefore in order while others will argue that deference between people is wrong and that all people deserve respect equally. If a decision is made on the correct interpretation, say, in some test case where a member of the society refused to doff his cap to a dinner lady because she 'was inferior', and the result is that the action was wrong because hat doffing was a required mark of respect, Dworkin says that the society has entered a 'post-interpretive' phase, in which 'interpretation folds in on itself' to change the practice.

How could we apply this method to the famous vehicle case? Well, what is the 'best sense' we can make of 'Vehicles are prohibited from the park'? It seems that the most natural thing we would want to do is look to a thing we call 'the intention of Parliament'; we might then go to some principle of construction of statutes that requires ambiguous penal statutes to be resolved in favour of a criminal defendant. This seems natural, but why? Dworkin's explanation is that we understand the language of the statute in the context of the theory of democracy (parliamentary supremacy; hence the attention paid to 'the intention of Parliament') underlying it. He says that barristers do this sort of thing all the time. We assume that we have to construct an understanding of the words of the statute that makes best sense of the words that the major institution of our democratic legal system has produced; making best sense means, for him, best *moral* sense, by which he refers to the way in which we suppose that all decisions relating to taking away freedoms from people, whether money for compensation or fines, or imprisonment, should be in accordance with morality.

15 The Judicial Process

Does this form of interpretation bear any analogy with interpretation in art? What would be the analogy with 'Vehicles are prohibited in the park'? The first thing to note is that no-one (except the rare Marxist) disagrees that this phrase states the law; rather, the difficulty lies in working out whether it excludes skateboards. Are there equivalent consensuses on what counts as, say, part of a novel? The answer must surely be yes; we all accept that Shylock is the name of the Jew in Shakespeare's *The Merchant of Venice*; no-one disputes that. However, people could dispute that *The Merchant of Venice* is a play, as opposed to an anti-Jewish tract. But that is not enough to ruin the analogy, because, as pointed out with the Marxist above, it is always going to be possible to dispute. After all, even clear statutes enacted by Crown-in-Parliament which *purport to bind Parliament's successors*, can be laid open to the same charge. What is the analogy with the vehicles through the park legislation and *The Merchant of Venice*? We can easily imagine two rival interpretations (and such interpretations are common and widely argued over). Some will argue that Shylock is mean, self-defensive and whingeing, citing various of his actions and drawing evidence from his use of language; others will argue that he has a soul and is sensitive to human suffering and joy, drawing similarly from the work.

Who is to say who is right? Perhaps the analogy breaks down here; after all, we have a judge to decide in the field of law. But it is only an analogy, after all. One of the things people feel about interpretation in the field of literature is that is subjective in a way that interpretation is not in law. But it is difficult to give a rational explanation of that feeling; literary critics as much wrestle with the problems of rival interpretations as do judges and barristers; certainly, literary critics do not sit back and say 'Well, it is *just* a matter of taste, either you like it or not'. To conclude, then, it seems as though there is a great deal to the analogy between legal argument and literary criticism.

C PRECEDENT

15.9 Introduction

In England, precedent is of much importance. Past precedents not only guide later decisions, but if appropriate within the hierarchy of courts, bind judges in later cases. This is the theory of stare decisis. In considering this doctrine the student might like to ask whether stare decisis is absolute and inflexible, or whether its rigidity is more apparent than real. As with the whole of this chapter, it is useful to know some case law.

15.10 Key points

a) *The English system of stare decisis*

   i) Decisions of superior courts bind lower courts in later cases.

   ii) The advantages of this system are certainty and uniformity.

b) *Comparison with civil law countries*

   i) Past decisions do not bind but are merely persuasive.

   ii) This system has more flexibility, although it sacrifices a degree of certainty and uniformity.

15.11 Analysis of question styles

This has not been a popular topic in recent years. Questions are likely to call for an evaluation of the theory of stare decisis, and comparisons with other legal systems are likely to be useful.

Jurisprudence: The Philosophy of Law

15.12 Question

A useful question for revision purposes might be:

'Nevertheless, the basic flexibility of the system is preserved, not so much by the formal limitations on the rule of stare decisis but by the relative freedom with which the courts may and often do determine the scope and limits of past precedents ...' (Lloyd: *An Introduction to Jurisprudence*). Discuss.

Written by the Editor

Skeleton Solution

Precedent – stare decisis – civil law countries – lack of flexibility? – ratio decidendi – obiter dicta – traditional view – *Donoghue* v *Stevenson* (1932) – Goodhart – Stone – no definition

Suggested Solution

In England precedents have great importance. According to the rule of stare decisis, the decisions of superior courts bind lower courts in later cases. There is thus a hierarchy of courts – for example the House of Lords is superior to the Court of Appeal. This contrasts with the place of precedent in civil law countries where past decisions are merely persuasive, not binding. The rule of stare decisis provides for much uniformity and certainty of decisions. It is, however, open to the criticism of extreme inflexibility, with the attendant risk of injustice in some cases. It will be shown that stare decisis does actually give judges a wide measure of flexibility, and that one of the major reasons lies in the definition of ratio decidendi.

As Lloyd points out, one of the functions of the judge is determining the 'scope and limits of past precedents' and thus which parts of an earlier case are binding on him. The binding part of a case is known as the ratio decidendi, as distinguished from the obiter dicta. The reason why this technique provides flexibility is that the definition of a ratio decidendi is uncertain; it is thus up to the judge to decide its exact scope.

The traditional view of ratio is that it is that rule of law enunciated by the judge to the extent that it is necessary to decide the case. But an examination of a well known case shows the unhelpfulness of this definition: in *Donoghue* v *Stevenson* (1932) was the relevant and necessary part Lord Atkin's 'neighbour principle' or merely a narrow principle of manufacturer's liability?

An alternative definition is that put forward by Professor Goodhart for whom a ratio is the decision based on the facts treated as material by the judge. There are difficulties with this – it may be difficult to tell which facts the judge took into account. Professor Stone takes a rather different view. For him there are two possible rationes – the prescriptive and the descriptive. The latter is ascertainable from the given decision but the former is how the courts treat the earlier decision in subsequent cases.

It should be pointed out, however, that none of these approaches tells us how a judge may decide the ratio of a case. All he can do is take as the ratio the principles that seem to him appropriate. It is this which gives flexibility. For example, judges in cases subsequent to *Donoghue* v *Stevenson* (1932) look the wider principle as being the ratio. Had they confined themselves to the narrower principle of manufacturer's liability, the law of negligence might have developed quite differently. It is therefore clear that I agree with what Lloyd says in the quotation.

15 The Judicial Process

D STATUTORY INTERPRETATION

15.13 Introduction

Once again it is useful to demonstrate points made about the three 'rules' of statutory construction by means of case law. The ever growing flow of statutory law, combined with the inherent ambiguity of many words and phrases, means that statutory interpretation is becoming increasingly important. Despite this, it is fair to say that this has not been the most popular examination topic in recent years.

15.14 Key points

a) *The canons of construction*

   i) The statute must be read as a whole.

   ii) Ejusdem generis.

   iii) Narrow construction of penal provisions.

   iv) Interpretation Act 1978.

b) *Presumptions*

   i) Against alteration of law.

   ii) Against imposition of no-fault liability.

   iii) Against ousting the jurisdiction of the courts.

   iv) Against depriving a person of a vested right.

c) *The three 'rules' of statutory construction*

   i) Mischief rule.

   ii) Literal rule.

   iii) Golden rule.

15.15 Analysis of question styles

Statutory interpretation has not been a particularly fruitful source of examination questions in recent years. Having said that, when it does arise the student should be able to attain good marks provided the basics of the above key points, and some illustrative case law, are known.

15.16 Questions

TYPE ONE

A fairly straightforward question concerning the three rules of statutory construction. The answer should be backed up by case law.

1) Which of the three rules of statutory construction do you consider to be the most accurate description of the way in which judges interpret statutes?

Written by the Editor

Jurisprudence: The Philosophy of Law

Skeleton Solution

Mischief rule – *Heydon's Case* (1584) – purposive – *Mandla* v *Dowell-Lee* (1983) – literal rule – *RRB* v *London Borough of Ealing* (1978) – golden rule – *R* v *Allen* (1872) – inconsistent approach – rules conflict – Rupert Cross.

Suggested Solution

The three rules of statutory interpretation which are most commonly suggested are the literal, the golden and the mischief rule. Although support can be found in the cases for all three rules, they are somewhat contradictory. It is thus proposed to consider which, if any, rule most accurately reflects the way in which judges interpret statutes.

The mischief rule was probably at the height of its popularity in the sixteenth century. In *Heydon's Case* (1584), the classic statement of the rule was laid down: there are four things to be considered when interpreting statutes: the common law before the Act; the mischief that the common law did not provide for; the remedy appointed for that mischief; and the true reason of the remedy. Thus interpretation is purposive. There is still some support for this rule today. For example, in *Mandla* v *Dowell-Lee* (1983) the House of Lords considered the purpose of the Race Relations Act 1975 before applying it to the facts of the case.

The mischief rule is not, however, the only approach used in recent years. In *RRB* v *London Borough of Ealing* (1978) for example, the literal approach to the Race Relations Act was taken. According to this approach the literal meaning of words must be taken – the intention of parliament is taken to be contained in those literal words. Clearly this approach stems from constitutional principles of the separation of power. One might query, however, whether there is usually only one 'literal' interpretation of words and phrases – words are often unclear or ambiguous.

The strictness of the literal rule has often been mitigated by the 'golden rule'. Where a literal interpretation results in a meaning which parliament could not possibly have intended, a secondary meaning can be taken. An example is *R* v *Allen* (1872) where the literal definition of bigamy in the Offences Against the Person Act 1961 was not applied since that would have led to the absurd conclusion that bigamy could never be committed.

From an examination of case law it becomes apparent that there is no one consistent approach to statutory interpretation. All three rules are sometimes applied although in many ways they conflict. For example, both the mischief and the golden rule are to some extent purposive, whilst the literal rule masks the statutory purpose. Professor Cross has put forward a pleasing formulation of what judges do. He suggests that the mischief and literal rules are mixed, and the element of context added. Thus judges look at the ordinary English meaning of words in the general context of the statute. That ordinary meaning may be displaced of the result would be absurd. Perhaps this is a better description of how judges interpret statutes than a strict adherence to one or other of the three rules.

2) 'But if codification comes, it may well be that ... the judges will continue, though perhaps less obviously, to be an important law-shaping force. Indeed I suspect that we must assess the future position of the judge as a lawmaker on the basis of the experience of other systems than upon a discussion of the technicalities of statutory interpretation.' (Lord Scarman). Discuss.

University of London LLB Examination
(for External Students) Jurisprudence and Legal Theory June 1983 Q5

15 The Judicial Process

Skeleton Solution

Judge – made law – legal codes – Law Commission – generality – interpretation of statutes – codes filled out by judicial interpretation – France – stare decisis.

Suggested Solution

Large parts of our present law are judge-made, either by development of the common law or by the interpretation and construction of statutes. If our law was codified, the various possibilities of that codification might well affect the judicial role in the 'legislative' area. Lord Scarman's statement suggests, somewhat obscurely, that if we do codify, the judge's position will be more akin to those in other countries which have codes now than to the present state of statutory interpretation in this country. As I shall attempt to point out below, I find the situation to be rather more complex than this, much depending on how the exercise of codification is carried out. I will start with a consideration of that question, and then, armed with different possibilities, will turn to the rest of Lord Scarman's statement.

Most countries do have a legal code of some kind, even if in only a limited area (eg constitutional law, through a constitution or Bill of Rights). Our law is generally uncodified, although certain areas set up and developed by statute only (many aspects of the welfare state; redundancy payments and unfair dismissal; some aspects of company law) might be seen as approximations to a code. The Law Commission was set up in the 1960s to aid the process of law reform by proposing new legislation and commenting on the old law; one of their aims is codification. The area they have chosen to start on is contract, but as yet there has been relatively little progress.

There are many problems to be ironed out and choices to be made before the work of codification can begin. 'Do we need a code?' might be the first question. Advantages of certainty, intelligibility to the average citizen, and clarity are claimed, but all must be doubtful. Technical legal concepts will always be technical and therefore to an extent unintelligible; there will always need to be a fairly detailed body of law in each area to achieve certainty, but tempered by a degree of flexibility and, to that extent, inherent uncertainty. Let us assume that a code is to be aimed for, we must next ask: what level of generality? Do we want a general code laying down general guidelines with details to be fleshed out, or a detailed code (with anomalies in the present law hopefully removed)? The problem with just having general guidelines is that the whole corpus of present detailed law is swept away, and the problem with having a detailed code is that development of the law will be difficult, as judges will be tied down to such an extent. Another alternative is a general code with a detailed commentary. This is just another variant of the detailed code if commentary is authoritative, because again the detail is there and binds the judges. The amount of detail given is obviously important to the judge's position after the code; also of importance is what content the code has, particularly whether the detail mirrors past detail from earlier cases (in which case the judges might feel they had a stronger right to interpret and develop it?), and whether the code allows for judicial interpretation and development, or not. Will judges just decide from case to case, or will the stare decisis doctrine be retained, whereby case rulings become binding over lower end co-ordinate courts?

Bearing in mind those possibilities, let us consider Lord Scarman's proposition that the judge's role should not be sought in the present technicalities of statutory interpretation. In fact much interpretation of statutes is not technical at all, but very straightforward; more difficult cases are, however, the subject of a series of canons and presumptions of construction, and of different approaches (literal, mischief, golden) to the construction of ambiguous and uncertain phrases and sections. Some of these rules will inevitably be relevant to any sort of code. If the code is a general statement of principle, judges will have to decide between attempting 'literal' approaches (ie following the exact wording) or more purposive approaches (ie attempting to discover what the framer's purpose was in using the particular phrase or section, and construing in the instant case to further that interpretation); although Sir Rupert Cross recently suggested that in present judicial practice these approaches were fused into a single one, of attempting to find the meaning of the phrase (etc) in its context. If the code is a detailed one, or comes with some kind of detailed commentary, it may well be that judges will follow that present practice and use all the minor canons and rules (eg eiusdem generis, presumption against liability without fault, presumption against ousting the jurisdiction of the courts) to interpret the detailed provision. It is a separate question (not related to technicalities of statutory interpretation) whether such decisions on the meaning of a particular part of the code would bind future judges under the stare decisis doctrine, as – it is submitted – decisions now on the meaning of a phrase in a statute bind.

Our analysis thus far suggests that Lord Scarman was incorrect in that at least part of the judicial role under a code would involve a continuation of some of the present technicalities of statutory interpretation. Lord Scarman suggests that the future position of the judge as lawmaker should be assessed rather on the basis of the experience of other systems. Most systems do have codes, and civil law systems are all based on codes. In those, the codes tend to be not detailed but general, and are filled out by judicial interpretation. The most obvious example is France, where the general provisions of the code are expanded and detailed by series of judicial decisions, backed up by the learned notes attached to the judgments. One major difference from our system is the lack of a system of stare decisis: decisions are not binding. However, series of decisions do carry great weight, as do decisions of the *Cour de Cassation*; and in England there are several ways in which flexibility is introduced (notably in choice of ratio, in distinguishing, and by the House of Lords using the 1966 *Practice Statement* allowing overruling of previous decisions). In any case, whether or not we have a system of stare decisis is not dependent on whether we have a code or not; even with a code, the judge's inherent feelings of stability could well lead to stare decisis being retained, so that decisions on the code must be followed. Only a deliberate change, either by the code or by a change in judicial practice, can bring about a non-binding precedent approach in this country.

Our conclusion must be that under a code, the judicial role in terms of lawmaking will depend on the amount of detail and the content of the code, and the retention or otherwise of stare decisis. If the code is a fairly general one, the judges will be called upon to fill out the details, relying on either a literal or purposive approach, but with the present very technical notes of statutory interpretation inappropriate (because of the absence of detail). Whether the present system of stare decisis will apply to the development, or whether the broader and more flexible civil law approach to precedent will take over, depends on the wording of the code, and the practice of the judges. If the code is a detailed one, one will continue to look at present rules and statutory interpretation. The experience of Continental and other judges on the basis of a general code in the absence of stare decisis will not be relevant.

Either way, enough has been said to know that the judges will continue to be an important lawmaking force even after codification takes place.

PART E

PREPARING FOR THE EXAMINATION

16 Jurisprudence – An Overview

16.1 Introduction
16.2 Analysis of questions
16.3 Questions

16.1 Introduction

There is nearly always at least one 'general' jurisprudential question on every examination paper. Such questions require an 'across-the-board' approach, and the student must think and plan carefully before putting pen to paper. It is often more difficult to achieve high marks on this type of question and some examples are thus helpful.

16.2 Analysis of questions

This type of question is usually very open ended. It will be up to the student to select the material used in the answer. Such questions illustrate the importance of considering jurisprudence as a whole, as opposed to as a collection of discrete topics.

16.3 Questions

The following are all examples of general questions:

1) What do you understand to be implied by the phrase 'equality before the law'?

University of London LLB Examination
(for External Students) Jurisprudence and Legal Theory June 1984 Q3

Skeleton Solution

Equality – process of law – application – process of lawmaking – relevant grounds for differences – minority groups – sociological studies – Marx – justice – Nozick – Dworkin – Rawls – end result.

Suggested Solution

The phrase 'equality before the law' immediately summons in my mind the picture of a prisoner before a court: if there is 'equality before the law' then that prisoner will be treated equally whether he is a peer or an ordinary working man, a policeman or a layman etc. The phrase, then, implies equality of respect in the process of law application. Its meaning goes further; it also implies – and this is a wider question – that all are respected equally in the formation of the law, in the process of lawmaking. I will look at the implication of these two meanings in turn.

First, then, equal respect in the process of law application. It is thought to be desirable that the law is applied equally to all. Of course, this is not limited to the rather narrow example which I gave at the start of this essay, the prisoner in the dock: it applies equally to the parties in civil actions, to witnesses and to the procedure before either criminal or civil trials. Is the law applied equally to all? We must make an initial and important point: equality of respect implies not the same treatment for all whatever the circumstances, but rather that any differences in treatment are justifiable on relevant grounds. It is justifiable to refuse a multi-murderer's application for bail on the grounds that he is dangerous, but not on the grounds that he is black and therefore racially inferior.

In our society, there are many areas in which the question of equal respect is important. Are minority racial groups treated equally by the law: are the police more likely to arrest and charge them, their legal advisers less likely to understand them, the courts less likely to believe them (as witnesses and defendants) and more likely to convict? In another area, are public officials and bodies equal before the law: are the courts more likely to believe a police officer than a member of the public, too sympathetic to a governmental plea of national security as a justification for an otherwise illegal act, more likely to hold an individual negligent than a public body unreasonable? Are they more sympathetic to elected bodies with a Conservative majority?

These and many similar questions can be asked: it is not my intention to answer them, they are used to show the types of questions implied by 'equality before the law'. Whether there is such equality in any particular society is a factual question. One important part of the answer will be sociological studies of the society in question to see if groups are – statistically at any rate – treated differently.

I said in my second paragraph that such equality of respect was thought to be desirable. In fact, this is an open question. A Marxist view might be that since law's purpose is the oppression of the masses, the application of law will inevitably involve discrimination against the masses and in favour of the owners and the state. Whether one accepts this depends on one's view of Marx: one thing which can and should be said in support of Marx's view is that the application of law in many countries, including the UK, does depend on wealth and colour. Lawyers are expensive in the UK; engaging in litigation in a costly business. Legal aid is, of course, available, but not all lawyers accept legal aid work (because it is relatively poorly paid) and it does not cover all cases (for example, it does not stretch to representation at many tribunals, including industrial tribunals). To get the best advice and representation, money is generally required. Further, there is enough evidence of racial discrimination in the legal profession and by the police to at least raise a prima facie suggestion that racial minorities are not equal before the law.

The above discussion was concerned with the application of law, as against the law itself. The phrase 'equality before the law' to me implied not only equality in law application but also in law formation. You will note that I do not mention equality in *law content*. The law will always distinguish between different groups, giving special powers to the police and public authorities and groups of individuals (companies, partnerships, universities, trade unions). It will always be possible to argue about whether the balance between groups has been struck correctly, whether there is sufficient justification for the differences in treatment between groups. The groups which are not given a particular advantage will complain that the law is not equal as to content, whereas the groups which have been given it will argue that the differences between the groups justified the difference in treatment.

The proper way to solve these arguments is to move to the more fundamental question of whether the *law formation* process treated the groups equally or not. This question is at the heart of discussions about justice, the just arrangement for society. Political philosophers of all persuasions claim that it is their theory of this arrangement that is the one which treats people equally. Even a philosopher like Nozick, who bases his 'minimal state' view on a libertarian basis, might claim that equality in the law formation involved not infringing on anybody's rights or liberties and thus would involve accepting his theory.

16 Jurisprudence – An Overview

More liberal writers like Rawls and Dworkin would argue that equality involves taking every person's interest into account. Dworkin sees equality of concern and respect in the decision making process as being the root of all liberal theory, including Rawls and the utilitarians. Basically, in the terms that we have been using in this essay, it means that in the law formation process the views of all groups are taken into account equally. The laws that result will – as we have seen – inevitably involve differences in treatment, but these will be justified; they will flow from a consideration of the correct law to pass in view of all the interests involved.

Dworkin's own view goes even further than this, in fact. The danger of this democratic law formation process based on utility is that it cannot distinguish between interests and 'prejudices': what if, for example, I think negroes should be presumed guilty in a criminal trial because I believe they are an inferior race? This, says Dworkin, is an 'external preference' (ie one solely concerning others: though in fact the distinction between these and acceptable 'personal preferences' is a difficult one) and such preferences involve treating others as less than equal. Such preferences should, therefore, be excluded. Dworkin would exclude them, saying that people have 'rights' against decisions likely to have been made on the basis of external preferences. For example, there would be a right to free speech since any decision to curb it would be made on the basis of external preferences against other people saying certain things.

Enough has been said to show that, for Dworkin, 'equality before the law' involves principally an interpretative process which looks at people equally. Rawls' 'social contract' view is, in this respect, similar. If the law formation process respects people equally (including, in Dworkin's view, respecting their 'rights') then they are equal before the law – and should not complain about the content of individual laws.

Some people would go even further, and say that 'equality before the law' involves not just the formation and application of the law but also its *result*. It is not enough for the law to be formed and applied 'equally', it must also result in people being, in some way, made equal. Whether this further equality is to be 'equality of opportunity' – a notion espoused by Rawls and by many people, Conservative and Socialist, in the UK – or 'equality of end result' as espoused by other Socialists – is a matter of dispute. The welfare state and perhaps, particularly, the provision of state education are examples of attempts to 'equalise'.

The phrase 'equality before the law' implies many things and raises many questions, in law application and law formation, as well as in a consideration of the end result. I have not discussed the latter in as much detail as the others because I see it as part of the overall process of law formation.

2) 'Social context plays a crucial role in nourishing ways of theorising about law. If the prevailing social context changes and people begin to experience life differently, there will be a corresponding shift in the way they see their world and the role of law in it. Previous theories of law will lose their appeal and new perspectives will increasingly seem true.'

How true is this claim?

University of London LLB Examination
(for External Students) Jurisprudence and Legal Theory June 1993 Q12

General Comment

This is a wide-open question and one that calls for some ingenuity to answer; usually you are either a person who can answer one of these or you are not. In a way, the question is very banal. Do people change their views about law because of a change in social context? One way to answer this would be to discuss some variation of the position of objectivity in legal reasoning. Obviously people change their views, for all sorts of reasons, but this no way establishes any such thing as the subjectivity of views about law. Another way would be to consider what different perspectives of the law are, with perhaps some emphasis on the idea that a 'critical' perspective would be better (or incomprehensible!) and thereby introduce a discussion on the CLS perspective on law. Yet another way would be to examine the economics-and-law movement and show how adherents see law from another perspective, one which is perhaps fuelled by commercial, utilitarian concerns. And another would be from the point of view of the commercial barrister; the high street conveyancer; the judge; the 'bad' man who only wants to know what he can get away with; the council estate worker; the racially and economically discriminated. It is, as you can see, a wide open question.

Skeleton Solution

The nature of the question – objectivity – different contexts – examples of opposing pictures of law: the western democratic versus Islamic law – law from the perspective of positivism – the meanings of 'liberalism' – law from the point of view of the 'morally concerned' – conclusion that all these ideas feed off a central paradigm: law from the point of view of morality.

Suggested Solution

The question can be answered at a simple level; it is clear that people change their views in response to the circumstances, the social context, in which they live. But often those views change in the following way; someone comes to see that the former way he saw things was *wrong*, the left-wing student in favour of abortion on demand who becomes violently anti-abortion on becoming a nursing sister on an abortion ward, for example, or the right wing law student who joins a legal advice centre and comes to the conclusion that most laws perpetuate an unjust class distinction. It does not follow that because people change their minds that somehow there is no *right* way to think about law, that there is not a 'correct' perspective from which to view law. Let's think about it; we all understand, for ourselves, our change of mind whereby we say that what we once thought to be wrong. Why can't we say that of a whole perspective we have of law? It is possible to argue that 'it is wrong – now – for that person, but not for anyone else', but that is too quick. If things were as subjective as that, why would a person bother to say 'I was wrong' as opposed to 'I've changed my views'? If things were really subjective, there would be no need to announce it to anyone that the former idea was wrong. It simply wouldn't be of any interest to anyone!

However, the question is more than one about the objectivity of reasoning (and so is less philosophical than it appears). It is about the interesting sociology of the different thoughts people happen to have about law. A good way of putting this point is to imagine the law as personified in the form of a cathedral; there is no one point whereby any person can look and see the cathedral in its entirety; there are only points of view – the aerial one, the one from the door, the crypt, the nave, the west wing, the pulpit, and so on. If we employ this analogy we can see that as a person moves from one context to another, he obtains a different view. Nevertheless, there is nothing wrong with saying that there is a cathedral 'objectively' there; rather it is just that there cannot be one definitive view of it. It is interesting to explore further this idea.

As two possible contexts, we could take a western democratic view of law and an Islamic view of law. The first is essentially liberal, in a very basic form of liberalism. Central to the idea is that of the 'rule of law', under which every person is subject to the laws and *free*, as an individual, to do what he likes *within* the confines of those laws, in particular, to work for the change of those laws but generally only through democratic means. In Hart's terms (but here he was talking of English positivism), it should be possible, through the rule of law doctrine, to drive a *wedge* between what the state requires by way of law (a matter, for Hart, of identification by the rule of recognition) and what the citizen thinks he must do as a matter of personal moral conscience. In Fuller's, or Dworkin's, terms, it means that the morality 'inherent in the law' is a liberal morality, one that sees human beings as independent judges of what counts as a good life *for them.*

In the most general terms, this is the context of Western Democratic thinking as espoused by Western Democratic legal systems (whether they live up to this ideal, to which they clearly pay lip service, is another matter). Economic libertarians have used the idea to their own advantage; thus they see the way open to economic exploitation; 'communitarians' have attacked the idea as being 'selfish, egotistical and ruthlessly individualistic'; defenders of the ideal claim, however, that liberalism, properly understood, could not allow exploitation (because liberalism's fundamental premise is that *people are important*) and that liberalism must show a concern beyond the selfish motives of individuals to require of individuals a concern for *other individuals*. Nevertheless, I suggest that it is essentially the emphasis on individualism that marks out, in the most general sense, the social context in which western democratic legal systems operate.

Let us contrast this view with the fundamentalist Islamic state. Here we have no wedge between individual conceptions of what is right and wrong and what the State thinks is right and wrong; there genuinely is no gap. What the State says *is* right for the individual, who lacks the same sort of status as citizen enjoys in the West. What does this mean? The religion, the morality, the law (state decision) are all one and the same thing. The individual who is brought up within this social context does not himself understand the distinction advocated by Hart; it means nothing to him that he may do one thing which is contrary to that demanded by the State, because the social context does not encourage him to draw that distinction; indeed, if the distinction were drawn to his attention, he would in all probability dismiss it as a wicked and blasphemous. It is not difficult to imagine being in such a country (incidentally, there is no fully Islamic state in the world at present). The novel by Margaret Attwood, *The Handmaid's Tale*, depicts such a society and the power of her book lies in the ease with which the rulers in that society manage in a very short space of time to encourage people to think in that way and lose their distinctive individuality.

How do we make sense of these two ways of looking at the world of law? Well, we must form a view. Very quickly, one might ask oneself head on: Which sort of society do I prefer? Of course, the answer doesn't lie in *just* preference; we could reject the Islamic type society after having been convinced by the arguments of either *Law's Empire* or *The Concept of Law*, on the grounds that we think that human beings are best when treated with respect towards individual decisions about how their lives should proceed. On the other hand, perhaps because we have a less rosy view of human nature, we might take the view that people are best when they are directed in their lives; that they are best when they *do not* make their own decisions for them. In this case we will prefer the Islamic-type legal system.

What does this line of thinking suggest? It raises the possibility that people can transcend their contexts (someone like Hart might be visionary in the Islamic-type state; someone like an Islamic jurist might be visionary in the western democratic state, succeeding in showing people how decadent was the 'virtue' that people had a 'right to go wrong') and produce a perspective on law that is independent. Further, it suggests that a natural line of imaginative thinking about law that transcends social context is that there is at least this much that is 'objective' about the production of a legal theory – and a point put very well by John Finnis, for example – that legal theorising about perspectives in law trade off one very central feature: that legal theorising is at heart a form of moral theorising.

3) 'Are legal philosophies like artistic creations about which some suggest that one can only say "I like it" or "I don't like it", or are there valid standards for criticisms of, or preference among, legal philosophies?' (Jerome Hall). What is your answer to this question?

University of London LLB Examination
(for External Students) Jurisprudence and Legal Theory June 1986 Q5

Skeleton Solution

Element of personal choice – also valid standards to guide that choice – purpose of legal philosophy – extent to which arguments stand up to critical scrutiny – results of experience and experiment – intuitive convictions – thus need for personal choice.

Suggested Solution

I will attempt to show that while there is an element of personal choice and taste in deciding between different legal philosophies, there are valid and acceptable standards available to guide that choice and, in particular, to assist in the rejection of unsatisfactory philosophies.

The first standard which can be used is to consider the purpose of a particular philosophy, the question being asked. For example, Fuller's 'inner morality of law' notion is derived from a viewpoint which sees law as an interaction between the governors and the governed, with the guidance of people's behaviour as law's main function. Hence, to the extent that the law falls short of Fuller's eight 'excellences' which constitute his 'morality', it is less law: Fuller allows for the existence of a legal system to be a question of degree based on the extent to which the excellences are achieved. Fuller's starting point is an interesting one; certainly it would not be accepted by many sociologists, who view law not in terms of interaction or consensus but more in terms of conflict between ruler and ruled. The choice between Fuller's aim of explaining law as interaction and the sociologist's alternative model can be made on the basis of an assessment of the evidence available in given societies and legal systems; it is capable of objective decision at least to an extent.

A second standard by which philosophies can be judged is the extent to which the claims and arguments underlying them stand up to critical scrutiny. Austin and Bentham based their legal philosophy on the notion of a law being the 'command of a sovereign', a view which has been subject to much criticism and in particular the irrefutable points made by Professor Hart in his *The Concept of Law* and elsewhere in his writings. For example, he forces us to reject the idea of a sovereign identified by habitual obedience as an explanation of authority within the legal system by the arguments raised in Chapter 4 of *The Concept of Law* concerning the succession of a new sovereign and the persistence of a past sovereign's law. The strength of Hart's arguments cause us to choose his, rather than Austin or Bentham's, explanations and provide us with benchmarks by which to criticise those earlier theories.

In similar fashion, logical arguments can be ranged against the legal philosophy known as 'American Realism'. The realists' concentration on dispute settlement as being the 'core area' of law ignores the great extent to which the aim of law is (and the working lives of lawyers

16 Jurisprudence – An Overview

are spent in trying) to prevent disputes ever arising. Also, the suggestion that disputes are settled not on the basis of legal rules ('paper rules', as some realists dismissively call them) but by the judge's prejudices, beliefs and feelings, can be seen upon empirical observation to be a vast over-simplification and distortion of the true picture.

That last point brings us to another standard by which theories can be compared: by the results of experience and experiment. The claim that law is mainly about courts is belied by the experience of most practitioners in trying to guard their business clients from ever getting to court: the claims of early legal anthropologists that primitive societies had no recognisable 'law' has been proved by empirical research to be incorrect: as Llewellyn and Hoebel showed in *The Cheyenne Way*, it is even the case that some primitive societies have procedures for deliberately changing the law, deliberate 'legislation'. This sort of empirical treatment is obviously most suited to the areas of study such as anthropology and sociology where law interrelates with the social sciences.

A final standard of criticism and preference which should not be overlooked is the extent (or otherwise) to which the conclusions of a philosophy match with our intuitive convictions. When studying the theory of Robert Nozick, for example, it is surely valid for us to consider whether or not we accept that any society organised in the way he suggests could conceivably deserve the label 'just'.

As this last standard shows, there is a narrow dividing line between a valid standard and personal choice or preference between viewpoints and philosophies. This is particularly so between theories which can co-exist without any logical contradiction. Despite Fuller's protestations to the contrary, his 'inner morality' can co-exist with Hart's positivist philosophy, as Hart himself has argued.

A further, more controversial, example is the possibility of co-existence of some central tenets of positivism (notably, that an unjust law is still a valid law) with natural law ideas – a possibility explored by Finnis in *Natural Law and Natural Rights*. This logical possibility of co-existence does not, in my view, rule out the necessity for a choice to be made, but rather accentuates it: one must still decide which of the two (or more) logically coherent philosophies is the correct one, the one which most closely captures the essence of law and the legal experience.

Valid standards are, then, available to criticise philosophies and to narrow the possibilities; but the need for a personal choice remains.

4) 'Law insists that force not be used or withheld, no matter how successful that would be to ends in view, no matter how beneficial or noble these ends, except as licenced or required by individual rights and responsibilities flowing from past political decisions about when collective force is justified' (Dworkin). Discuss.

University of London LLB Examination
(for External Students) Jurisprudence and Legal Theory June 1987 Q5

Skeleton Solution

Use of force and the rule of law – Kelsen – monopolisation of force – meaning of 'rule of law' – Rawls and civil disobedience – theory of justice – revolution – legitimation of revolution – *Mitchell* v *DPP* (1986) – Marxist justification of force – force not dependent upon licence.

Jurisprudence: The Philosophy of Law

Suggested Solution

This is a question that covers such a large part of the course and is cast so wide that it is almost incapable of a concise answer, particularly under examination conditions. I would take this question to be addressing the issue of the use of force with regard to the rule of law and the circumstances, if any, under which force may be used.

Kelsen observed that a legal system could not exist unless the state had monopolised the use of force. The validity of this observation can be seen with regard to the present situation in Lebanon where the state has been unable to monopolise the use of force. There the whole system has broken down and it would not be appropriate to describe that place as having an efficacious legal system. That is certainly an important and useful observation, the making of which is less obvious than the statement of which. Once there is a monopolisation of force it then becomes possible to speak of the rule of law.

The point about the rule of law is that the rulers are to be bound by the same law as the ruled. This was noted by Lord Denning in *Gouriet* v *UPW* (1978) in which he quoted Thomas Fuller who said 'be you ever so high the law is above you'. All men are ruled by law including the rulers. This would be a criticism of Austin's view that there could be no limits placed on the sovereign and led him to deny that constitutional conventions were law. The question then arises as to what amounts to the rule of law.

In his volume on *Taking Rights Seriously*, Dworkin argued that law could not be neutral. For him the law must state, in its greatest part, the majority's view of the common good. The institution of rights is therefore crucial because it represents the majority's promise to the minorities that their dignity and equality will be respected. He continues that when the divisions among the groups are most violent then the promise to respect rights, if law is to work, must be most sincere. Dworkin continues that if the government will not take rights seriously then it will not take law seriously either.

A conception about the rule of law would require that individuals not take matters into their own hands. That would return man to a state of nature without the benefit of social organisation. Any force would need to be institutionalised and centralised along the lines noted by Kelsen. Nonetheless, as Rawls identified in *A Theory of Justice*, it would be possible to justify civil disobedience in terms of a conception about justice that authorised civil disobedience in order to ensure that the constitution was conformed to. There would here be no already established right or responsibility although the words of Lincoln's first inaugural address to the effect that the government belongs to the people and they may change it or if it will not change then they may exercise their revolutionary right to remove it. This view is inspired by the social contractarian natural rights view that believes that the rulers hold their position on trust to respect rights of the people and that if they are in breach of that trust then they may be removed by force if necessary. Whether these natural rights are the subject of already established rights remains a moot point. It also remains quite moot if one adopts Kelsen's point about the validity of a successful revolutionary change depending on might being right in the gaining of total efficacy. This would allow for an ex post facto legitimation of a violent change that when effected was otherwise illegal according to the ousted regime. The source of the right to revolt thus becomes crucial.

In the Grenadan Court of Appeal in *Mitchell* v *DPP* (1986) the court seemed to be laying down a more substantive test than was found in Kelsen for the legitimation of a revolutionary change when they stated that legitimacy would not be accorded to a regime that was undemocratic or oppressive or whose mandates were not obeyed through general popular support but through coercion. It is clear that that court was concerned to withdraw legitimacy from the revolutionary regime removed by the Americans and hence developed criteria in addition to the Kelsenian in order to achieve their end. They may also have opened Pandora's box in that they, by implication, have stated that if a revolution achieves these aims then it will be legitimated. Thus the use of force to achieve these ends is legitimate. Eekelaar went even further in a recent article on revolutionary legitimacy wherein it was stated that a revolution should, in order to attain legitimacy, achieve respect for group and cultural rights such as self determination. This implies that the use of force in order to achieve these ends is legitimate.

A Marxist approach would develop this point further and would insist that force be used in order to resist the institutions of the capitalists and to bring forward the communist revolution and the day of the classless society. The ends would justify the means employed. These means would, if tactically appropriate, include the use of force in circumstances where it was clear that law as a tool of the dominant class would not be legitimate.

We can therefore conclude that there would be circumstances where force may be used that would not be dependent upon license.

17 University of London LLB (External) 1996 Questions and Suggested Solutions

UNIVERSITY OF LONDON
LLB EXAMINATIONS 1996
for External Students
PART II EXAMINATION (Scheme A)
FOURTH YEAR EXAMINATION (Scheme B)
GRADUATE ENTRY LEVEL II (Route A)
GRADUATE ENTRY THIRD YEAR (Route B)

JURISPRUDENCE AND LEGAL THEORY

Monday, 3 June: 2.30 pm to 5.30 pm

Answer *ONE* question from Part A (the set book) and *THREE* questions from Part B from the following TWELVE questions

PART A (the set book)

1   '[The judge's] statement that a rule is valid is an internal statement recognising that the rule satisfies the test for identifying what is to count as law in his court, and constitutes not a prophecy of but part of the *reason* for his decision'. (Hart)

    Discuss.

2   '*The Concept of Law* is primarily aimed at historians or sociologists who want clear criteria of what it means to say a legal system exists and has no direct use to lawyers who want to know what "the law" is on some point.'

    Discuss.

3   What is Hart trying to establish with his theory of the 'minimum content of law'? Does he succeed in your view?

PART B

4   EITHER

    a) 'The pure theory of law ... establishes the law as a specific system independent even of the moral law. It does this not ... by defining the legal norm as an imperative, but as an hypothetical judgment expressing a specific relationship between a conditioning circumstance and a conditioned consequence.' (Kelsen)

    Explain and discuss critically with particular reference to the practical implications of his theory.

    OR

    b) Explain critically Kelsen's idea that legal validity depends upon a 'transcendental epistemological postulate'.

5 Is Hart fair to Fuller when he criticises Fuller's eight principles of the 'inner morality' of law as being analogous to principles of the 'inner morality' of the poisoner's art?

6 State what, in your view, is the most convincing form of utilitarianism. Can it account adequately for the existence of moral rights? Does it have to?

7 'Analysing the content of Austin's theory of law can proceed without locating it within the historical and social conditions which gave rise to it, but appreciating the meaning of the theory cannot.'

Discuss.

8 To what extent does Dworkin's image of legal development as similar to constructing a chain novel illuminate important features of the legal process?

9 'The CLS movement seems incoherent and lacking in positive ideas because western countries are experiencing a crisis of confidence in their institutions and have lost faith in the image of law as a coherent and rational body of doctrine. The approach of the movement is actually a passionate appeal to analyse the huge variation in law's roles and effects while placing the human actor at the centre of law.'

Discuss.

10 'While the specific predictions and empirical statements of Marx and Engels on law were rooted in the nineteenth century and have been largely disproved by history, many of the concepts and tools of analysis they created remain of vital importance for our understanding of law in society today.'

Discuss.

11 'Feminist jurisprudence does not so much claim that traditional jurisprudence was wrong, but demonstrates that women have been in a radically different social relation to the law than men.'

Discuss.

12 'All theories of natural law have relied upon some thesis that value is inherent in nature. Since that thesis is plainly wrong, all theories of natural law are incoherent and illogical.'

Discuss.

Jurisprudence: The Philosophy of Law

QUESTION ONE

'[The judge's] statement that a rule is valid is an internal statement recognising that the rule satisfies the test for identifying what is to count as law in his court, and constitutes not a prophecy of but part of the *reason* for his decision'. (Hart)

Discuss.

University of London LLB Examination
(for External Students) Jurisprudence and Legal Theory June 1996 Q1

General Comment

This question examines Hart's attitude to the predictive theory of obligation. It is necessary to consider what the rule of recognition is, together with analysing what are internal and external statements of law. The essay requires careful thought as it is easy to lose sight of the crux of the matter – one judge's decision says nothing about the behaviour of other judges.

Skeleton Solution

Test provided by the rule of recognition – meaning of an internal statement – question of validity and external statements – comparison of rule of recognition and the basic norm or grundnorm.

Suggested Solution

Professor Hart offers an illuminating discussion about the day-to-day life of a legal system in his book *The Concept of Law*; at the heart of a legal system is the rule of recognition which contains the criteria of validity of all rules of the system. The rule of recognition is seldom formulated expressly as a rule, though occasionally courts declare the importance of one criteria of law relative to another. For example, in the United Kingdom courts declare Acts of Parliament supreme over other sources of law. Mostly the rule of recognition is unstated, but its existence is shown in the way in which rules are identified and applied by courts and other officials.

There is a difference between the use made of the rule of recognition by courts and the use made of the rule by others. The crucial difference is that when courts reach a decision on the basis that the criteria provided by the rule have identified as a member of the legal system that decision has special authoritative status.

Hart likens the rule of recognition to the scoring of a game like cricket or football. The general rule defining the activities which constitute scoring (runs, goals, etc) is not formulated in the course of the game, yet it is used by the umpire, referee and players in identifying the particular phases of the game which count towards winning. It is important to note that the declarations of the umpire or referee have special authoritative meaning attributed to them by other rules. The difficulty with this analogy is that rules of cricket or football, although not formulated in the course of the game, are set by the governing bodies of the respective sports – so presumably Hart is saying that because the rules of the game have already been set by a governing body the referee, umpire or players can positively identify them by using what could be called a rule of recognition.

When unstated rules of recognition are used by courts and others in the identification of rules of a legal system, it is said that such usage is characterised by the internal point of view. This means that those who use the rules of recognition show their acceptance of them as guiding rules. This acceptance of the rules of recognition as guiding rules is accompanied by a particular kind of expression used not only by judges but also by ordinary citizens living under a legal system when they have identified any rule of the system. Thus an expression like 'it is the law that parking on a red line is punishable by a fine' or 'out' or 'goal' is the language used by someone who assesses a situation by reference to rules which are commonly acknowledged as appropriate for this purpose.

The language such a person uses is called an internal statement in that it manifests the internal point of view and is naturally used by people who accept the rule of recognition and apply it in identifying some specific rule of the system as valid. The internal statement is to be contrasted with the external statement which is made by the outsider or observer who says, for example: 'In the United Kingdom it is accepted as law whatever the Crown in Parliament enacts'. This is the language of an observer who does not accept the rule of recognition, but states that it is a fact that others in the United Kingdom accept it.

The internal statement governs the question of the validity of a rule of the legal system. The internal statement says that a particular rule of a legal system is valid. This means that it is recognised that a given rule passes all the tests provided by the rule of recognition, and is thus a rule of the legal system.

When one makes an internal statement about the validity of a particular rule of a system, one may be said to presuppose the truth of the external statement of fact which says the legal system is generally efficacious. The catch here, however, is that it would not be wholly correct to say that any time anyone makes an internal statement it means the legal system is generally efficacious. There may be rules of the legal system which are obsolete or dormant but still remain rules of the system. The efficacy of a system cannot be measured by such obsolete or dormant rules.

There is a common theory known as the predictive analysis of obligation which says that the internal statement that a given rule is a valid rule of the system and the external statement that the system is generally efficacious assert the validity of a rule, and so predict its enforcement by judges or other officials. The predictive theory is advanced to avoid metaphysical interpretations: either (a) that the statement which says a rule is valid suggests some mysterious content that cannot be detected; or (b) it predicts the future behaviour of officials of the system.

What the predictive theory does is to mistake the specific character of an internal statement, and treat it as an external statement about official behaviour. Therefore, when a judge makes an internal statement about the validity of a rule of the legal system in a judicial decision, the judge presupposes but does not state the general efficacy of the system. Neither does the judge predict his or her own and others' official behaviour. Accordingly Hart says the judge's 'statement that a rule is valid is an internal statement recognising that the rule satisfies the test for identifying what is to count as law in his court, and constitutes not a prophecy of but part of the *reason* for his decision'.

As far as the judge's internal statement and validity are concerned, the judge only remarks that a particular rule identified by the system's rule of recognition is valid because it satisfies the criteria provided by the rule of recognition. This is why that rule forms part of the reason for the judge's decision. It is not a prophecy or a prediction of the judge's own or others' future actions.

Jurisprudence: The Philosophy of Law

The rule of recognition can be compared with Kelsen's basic norm. Kelsen's basic norm supplies the criteria of validity of all norms in a legal order. Similarly the rule of recognition supplies the criteria of validity of all rules in a legal system. However, whereas Kelsen's basic norm is a theoretical construct, a fiction, Hart's rule of recognition is a fact as well as law. The basic norm is presupposed in our juristic thinking, and stands behind the historically first constitution with which people ought to behave in accordance. There is nothing in both Kelsen and Hart which says that because a judge pronounces a rule valid because it satisfies the criteria supplied by the rule of recognition, or that it is validated by a higher norm, the judge's decision is a prophecy or a prediction of the behaviour of others in future.

The predictive theory's mistake is to treat a judge's internal statement about legal validity as a prediction of the general efficacy of the legal system, and to a larger extent a prediction of what others may do. Hart refuses this and says the judge's internal statement is about what he or she through the criteria supplied by the rule of recognition identifies as law to count towards a decision in a case.

QUESTION TWO

'*The Concept of Law* is primarily aimed at historians or sociologists who want clear criteria of what it means to say a legal system exists and has no direct use to lawyers who want to know what "the law" is on some point.'

Discuss.

University of London LLB Examination
(for External Students) Jurisprudence and Legal Theory June 1996 Q2

General Comment

It is easy to misinterpret this question. It is not simply asking you to reflect on Hart's famous statement that his work, *The Concept of Law*, is 'an essay in descriptive sociology'. It is also easy to make the mistake of thinking that 'an essay in descriptive sociology' is of more relevance to sociologists and historians than lawyers. Using Hart's methodology you can establish the relevance of his work to the legal practitioner.

Skeleton Solution

Consideration of Hart's stated aim in the preface of *The Concept of Law* that his work is an essay in descriptive sociology – Hart's methodology – his elements of law – the existence of a legal system – virtues of legal positivism – wider concept of law – hard cases – Dworkin.

Suggested Solution

Hart's claim in the preface to *The Concept of Law* (2nd ed 1994) that his work is an 'essay in descriptive sociology' suggests that he wants to describe an entity which he regards as existing 'out there', just as a sociologist or a historian would report or describe an event that happened somewhere. It can be said, therefore, that Hart probably wants his 'essay in descriptive sociology' to be a description of a legal system.

To achieve this end he employs a methodology which uses strands of description and prescription to help our consciousness, and provide a view of the law which he highly recommends to us in our search for practical solutions to problems: keep law and morality separate and distinct. Hart's methodology, which is variously called the 'existence thesis' or 'development thesis', shows Hart's purpose in producing a theory of law that helps society. He imagines a pre-legal society with only primary rules of obligation. The rules contain restrictions on the free use of force or violence, theft and deception to which human beings are tempted, but which must be suppressed if they are to live in close proximity with one another. Such a society may show tension between those who voluntarily accept rules and those who do not. The rules of the group do not form a system but are simply a set of separate standards without any common identifying mark. Such a society, according to Hart, has three defects which are:

a) uncertainty about which rules are members of the system – which rule is a moral rule and which is legal;

b) static nature of rules: the society is rigid through lack of any means of quickly changing rules and introducing new ones;

c) inefficiency: when disputes arise through myriad social pressures it is impossible to find what rules are applicable.

To cure these defects in the pre-legal society, Hart recommends remedies which will cure them: (a) the rule of recognition; (b) the rule of change; and (c) the rule of adjudication.

The rule of recognition will specify features which a rule has to possess to be taken as conclusive affirmation that it belongs to the group. The rule of recognition may be no more than an authoritative list or text of the rules to be found in a written document. What is important is that there is now a reduction into writing of hitherto unwritten rules, which becomes a reference point and is authoritative.

The second defect, the static nature of rules, is cured by the introduction of the rule of change to deal with the slow process of growth within society. This empowers an individual or a body of persons to introduce new primary rules for the conduct of the group. To Hart, it is in the 'rules of change' that the process of legislative enactment and repeal is to be understood. The rules, besides specifying the person or persons to legislate, also define the procedure to be followed in legislating.

The third defect is that of inefficiency of the diffuse social pressures by which rules are maintained in a simple society. There is a waste of time in such a society through lack of organisation in catching and punishing wrongdoers. The remedy for this regime is to introduce 'rules of adjudication'. These are secondary rules empowering individuals to make authoritative determination of questions about breaches of rules. The secondary rules of adjudication define the procedures to be followed and also define the concepts of judge, court, jurisdiction and judgment.

The remedy for each of the three defects, as has been noted, consists in supplementing the primary rules of obligation in the simple society with secondary rules. The introduction of each remedy for a defect might be considered a step from the pre-legal into the legal world. Each remedy has its own elements which permeate law. Together the three remedies are enough to convert the regime of primary rules into what is indisputably a legal system.

This is the existence thesis of a legal system which at first sight is enough to support the suggestion that Hart's primary aim in *The Concept of Law* is to proffer the criteria or test that will enable the sociologist or the historian to recognise legal systems in any political system.

It would, however, not be correct to say that is the primary aim of *The Concept of Law*. To say that is to ignore Hart's other purpose, which is to distinguish between the state and the individual. To Hart, law is the demand of the state 'out there' which is separate from the individual as a moral being. In chapter 9 of *The Concept of Law*, he introduces the narrow concept of law which says the certification of something as valid is not conclusive of the question of obedience. In saying that law is the demand of the state 'out there', Hart seeks to emphasise legal positivism's claim that law is separate from morals. The 'wider concept of law' includes morally repugnant laws and is distinguished from the narrow concept – the natural law concept – which forbids morally unjust laws.

It can, therefore, be said that Hart emphasises positive law, the kind of law which is sought by lawyers who want to know what 'the law' is on some point. The law is the black letter rule. The lawyer who wants to know what the law is on some point must simply work out the black letter rule – check the sources of law to find out what the law says on the issue. As Hart says, the existing law is the demand of the state 'out there', so morality must be separated from questions of law.

Hart has a dual purpose which I believe he fully succeeds in establishing. He succeeds in his first purpose of offering sociologists and historians a test for recognising the existence of a legal system, and he succeeds in the second purpose of offering a practical help to the lawyer who wants to know what 'the law' is on some point. The practical advice to the lawyers from Hart's legal positivism is clear – the law is the demand of the state 'out there' which must be separated from our individual consciences. The rule of recognition was introduced to clear the air, to positively distinguish legal rules from what are not legal rules, to introduce certainty into the law. The rule of recognition possesses the criteria of validity of rules of the system so that the practitioner will be able to know positively what the law says on some point. Hart's legal positivism is therefore of practical help to the lawyer.

The only unfortunate thing about Hart's positivism is his analysis of hard cases. His analysis does not match the way barristers speak or argue in court. Hart says in hard cases there is a gap in the law since the law here is indeterminate, inconclusive or there is a gap in the law. Hart believes that the judge has to legislate to fill in the gap in the law when deciding cases. This means that in hard cases, there are no laws until the judge makes a decision. Dworkin disputes this view of law presented by Hart. To Dworkin the law is always complete without gaps. The law is explained, justified and underlain by principles so in hard cases there is always law to be consulted.

Dworkin's argument supports the way barristers speak and argue cases. The barrister always cites an existing law and never says there is no law to be consulted because of gaps in the law. Following Hart's account of hard cases it seems the barrister will not be able to know what 'the law' is in a hard case until the judge makes a decision. The barrister, from experience, might disagree as he or she, following Dworkin's approach, can always argue what 'the law' is on an issue.

Hart succeeds in *The Concept of Law* in doing two things: firstly, providing us with a methodology for recognising the existence of a legal system, which helps everybody including the sociologist and the historian; and secondly, providing the legal practitioner with the tool for recognising and distinguishing between law and morality. The rule of recognition helps the practitioner in identifying statutes and precedents – what 'the law' is on any issue.

17 University of London LLB (External) 1996 Questions and Suggested Solutions

QUESTION THREE

What is Hart trying to establish with his theory of the 'minimum content of law'? Does he succeed in your view?

University of London LLB Examination
(for External Students) Jurisprudence and Legal Theory June 1996 Q3

General Comment

The first thing to remember in answering a question on Hart's minimum content of natural law is that Hart is a positivist. Ask 'what is a positivist doing talking about a minimum content of natural law?' It will then be clear to you why Hart says that natural law contains a core of good sense which human beings must respect as long as we are what we are and propose to establish a viable society.

Skeleton Solution

The teleological conception of nature – Hart's positivism – his preparedness as a positivist to concede only the minimum ground to natural law – law and morals must have specific content – Fuller – Finnis – conclusion.

Suggested Solution

Hart's legal positivism is here defined to mean that 'it is in no sense a necessary truth that laws reproduce or satisfy certain demands of morality, though in fact they have often done so'(Hart, *The Concept of Law* (2nd ed 1994) p181). This contention of positivism entails a fundamental break with the natural law tradition which denies the 'separation thesis'.

According to the natural lawyer, in attempting to answer the question 'what is law?', one must look at the content of law, and any law which is against morality or natural justice is invalid. Hart responds that there are many different types of relation between law and morality. He says it cannot be seriously disputed that the development of law has been profoundly influenced both by the conventional morality and ideas of particular social groups, and also by forms of enlightened criticisms of people whose morality transcends current morality. However, he says, it is possible to take this truth 'illicitly' for a different proposition, namely, that a legal system must exhibit some specific conformity with morality or justice or must rest on a conviction that there is a moral obligation to obey it. Admitting that this proposition may be true, Hart says 'it does not follow that the legal validity of particular laws used in a legal system must include, tacitly if not explicitly, a reference to morality or justice' (Hart, ibid, pp181–182).

Natural law says that morality is bound up with the law. Hart's answer is that there is no need for law to have a 'further necessary content' but that law and morals must have a 'specific content' of natural law. Hart attacks the natural law teleological conception of nature, which espouses the idea of the ultimate end or goal for human beings. To Hart this is a grand design. The proper goal or end for human beings is survival. This is his basic assumption. His contention is that most men most of the time will want to continue to survive; the social arrangements men make are to this end. Among these social arrangements we wish to know whether there are some which may 'illuminatingly be ranked as natural law discoverable by reason, and what their relation is to human law and morality' (Hart, ibid, p188).

Following from this point Hart makes some generalisations which he says are truisms or facts

203

Jurisprudence: The Philosophy of Law

about human nature; there are certain rules of conduct which any social organisation must contain if it is to be viable. Such rules constitute the 'common' element in the law and conventional morality of all societies where there are forms of social control. In both law and morals is found much that is relevant to society, and which is universally recognised principles of conduct which may be called the minimum content of natural law.

According to Hart, there are five truisms or facts of the human condition which necessitate the specific content of natural law, and not the further necessary content favoured by natural lawyers. The five truisms or facts of the human condition are:

a) Human vulnerability: all men are vulnerable – even the strongest man has to sleep sometimes, and becomes vulnerable whilst asleep so there must be restriction on the use of violence or the infliction of bodily harm and killing.

b) Approximate equality: human beings differ from each other in physique, agility and capacity but no one is superhuman so for life to be less nasty, less brutish, and less short, aggression must be restrained. There must be co-operation between people for the benefit of all.

c) Limited altruism: since human beings are neither angels or devils, selfishness must be controlled so there must be co-operation between people in a community.

d) Limited resources: because of the scarcity of resources there must be rules to regulate property and prevent people stealing from others.

e) Limited understanding and strength of will: people obey rules for a variety of reasons which may be selfish or public spirited. It is necessary to make laws to curb the excesses of human beings.

Due to these five facts of human condition it is a 'natural necessity' to have minimum forms of protection for persons, property and promise which are indispensable features of law. To Hart, this is the common ground, the minimum connection that exists between law and morality, for example, theft and murder. He says it is false to say moral judgments are irrelevant. If persons, property and promise are to be protected then both law and morality must have a specific content of natural law.

Professor Lon Fuller in the *Morality of Law* says that Hart's minimum content of natural law says nothing about who should be included in the community that seeks the realisation of the commonly-shared objective of survival. There is nothing about who is to survive. Hart will respond that it applies to members of the group collectively. Professor Fuller also takes Hart to task for saying that an overwhelming majority of people wish to live even at the cost of hideous misery. To Fuller this is a dubious claim, which undermines any assertion that survival is a necessary condition for the attainment of other ends. To Hart survival is the chief aim of human activity. Professor Fuller disagrees with this and I share his opinion.

It was Aquinas who said if the chief aim of a captain was to preserve his ship he would keep it in port forever (Aquinas, *Summa Theologica* Pt I–II, Q2, Art 5). Fuller doubts whether Hart's search for a 'central indisputable element' in human endeavour can be successful. To Fuller, if we were to select the principle that supports and pervades all human endeavour, communication with our fellow human beings is the highest and he doubts whether most of us would cherish surviving in a kind of vegetable existence in which we cannot meaningfully articulate our thoughts.

Finnis, on the other hand, says human beings want to flourish, not merely to survive, so why should there be only a minimum content of natural law. Why not more? Even though Hart

17 University of London LLB (External) 1996 Questions and Suggested Solutions

does not say that even if his analysis of human society is accepted it will inevitably lead to a system of even minimal justice in any given society, his analysis is too narrow. Since human beings do not want just to survive but to flourish, why should there not be a further necessary content of natural law as natural law's teleological conception of nature envisages? Hart does not succeed in establishing why law and morals must have specific content. The social arrangements we make in society are not merely to aid the goal of survival but the myriad aims and aspirations we have. If law must have some moral input then the idea of law having whatever moral content is required to anchor such aspirations must be more appealing than the idea that since survival is the only human goal moral input in law must be limited to protecting persons, property and promise. If law coincides with morality in some respects why should it happen only to protect persons, property and prevent breaches of contract? Why should law and morality not coincide in other areas of human endeavour?

Imagine a fundamentalist society where the source of law is the Bible or the Koran; citizens in such a society live by the teaching in the scriptures and consider law and morality synonymous since the scriptures form the constitution of their community. Apart from the prohibition of murder, theft and breaches of contract, the scriptures also teach procreation, observance of the Ten Commandments or Sharia law, loving one's neighbour as oneself, seeking the Kingdom of God and they generally proclaim that the raison d'être of human beings on earth is to serve God.

Citizens of such a society will not see a need to limit the interface of law and morality to protecting persons, property and punishing breaches of contract. With law and morality being synonymous, citizens will expect that the aspirations in the scriptures are met, and will expect both law and morality to underpin all of the aspirations – just as the teleological concept of nature says. Citizens would expect, for example, to follow the moral exhortation in the scriptures and make a pilgrimage once in their lifetime. To such people survival is not their only goal. They would expect more from law than merely a culturally specific agenda to protect persons, property and promise.

It is arguable that welfare laws, divorce law (adultery is one fact that can lead to divorce), the duty of care concept and the neighbour principle in tort law have moral undertones, and show that law does coincide with morality in other respects.

Hart is not successful in proving survival is the main goal of human activity, and that morality coincides with law only to prevent murder, theft and breaches of contract. There is more to human endeavour which is supported and buttressed by the moral input of law than Hart admits. Although Hart's minimum content of natural law is a restatement of natural law, his version is too restrictive as law coincides with morality outside his minimum content.

QUESTION FOUR(A)

'The pure theory of law ... establishes the law as a specific system independent even of the moral law. It does this not ... by defining the legal norm as an imperative, but as an hypothetical judgment expressing a specific relationship between a conditioning cir-cumstance and a conditioned consequence.' (Kelsen)

Explain and discuss critically with particular reference to the practical implications of his theory.

University of London LLB Examination
(for External Students) Jurisprudence and Legal Theory June 1996 Q4(a)

Jurisprudence: The Philosophy of Law

General Comment

Questions on Kelsen always appear in the examination paper in one form or another. This question invites you to think about the nature of Kelsen's ought propositions. What must be kept in mind is that Kelsen intends his ought statements not to be an imperative like the command theory but as a hypothetical judgment. Ask yourself whether there are occasions when judges do not apply the law for any reason.

Skeleton Solution

The nature of Kelsen's pure theory of law – law as an independent entity – methodology – difference between science of law and other sciences – difficulties of drawing a strict line of demarcation between science of law and other sciences – question of probability.

Suggested Solution

Kelsen's pure theory of law establishes the law as an independent entity devoid of any impurities. His aim is to free law from the value judgments common to other sciences; his pure theory seeks to free the science of law with a methodology that eschews any reliance on politics, ethics, theology, psychology or biology.

By establishing the independence of law, Kelsen seeks to liberate law from its traditional association with morals. Natural law makes morals part of law, and this makes the legal norm an imperative. For example, the traditional association of law and morals makes 'thou shall not kill' a legal norm as well as a moral imperative. Law and morals are interlinked. To Kelsen, law's liberation from morals means the pure theory is to be seen as a theory of positive law. The pure theory does not question the requirement that law must be moral. It questions the view of natural law that law is part of morals and every law must therefore have some moral input. The quotation in the question shows that if the moral law is imperative Kelsen's legal norm is not, so there is a difference between the moral norm and legal norm. The difference is shown by separating law from other sciences which explain causal, natural processes.

The law of nature links a particular circumstance – the cause – to a particular effect. Law links the legal condition (a conditioning circumstance) to the legal consequence (a conditioned con-sequence). There is a relationship here. With the law of nature the link is explained by the principle of causality: if A, then B. The pure theory, on the other hand, says that law has a 'specific relationship' which is a special and peculiar principle of law. Law, then, is a hypothetical judgment, an imputation, because when a conditioning circumstance (delict) happens it says nothing with regard to value, the moral or political value of the ensuing relationship.

According to the pure theory, the legal rule says: 'if A is then B ought to be'. The ought is a pure a priori category which expresses no moral or political value between A and B. Kelsen says there is no cause and effect between A and B. The example Kelsen gives is that punishment does not always follow a delict as cause upon effect. The legal rule, therefore, only expresses a hypothetical judgment, eg: 'if someone steals he ought to be punished'. The ought statement is the hypothetical judgment because A may steal and not be punished. Here the law is not followed so there is no cause and effect. There is no imperative analogous with a moral norm. To Kelsen the ought category of law indicates the 'specific sense' in which the legal condition and the legal circumstance are understood in the legal rule.

17 University of London LLB (External) 1996 Questions and Suggested Solutions

What Kelsen is saying is that by being a hypothetical judgment the rule of law is different from the rule of nature because while natural science describes its objects by the principle of causality, law describes its objects by the principle of normativity or imputation. Therefore, a normative rule is valid even if it is unenforced. For example, a normative rule which says 'if someone kills he ought to be punished' is still valid even if in a given case someone who murders is not punished. This is because an 'ought' statement which is a hypothetical judgment (explains why the killer in this case is not punished) is different from an 'is' statement which says if someone kills he is actually punished.

The difference between a legal norm and the law of nature is not seen by examining the elements that connect them but by the manner of their connection. Whereas the rule of law connects the conditioning circumstances and the conditioning consequence with an 'ought', the law of nature connects two elements by an 'is'.

There is a difficulty in drawing a strict line of demarcation between a rule of law and a law of nature as presented by Kelsen. He agrees that both a legal norm and a law of nature follow hypothetical judgments attaching certain consequences to certain conditions. If both have this logical form how can he make any watertight compartment between the two? He says the difference between the rule of law and the law of nature as far as connection between the two elements is concerned is that whereas the rule of law uses 'ought' to connect two elements, the law of nature uses an 'is'. However, if punishment ought to follow upon the commitment of a delict by someone is this not the same as causality? If both a legal norm and a law of nature employ hypothetical judgments, is it then not correct to say that if a law of nature is characterised by probability (in that there is nothing absolute about a law of nature which cannot be contradicted by another law of nature), is it also not the case that a legal norm can be contradicted by another legal norm?

Kelsen is not convincing about the specific relationship between a conditioning circumstance and a conditioned consequence as far as law is concerned. Punishment may not follow upon a person committing a delict but that may be because another legal rule rescues the person from punishment. For example, the law exempts children under 10 years of age from punishment. If a child in this age group escapes punishment it is because the law exempts the child, and it is misleading to say the law was not enforced because it is only expressed as an imputation. If the logic of this argument is followed then the pure theory cannot establish any binding force in law.

The problem with the pure theory is that Kelsen sees law as a hypothetical judgment. If a law says 'if someone steals he ought to be punished', and a thief escapes punishment, it is not the case that the judge deciding the case sees the law as a hypothetical judgment but that in all probability the thief was able to rely on another law as a defence or that the thief was let off on a technicality. It is not that because the thief escapes punishment because the judge chooses not to enforce the law without reason. In practice the pure theory, by relying on hypothetical judgment will admit value judgment, moral or political. The pure theory may properly be called a theory of positive law in that it seeks to separate what is a legal rule from what is a moral rule, yet describing a legal rule as a hypothetical judgment has its own problems in practice if not in theory. The practical implication of this theory is that a legal rule has no force until enforced by a judge or an official.

QUESTION FOUR(B)

Explain critically Kelsen's idea that legal validity depends upon a 'transcendental epistemological postulate'.

University of London LLB Examination
(for External Students) Jurisprudence and Legal Theory June 1996 Q4(b)

General Comment

Your knowledge of Kelsen's theory must be comprehensive enough to give you the confidence to tackle this question. If Kelsen's grundnorm or basic norm is not validated by any other norm but must, as he says, be presupposed in our juristic thinking, is one not right in arguing that Kelsen's grundnorm, like a phantom, can be based on anything?

Skeleton Solution

The idea of the norm and legal validity – the idea that a higher norm validates another norm – hierarchical structure of norms – the basic norm or grundnorm – Kantian epistemology – criticism by Julius Stone – Kelsen's response – Hart's criticism of the basic norm – MacCormick.

Suggested Solution

The law is a legal norm in Kelsen's pure theory of law. A legal norm is valid and the reason for its validity is that it is validated by a higher norm. This means that norms are in a hierarchical structure, and we trace the reason for a particular norm's validity up the hierarchy.

However, the search for validity cannot go on indefinitely. For example, if we want to trace the validity of a local authority bye-law we trace it up the hierarchy to a statutory instrument whose validity can be traced to an enabling Act of Parliament; the validity of the Act of Parliament can be traced to a constitution which empowered legislators to make law. The first constitution sits at the apex of the hierarchy. How does the first constitution achieve its validity? Here Kelsen says the final norm is presupposed because it is not created by an authority whose competence will have to be anchored on a still higher norm. Though the legal validity of this final norm cannot come from another higher norm, its validity cannot be questioned. This presupposed final norm is called the basic norm or grundnorm. All norms whose validity can be traced to the same basic norm form a system of norms – this becomes a normative order.

Kelsen's idea is that in tracing the validity of a norm we eventually arrive at a historically first constitution whose validity could not be traced to a positive law created by a legal authority. For example, the historically first constitution may have been promulgated after a successful revolution. This revolution may have breached a legal order based on a constitution. Therefore, in considering a particular national legal order, validity is traced to a presupposed basic norm. That is how a constitution imposed by a revolutionary regime can be said to be binding. The presupposed basic norm is important in that the validity of the constitution makes it possible to interpret acts made or done under it or its application of valid rules, as well as acts performed according to valid rules.

To help us understand what the basic norm is, Kelsen says it must be kept in mind that it refers directly to a specific constitution which is established by custom or is of statutory creation and is by and large effective. It is only by presupposing the basic norm that we are able to interpret the subjective meaning of an act made under the constitution as an objectively valid norm. To interpret the subjective meaning or constitution-created acts as objectively valid norms, Kelsen employs Kantian epistemology which asks:

'How is it possible to interpret without a metaphysical hypothesis, the facts perceived by our senses, the laws of nature formulated by natural science?' (Kelsen, *Pure Theory of Law* (1967), p202)

Drawing on this, Kelsen asks:

'How is it possible to interpret without recourse to meta-legal authorities like God or nature, the subjective meaning of certain facts as a system of objectively-valid legal norms describable in rules of law?' (Kelsen, ibid, p205)

The pure theory's epistemological answer is that it is by presupposing the basic norm that one ought to behave in accordance with the constitution. The function of the basic norm is to underwrite the objective validity of a positive legal order, and it does this by interpreting the subjective meaning of acts of human beings by which the laws of an effective legal system are created as their objective meaning.

Problems raised by commentators about the pure theory of law have centred on the idea that the validity of a norm depends on a 'transcendental epistemological postulate'. According to Professor Julius Stone, the basic norm conceals

'an ambiguity, swinging between, on one hand, a norm that is at the top of the pyramid of norms of each legal order, and on the other, some other norm which remains outside this pyramid, and is wholly meta-legal, and amounts to a general presupposition requiring that in each and every legal order "the constitution" shall be obeyed'.

Kelsen's response is to emphasise that the basic norm is only presupposed in juristic thinking as the constitution in a legal-logical sense. This distinguishes a constitution presupposed in juristic thinking in a legal-logical sense and a constitution in a positive legal sense. This means that the basic norm presupposed in a legal logical sense in juristic thinking is not created by the real act of will of a legal organ. Kelsen says the basic norm is meta-legal if we say that it is not created by a positive law, and it is 'legal' if we are to understand things with legal significance; so the basic norm presupposed in juristic thinking has the function of interpreting the objective validity of the requirement of a community's constitution.

At first sight it would seem that Kelsen's Kantian epistemology is false in the sense that, as Professor Stone points out, the juristic thinking employs a meta-legal concept or value judgment not created by any positive law. This way Kelsen's epistemology relies on some meta-legal authority, possibly nature.

Professor Hart's criticism of the pure theory is that to say that a rule is valid is different from Kelsen's idea of validity. According to Hart a rule is valid if it passes the test of validity provided by the rule of recognition. Kelsen's response is to ask when one looks back to the ultimate constitution or to Hart's rule of recognition what is it that makes this rule of recognition valid? Hart dismisses such a question. To him questioning the validity of the rule of recognition is just like asking whether the metre-bar in Paris used for measuring metre lengths is itself a metre in length.

To Hart the validity of the rule of recognition is a fact. This can be demonstrated by pointing to how officials identify the law. When officials identify rules of their systems it means they accept and use the rule of recognition. Kelsen's reply will be that since the rule of recognition is not created by any positive law it is also 'meta-legal' or at best presupposed. Kelsen can say that, like the rule of recognition, when officials of a system identify rules and apply them, it is because they have presupposed a basic norm and can trace individual norms to a basic norm. To Kelsen the basic norm is a theoretical construct, performing a theoretical function. It becomes the norm that stands behind the historically first constitution.

MacCormick in *H L A Hart* (1981) supports Kelsen and says the pure theory of law aims to establish what makes possible knowledge of the law as an objective normative order. To MacCormick, there is a presupposition of a non-positive basic norm according to which the human act of creating the historically first constitution of a legal order is valid.

The idea of the presupposed basic norm giving validity to all other norms in the legal order makes sense if we think that after a revolution a new regime makes a new constitution and the legal order of that particular territory is in general effective due to validity given to the constitution. Since the basic norm is a fiction, a theoretical construct, it remains free of any value – this is why the validity of norms in the legal order depends upon a transcendental epistemological postulate.

QUESTION FIVE

Is Hart fair to Fuller when he criticises Fuller's eight principles of the 'inner morality' of law as being analogous to principles of the 'inner morality' of the poisoner's art?

University of London LLB Examination
(for External Students) Jurisprudence and Legal Theory June 1996 Q5

General Comment

This is a popular topic in the positivism/natural law separation of law and morality debate. What makes a good legal system? If the Mafia was to take over the United Kingdom, abolish Parliament and the judiciary and appoint its henchmen to make and enforce Mafia laws would there be a legal system properly so-called?

Skeleton Solution

Background of Hart/Fuller debate – Hart's positivism as a response to Gustav Radbruch – Fuller's reply – the eight principles – Hart's counter-attack – evaluation and conclusion.

Suggested Solution

The background of the Hart/Fuller debate is rooted in the nature of the Nazi legal system. It was widely believed by natural lawyers that the evil nature of the Nazi legal system and the Nazi regime generally was partly supported by positivism. Gustav Radbruch, a positivist who lived through the Nazi atrocities, felt that the obnoxious acts of the Nazi regime would not have happened but for positivism. He renounced positivism and supported natural law principles. Radbruch's attack on legal positivism, and in particular his suggestion that positivism contributed to the Nazi atrocities, did not go unanswered.

Professor H L A Hart felt the attack on positivism was uncalled for and unjustified so he launched a defence of positivism. In an article, 'Positivism and the Separation of Law and Morals' ((1958) 71 Harvard Law Review 593–629), he defends his positivist thesis. The positivist slogan 'law is law' can be answered with a utitilitarian riposte that 'law may be law but too evil to be obeyed'. This is an evaluative statement which people can agree with as the statement separates law from morality. It is a completely different scenario to say that 'this law is invalid because it is too evil'. People who accept the validity of any law will find it difficult to accept this as they believe laws duly passed by lawfully-constituted authorities are valid laws.

Fuller disagrees with Hart and in his response 'Positivism and Fidelity to Law – a Reply to Professor Hart' ((1958) 71 Harvard Law Review 630–672), he criticises Hart for failing to take into account the nature of law. To Fuller, law aspires to morality. Referring to Hart's union of primary and secondary rules, he says such rules are fundamental rules of a legal system because they are rules not of law but of morality. They derive their efficacy from a general acceptance which in turn rests ultimately on a perception that they are right and necessary. It is fair to say that Hart will respond to Fuller's claim that there can be legal systems based on fear, but that does not mean people accept rules because of morality. To Fuller, law contains its own implicit morality and this morality must be respected if we are to create anything called law, even bad law. This is because, as he says, the authority to make laws must be supported by moral attitudes that accord it the competency it claims. This explains Fuller's position on the Nazi legal system.

It is against this background that Fuller propounds his eight principles which he calls the 'inner morality of law'. He says that for positivism to present the formal characterisation of human institutions like a legal system independent of their purposes is unjustified. To him the characteristic features of a legal system exist because they are related to the purpose of legal systems and this purpose is inherently a moral one. Thus an understanding of what law is *cannot* be separated from an understanding of what law ought to be in so far as an understanding of what law is involves an understanding of the moral aspirations that are implicit in the concept of law itself.

In his work *The Morality of Law* (1964), Fuller gives the eight principles which to him form the minimum features which together amount to a moral ideal which explains the purposive nature of law. The eight principles are:

1. rules must be general; meaning they must apply to all and not only a section of the population;

2. they must not be retrospective but prospective; this will eliminate unfairness in law;

3. rules must be published; this means making enacted rules public to avoid corruption;

4. rules must be intelligible; meaning people should be able to understand them;

5. rules must not be contradictory; meaning rules made should not make contradictory claims on people, for example: a law proclaims equality of sexes and yet bars women from holding public offices.

6. compliance with rules is possible; meaning people like the vulnerable in society should not be saddled with responsibility when they lack the necessary physical or mental capacity;

7. rules must not be constantly changed; meaning since people want certainty in the rules to enable them to pursue their goals and ambitions constant changes of rules will badly affect them;

8. there must be congruence between the rules declared and the rules as applied; meaning rules must not say one thing while officials do the other.

Failure to comply with any one of the eight principles results in something that is not law at all.

Fuller calls the eight principles 'the inner morality of law'. Following the eight principles shows 'fidelity to law'. To Fuller the 'inner morality of law' is a morality of aspiration, so the eight principles should be thought of collectively as a moral aspiration for legal systems.

Hart's response to Fuller is that his eight principles are nothing more than principles for good and effective law making. To Hart, law is an instrument that can be used for good as well as bad purposes and its efficacy is not linked with morality. An example can be cited of the apartheid South African legal system. Laws made under the apartheid system were consistent with Fuller's principles yet many people regarded the apartheid legal system as amoral.

To Hart, Fuller has no justification for calling his eight principles the 'morality' of law. He says we can describe certain principles for effective poisoning which may read as follows:

a) administer a large dose but not large enough to kill;

b) choose a poison that can be masked so that it is undetected;

c) aim not to kill instantly;

d) choose a poison which is tasteless and odourless.

According to Hart, we could call the above steps 'principles' of a poisoner's art but it would be absurd to call these 'principles' the 'inner morality of poisoning'.

It is arguable that a government can rigidly follow Fuller's eight principles and yet pass obnoxious laws. This is what leads Hart to say an 'inner morality of law' is compatible with great iniquity. I do not think, however, that Hart is fair to Fuller at all. The fact that some regimes knowingly subvert the rule of law does not mean that law has no moral value. It can be said that consistency with the eight principles makes extreme forms of repression very difficult, though there still would remain unanswered questions about justice.

Fuller is concerned about the proper purpose of a legal system. He says that if a person describes a legal system, the person actually evaluates the degree to which that system is successful in achieving its purpose. To him, therefore, legal morality is a kind of morality intrinsic in law. Fuller's morality is based on goals that a legal system ought to aspire to in order to achieve procedural justice. Using Fuller's eight principles, we may ask if laws are to be effective should they not be published, made prospectively, not contradictory, intelligible, and must official actions and decisions not conform with the published law?

Fuller's response to Hart's poisoner's art attack is that evil aims lack the coherence moral aims have, and that paying attention to the coherence of law will ensure the morality of law. Is this not an overstated point Fuller is making? As Hart has forcibly pointed out, evil aims can equally be 'coherent', and having coherent principles toward a desired goal does not establish the morality of any practice. Indeed, there was coherence in the Nazi legal system and in the apartheid South African legal system.

Although Hart's poisoner's art response is very stimulating and instructive, I believe he misses the point of Fuller's argument. Fuller's 'inner morality of law' calls for procedural justice and fairness in any legal system. I believe this is a worthy idea. I do not think anybody would disagree with a demand that frankness and openness become virtues of a legal system. If Fuller's eight principles of 'inner morality of law' lead to transparency in a legal system I think that that itself has a utility value which gives it its moral status.

17 University of London LLB (External) 1996 Questions and Suggested Solutions

QUESTION SIX

State what, in your view, is the most convincing form of utilitarianism. Can it account adequately for the existence of moral rights? Does it have to?

University of London LLB Examination
(for External Students) Jurisprudence and Legal Theory June 1996 Q6

General Comment

This is a straightforward question on utilitarianism. To gain good marks, however, the candidate has to demonstrate an understanding of the utilitarian principle and its practical meaning. What does it mean to say a particular law has a utility value either for the majority or minority members of community?

Skeleton Solution

Classical utilitarian doctrine – theory in perspective – individual rights as moral rights – Dworkin's rights thesis – conclusion.

Suggested Solution

The father of utilitarianism, Jeremy Bentham, says in his book *An Introduction to the Principles of Morals and Legislation* (1823) that

'nature has placed mankind under the governance of two sovereign masters, pain and pleasure. It is for them alone to point out what we ought to do, as well as determine what we shall do'.

Bentham advances the principle that the proper basis for morality and legislation is to use the felicific calculus to test the rightness or wrongness of any action private or public.

He says the maxim 'the greatest happiness of the greatest number' provides the criterion for testing the morality of the utilitarian principle. This principle, therefore, is about seeking the greatest or highest welfare of the greatest number of people. To achieve this he recommends that:

a) since men want happiness they must approve a principle which says that they ought to have what they want;

b) acceptance of the principle of utility reduces disagreements about future matters of fact, thereby making morals and legislation scientific;

c) given that men are motivated by pain and pleasure, properly drafted legislation can produce a coincidence between the interest of the individual and the interest of the community. Recognising the rewards and punishments laid down by the law, a person will be able to draw the necessary conclusions about the rightness or wrongness of any proposed actions, that is, the effects of his or her actions upon his or her own happiness as well as that of the entire community.

With these recommendations in mind, Bentham advocates that the obligation to obey the law is based on the promotion of the collective good. He says, therefore, that 'the evil of punishment must exceed the profit of the offence'.

The attractiveness of the moral principle enshrined in the principle of utilitarianism is instructive. The jurist sees the law as a mechanism which operates for the good of the whole

Jurisprudence: The Philosophy of Law

society. If the good of the whole society is of the essence, then the utilitarian will argue that the moral worth of the principle in recognising that action be taken in the interest of the moral rights of the majority is worthy of attention.

Professor Dworkin in *Taking Rights Seriously* (1978) says the moral appeal of utilitarianism rests on the fact that in coming to a judgment about general welfare, each person's interest counts equally. To Dworkin, people must be treated with equal concern and respect when political decisions are taken that will affect them. This idea finds expression in utilitarianism in the sense that each person's interest counts equally in the utility calculations. However, Dworkin favours a version of utilitarianism which allows an individual's rights to trump general welfare.

Dworkin's position follows from the criticism that even though classical utilitarianism is said to be a moral principle in that the rights of the majority are protected and promoted, the rights of the minority are sacrificed in the process. It becomes a question of the rights of the majority against the rights of the minority.

The flows in the utilitarian doctrine can be stated to lie in the felicific calculus used to measure pleasure and pain. How does one measure pleasure and pain using a felicific calculus? We are dealing with intangibles which are subjective elements, and it is difficult to measure pain and pleasure in any objective way. Having said this one is conscious of the fact that legislation made by legislatures is based on a utility calculation, using the greatest happiness of the greatest number maxim of Bentham. To Bentham good legislation can be made using the felicific calculus. It is arguable that if the motive behind law making is to seek the interest of the whole community, then utilitarianism accounts for the moral rights of the majority of citizens, say the right to life of everyone.

The very idea that classical utilitarianism accounts for the moral rights of the majority throws into question the moral rights of the minority. If the majority has a moral right to life, does it mean the sacrificing of the moral right of the minority to achieve a similar end? Because of this, classical utilitarianism is criticised for not catering adequately for individual moral rights as against the collective moral rights.

An argument can be raised on the moral worth and autonomy of the individual which means that people should not be treated merely as aggregate numbers in some grand calculus of general social benefits. According to Kant, human beings are not means to an end but ends in themselves. John Rawls' idea (Rawls, *A Theory of Justice* (1972)) of trading one person's welfare for another's offends peoples' moral intuition. For Rawls, classical utilitarianism cannot satisfy the requirement of moral justice because of its ability to sacrifice the interests of the individual for the collective welfare.

This idea that the individual is an autonomous moral agent has been questioned by many philosophers. They say this view must be modified in order to account for an adequate conception of political society. They ask whether the integrity of individuals in an imaginary state of nature can really be preserved on the transition to a political society, and that whether it is enough to view society merely as the sum of the individuals within it, its creation forming no extra or incompatible rights or obligations as Robert Nozick suggests in *State, Anarchy and Utopia* (1974).

A response to this well-known argument is that although an individual is a member of a political society, the individual has a moral right to be treated with equal concern and respect, and exemplary sentences, eg 'sacrificing' one offender in the hope of deterring others, are morally objectionable, as they condemn an individual in order to achieve a social goal.

17 University of London LLB (External) 1996 Questions and Suggested Solutions

Professor Hart (Hart, *Prolegomenon to Principles of Punishment: In Sentencing*, eds Gross and Von Hirsch), in tracing the utilitarian value in sentencing, says the primary operation of criminal punishment consists of announcing certain standards of behaviour and attaching penalties for deviation, and leaving the individual to choose (just as Bentham advocated with the felicific calculus in calculating pain and pleasure). Hart says this is a method of social control which maximises individual freedom – which itself has a moral worth – within the framework of the law. That classical utilitarianism is not satisfactorily convincing, in that it does not adequately account for individual moral rights, is shown by Hart's call that the state must forbid the use of one human being for the benefit of others except for the individual's voluntary actions against them (Hart, ibid).

The arguments marshalled above accept that the classical utilitarian doctrine is convincing and show that classical utilitarianism, as espoused by Jeremy Bentham, is a moral doctrine. It considers the moral rights of the whole community, not individuals. This is as far as it goes. It has also been shown that the moral rights which the principle recognises are the moral rights which the majority enjoys, and that in achieving this the moral rights of the minority are sacrificed. However, it is arguable that the moral rights of the individual must be protected. This places the moral rights of the majority in conflict with those of the minority. It cannot be right that a theory can be made to apply unequally to people in a society. Whether it is for better or for worse, the classical utilitarian doctrine does account for the existence of moral rights.

However, I am of the view that the classical doctrine does not adequately account for moral rights if it trades off the welfare of some people for the benefit of others. If we accept that apartheid is an evil system it cannot be justified that a law will enshrine the right of the majority to treat the minority who are of different racial background obnoxiously simply because it increases the general happiness or welfare of the majority. Is the end a good in itself? What about the misery of the minority? This is why classical utilitarianism cannot adequately account for the moral rights of people.

But does it have to account for moral rights at all? Indeed it does – since human beings are autonomous moral agents any theory that seeks to promote their general interests and welfare must recognise the moral worth of the individual. Professor Dworkin advocates that in a majoriterian democracy where decisions are taken in the interests of the majority, the rights of the minority must be protected and the interests of the majority must be subjected to considerations of individual rights. To Dworkin, rights are species of moral rights, and respecting them is consistent with treating people with concern and respect. I agree totally with this view.

QUESTION SEVEN

'Analysing the content of Austin's theory of law can proceed without locating it within the historical and social conditions which gave rise to it, but appreciating the meaning of the theory cannot.'

Discuss.

University of London LLB Examination
(for External Students) Jurisprudence and Legal Theory June 1996 Q7

Jurisprudence: The Philosophy of Law

General Comment

Questions on Austin are popular among candidates. This particular question invites the candidate to consider whether it is possible to appreciate the meaning of Austin's theory without placing it within the context of the historical period that spawned it. You should not simply give an account of Austin's theory. Remember the question: does it matter to place it in its historical context?

Skeleton Solution

Austin's positivism – command theory – reasons for his stance located in historical and social conditions of his time – analysis of theory – appreciation of theory – conclusion.

Suggested Solution

John Austin establishes his positivist credentials with his opening line of *The Province of Jurisprudence Determined* (1954):

'The matter of jurisprudence is positive law: law, simply and strictly so-called; or law set by political superiors to political inferiors'. (p9)

To Austin, laws made by men for men are positive laws and natural law or law of nature is positive morality (Austin, ibid, p11).

The historical and social conditions which gave rise to Austin's positivism could be said to be the prevalence of natural law doctrine that emphasised law as the law of nature, with which all laws made by men must conform in order to be valid. Austin was minded to propound a theory which stressed that all law was positive law in the sense that it was an expression of the will of a supreme authority. In other words, Austin recognised that what was needed was to advocate a view of law as a series of rational commands given by human beings with sanctions attached for non-conformity. Even though Austin did not explore fully the meaning of the word 'command', he believed his problem was solved by linking 'command' to the universally recognised doctrine of legal sovereignty.

Austin defines law as the command of a sovereign who is habitually obeyed. As noted above, Austin's problem was to link the word 'command' with legal sovereignty. In this suggested solution analysis of Austin's work will be limited to 'command', 'habitual obedience' and his sovereign.

Austin said in his first lecture that

'Frankness is the highest compliment ... I therefore entreat you, as the greatest favour you can do to me, to demand explanations and ply me with objections – turn me inside out'.

No doubt he has been very much obliged over the years with withering criticisms. Jolowicz (Jolowicz, *Lectures on Jurisprudence* (1963), p1) says that 'Austin's doctrine forms a very good target – we must set it up and see it clearly in order to throw bricks at it'.

Karl Olivecrona makes the point that law is not identical with the declaration of will as Austin's theory says (Olivecrona, *Law as Fact* (1971), p32). Professor Hart says in *Essays in Jurisprudence and Philosophy* (1983) that the definition of law as a command is inadequate, saying a legal system, even a simple one, is distorted if presented as a command. Asking the question 'what is a command?', Hart says it is

'simply and expression by one person of the desire that another person should do or abstain from some action, accompanied by a threat of punishment which is likely to follow disobedience (Hart, *The Concept of Law* (2nd ed, 1994), p59).

Accordingly to Hart, the command theory was simply a trilogy of command, sanction and sovereign, which he likened to a gunman threatening his victim for money: the gunman enforces conduct which differentiates 'obliging' from 'obligation'. To Hart, if one is under an obligation one has a legal duty to perform, whereas a gunman merely obliges conduct by threats; law, therefore, is 'surely not the gunman situation writ large and legal order is surely not to be thus simply identified with compulsion'. Even placing Austin's theory in its historical and social conditions it is difficult to appreciate why he thought law was a 'command'.

On the question of habitual obedience to a sovereign, Hart says it is wrong to think of a legislature with changing membership as a group of persons habitually obeyed. Hart would point to the legislatures in, say, the United Kingdom and America, and ask: 'since newly elected members had not known anything called habitual obedience how can they be called sovereign within Austin's definition?' He agrees that the idea is only suitable to a monarch sufficiently long-lived for a 'habit' to grow. Taking issue with the idea of the legally-untrammelled will of the sovereign who is above the law, Hart points out that legislators cannot make laws unless they comply with fundamentally accepted rules specifying the essential law-making powers. The point is that if legislators have to follow rules when making laws then their sovereignty is limited. Hart also brings home the point that procedural rules are not commands habitually obeyed, nor can they be expressed as habits of obedience to persons. Furthermore, he points out that other legal rules in society have quite different functions. They enable and empower people; they create rights such as rules enabling individuals to make contracts, wills and trusts (Hart, ibid, p62). Hart quotes with approval Hagerstrom's analysis (Hagerstrom, *Inquiries into the Nature of Law and Morals* (1953) p217) that if laws were merely commands, the notion of an individual's right was inexplicable, for commands are something we either obey or disobey and are not right-conferring.

With reference to Hart's remarks on law being the command of a sovereign, I believe he has failed to direct his analysis to the fact that the body politic may not habitually obey a particular person or body of persons as the sovereign, but rather the institution they represent. In the United Kingdom for example, people have habitual obedience to the Crown, an institution, and not the person of a King or Queen, so the institution is continually obeyed even when a new King or Queen is crowned on the death of the previous incumbent. As far as Parliament is concerned, it is composed of members of whom at least some vote against particular bills during the process of law-making in Parliament. Are such members said to have commanded anything as the sovereign? The fact that there is often a division in Parliament during the process of law creation reinforces the argument that sovereignty resides not in the Members of Parliament, but in the institution called the Crown-in-Parliament which is habitually obeyed. Again, however, when one reads Austin's theory against its historical and social conditions, it is difficult to appreciate the theory as clear-headed. Austin says that the House of Commons is merely trustee of the people's power so sovereignty resides in the Crown, the Lords and the electorate. Austin believes that in the United States sovereignty of each state and the federal union resides in the states' government forming one aggregate body; however he promptly contradicts himself by saying he means the body politic, in other words the electorate.

To Austin the sovereign is indivisible and illimitable. It is wondered if he was of the opinion that sovereignty in the United States resides in the aggregate body of the states, how is it that the electorate forms part of the sovereign? How can the bulk of the people be in a habit of obeying itself? Hart is right to say this is a picture of society divided into two halves, the sovereign giving orders for the subjects to habitually obey, but the blurring factor here is we have a society where the majority gives orders for the majority to obey.

Austin may reply that the majority has both private and public capacities. When it gives orders, it does so in its official capacity, and it obeys the orders in its private capacity. This leads to the absurd situation of the electorate undergoing metamorphosis, and Hart rightly asks when does the metamorphosis happen?

There are inadequacies with Austin's command theory, and as the quotation in the question states, analysing the context of the theory can proceed without locating it within the historical and social conditions that produced it. The argument to be made here is that the institutions which he was writing about are still very much part of the constitutional firmament of both the United Kingdom and the United States of America, just as they were part of the constitutional set-up of these countries at the time he was writing. It is a valid argument that there is a clear lack of thoroughness with the theory and that has nothing to do with the historical and social conditions of the time he was writing.

It is appreciated that Austin wanted to propound a theory that required empirical explanation of law without metaphysics. He found it necessary to separate what was a legal rule from what was a moral rule, and he needed to think of a prior command, a sort of order given by human beings to be obeyed by human beings, and he linked all this to the legal concept of sovereignty. However, this does not mean that he could not have done better than presenting law as the command of a sovereign.

As Hart says, it is better to offer a theory that does not trace law to any particular author. Thus describing law as a system of rules should be enough. Hart accuses Austin of propounding a theory on the back of definition. I believe this is a valid criticism of Austin's work. Austin himself said that frankness is the highest compliment he could be paid and invited readers to turn him inside out. I join in obliging him. The historical and social conditions prevailing at the time he was writing cannot be used as an excuse for the flaws in his theory. Appreciating the theory does not require it to be located in any historical or social conditions. The institutions which Austin wrote about are still with us – very much part of the constitutional make-up of both the UK and USA. That is why his theory can still be criticised today by referring to these same institutions he used as paradigms.

QUESTION EIGHT

To what extent does Dworkin's image of legal development as similar to constructing a chain novel illuminate important features of the legal process?

University of London LLB Examination
(for External Students) Jurisprudence and Legal Theory June 1996 Q8

General Comment

To gain good marks for this question the candidate must exhibit a good grasp of Dworkin's idea of interpretation. This is not a question to be treated casually. Do not attempt it if you do not understand Dworkin's idea of constructive interpretation.

Skeleton Solution

Dworkin's idea of interpretation – law as integrity – the chain novel analogy – Hercules methodology.

17 University of London LLB (External) 1996 Questions and Suggested Solutions

Suggested Solution

Dworkin's idea of interpretation is about legal reasoning in the judicial process. There are three stages of interpretation in the legal process:

a) the pre-interpretive stage;

b) the interpretive stage; and

c) the post interpretive stage.

At the pre-interpretive stage, the judge considers the pre-interpretive legal data. This means the judge is bound to consider the actual legal materials at his or her disposal. Some interpretation is required even at this stage to find what legal materials to consider. This is about considering the relevant existing law.

At the interpretive stage, the judge constructively interprets the legal material. He or she makes the best possible sense of the legal material. This is Dworkin's best light thesis. The interpreter of the legal materials (the judge) questions and examines the issues in the light of his or her constructive interpretation of the law. To Dworkin, this constructive interpretation leads to the morally best interpretation of the law.

At the post interpretive stage, changes, if any, are announced, and the existing law is overruled if necessary.

Let us assume that someone is required to interpret a particular communal practice. It will help to assume that the community we are concerned with is a distinct person with opinions and convictions of its own, a group consciousness of some sort, and that assumption means that the interpreter must judge and dispute the opinions of a person, and not simply discover and report. He or she must distinguish between the opinion the group has about what is needed, which he can find out by reflecting on its distinct motives and purposes, and what the interpreter thinks the practice really requires.

The idea of interpretation is linked to Dworkin's idea of law as integrity. For interpretation to be successfully carried out the judge must accept law as integrity. Integrity says law must speak with one voice. Judges must assume that the law is structured on coherent principles about justice, fairness and procedural due process, and that in all fresh cases that come before them they must enforce these so as to make each person's situation fair and just by the same standard (Dworkin, *Law's Empire* (1986), p243). Law as integrity rejects the positivist 'law is law' as well as the cynicism of the realist school.

To Dworkin, the unifying force of judicial practice is integrity, which is a public virtue comparable with justice and fairness. It demands that the judge justify his or her decisions by making them conform to the entirety of the law which has a life of its own.

It is against this background that Dworkin's image of legal development is compared to the construction of a chain novel. Dworkin says that judges, like novelists, undertake constructive interpretation when they undertake legal reasoning in judicial practice. The aim of constructive interpretation is to discover the intention of an author, not because the aim is to discover the purposes of the former author, but to impose purpose over the test or data being interpreted (Dworkin, ibid, p228). To Dworkin, since all constructive interpretation shares this feature, which is normative, it explains why judicial interpretation can be compared with the constructive interpretation of a novel by a novelist. Judges are authors as well as critics, and a judge adds to what he or she interprets; future judges are confronted with what the previous judge has done.

Jurisprudence: The Philosophy of Law

The comparison between literature and law leads to Dworkin's idea of chain novel. In this enterprise a group of novelists are expected to write a novel seriatim. Each novelist in this chain is supposed to interpret the chapter given to him or her in order to write a new chapter, which is passed on to the next novelist. This goes on down the chain. The job of each novelist is to write his or her chapter so as to make the novel under construction the best it can be, and Dworkin says the complexity of this enterprise is similar to the complexity of legal reasoning in deciding cases under law as integrity.

Each novelist's aim is to make a single novel with the material supplied, and the single novel will have to encompass what he or she adds to it, and within limits, what future authors would want or be able to add. He or she must endeavour to make the novel the best novel constructed by a single author rather than make it seem the work of different authors. The novelist has to make a judgment or a series of judgments as he or she writes and rewrites. He or she has to decide on a *working theory* about the novel's characters, plot, theme and aim in order to come to a certain decision about what would constitute continuing a chain novel and starting a new one.

If the novelist is a good critic, his or her views will be various and complex because the value of a good novel cannot be encapsulated from a single view point. There are two dimensions which the novelist considers to structure any interpretation he or she adopts. The first is the dimension of fit. The chain novelist cannot make any constructive interpretation unless he or she believes the material given him or her was not written by a single author. Any interpretation which he or she adopts must flow from the text supplied. The second dimension says that the novelist is required to judge which of the available interpretations makes the work in progress best, all things considered. The novelist might find that he or she has written a rather different interpretation, or may find it impossible to sustain the existing theme. In this case, the novelist will reconsider other interpretations which he or she at first rejected, and at all times return to the text to reconsider the interpretation that construes its best meaning.

Someone may accuse the novelist of rewriting the 'real' novel to produce a different one that he or she likes; that the 'real' novel can be discovered in some other way than by the novelist's method. Such a person can be said to have misunderstood not only the chain novel enterprise but the nature of literary criticism.

To Dworkin, judicial reasoning is exactly the same as the chain novel process; that cases which come before judges must be treated like the chain novel analogy. The judge, like the novelist, must undertake constructive interpretation of the legal data and follow the two dimensions, like the novelist. First is the dimension of fit. The judge similarly cannot make any constructive interpretation unless he or she believes the legal data before him or her does not come from a single author. Here the judge will think that the legal materials come from the legal system generally. The different judges in the legal system represent the different authors. Any interpretation the judge adopts must flow from the text supplied. This accords with Dworkin's idea of interpretation. The stage where the judge begins with the text is the pre-interpretive stage. At the interpretive stage, the judge considers possible inter-pretations to adopt.

It is here that the second dimension which the novelist follows applies to the judge. The judge is required by the second dimension to decide which of the available interpretations makes the decision the best one. When the novelist has produced the finished work, the novel gets handed to his or her successor down the chain. This represents the post interpretive

17 University of London LLB (External) 1996 Questions and Suggested Solutions

stage in Dworkin's theory. When the judge has made a decision it is handed down the chain to other judges to consider as precedent.

A judge deciding a common law case like *McLoughlin* v *O'Brian* (1983) must think of himself or herself as an author in the chain of common law. The judge is faced with existing precedents which deal with problems analogous to the case under consideration. The judge must think of the precedents as part of the long story which he or she must interpret, and then continue using his or her own judgment to make the unfolding story as good as can be. Like the novelist, the judge during legal reasoning constructs the precedents in the best possible light, and best here means morally best.

The judge's decision, which is his or her post interpretive conclusion, represents an interpretation that fits and justifies the practice that has gone on before, as far as possible. Just like the interpretation in a chain novel for which each interpreter considers the enterprise as a delicate balance between different types of literary and artistic attitudes, so with law, judges consider the practice as a delicate balance between different political convictions.

As an example of how a judge acts like the chain novelist in judicial practice, Dworkin offers Hercules, a superhuman, patient and intelligent judge who accepts law as integrity and who, like a chain novelist, has to decide a hard case like *McLoughlin* v *O'Brian*. Like the chain novelist, Hercules will first construct a moral theory of the system, draw up a list of different interpretations from the precedents, and go through the list until he comes to a decision as to which interpretation best fits the settled law and provides the best justification of it. This means that the judge's constructive interpretation of the existing precedents best fits the law and provides the morally best interpretation of them.

Dworkin's chain novel idea certainly throws light on judicial practice in the common law, especially in hard cases. The chain novel analogy mirrors judicial interpretation of the legal data, illuminating the process in a way which even the non-lawyer will find helpful.

QUESTION NINE

'The CLS movement seems incoherent and lacking in positive ideas because western countries are experiencing a crisis of confidence in their institutions and have lost faith in the image of law as a coherent and rational body of doctrine. The approach of the movement is actually a passionate appeal to analyse the huge variation in law's roles and effects while placing the human actor at the centre of law.'

Discuss.

University of London LLB Examination
(for External Students) Jurisprudence and Legal Theory June 1996 Q9

General Comment

Do you believe the Critical Legal Studies movement is incoherent and lacks positive ideas? There is no one right or wrong approach to answering this question. Your approach will depend on your stance on the CLS movement.

Skeleton Solution

Analyse question – crisis of confidence in institutions of western countries – law as a coherent body of doctrine – the nature of the CLS attack – Robert Unger as a paradigm – summary and conclusion.

Jurisprudence: The Philosophy of Law

Suggested Solution

The question raises issues about the contribution of the Critical Legal Studies (CLS) movement to legal thought or legal science. The immediate question that comes to mind on reading the statement in this question is whether the emergence of the CLS movement is attributable to any crisis of confidence in Western countries, their legal systems in particular and their political institutions in general.

In Western democracies where the rule of law is a way of life, is it the case that there is so much uncertainty in the law, and so much disillusion with legal systems, that the institutions of the state feel under attack? It is against the background of solid guidance an institution like a legal system offers in a society that we must discuss the CLS movement's approach to law and legal practice in western countries.

The CLS movement emerged in America in the 1970s. It is thought to be the successor of American Realism. The movement's dominant themes are sceptical about law as an institution. In an article, 'The Critical Legal Studies Movement' ((1983) 96 Harvard Law Review 563), Roberto Unger says that the movement has undermined the central ideas of modern legal thought and put another conception of law in their place'. To the CLS movement, the law is contradictory, indeterminate and oppressive. In any society if law exhibits these faults it is inevitable that some kind of movement will rise to call for reforms.

Let us take the issue of the indeterminacy of law. The CLS movement argues that 'legal reasoning' is nothing but an exercise in the use of abstract doctrines with no way of proving which side is right or wrong. Lawyers and judges, as the actors at the centre, can manipulate doctrine after their own purposes, and a judge could arrive at a decision either way using the same doctrine. In other words, a judge could arrive at a decision for both sides of an argument using the same legal text. Many lawyers believe that legal rules determine the result of a case even though the nature of the adversarial legal system is such that one can make an argument for both sides of a dispute. For example, whereas a lawyer can prosecute for fraud and tax avoidance, the same lawyer can advise clients on insurance, VAT, tax laws, and how to regulate one's affairs within the law. The lawyer works on the basis that there is regularity within the law, both short and long term. The CLS movement will say that the lawyer is wrong in believing there is regularity in the law since no system of rules provides determinacy.

This argument can be rebutted. Professor Hart in *The Concept of Law* (2nd ed 1994) says the rule of recognition was introduced to clear the air, to show what is law and what is not, to determine conclusively what rule is a member of the system. When lawyers and others say 'it is the law that ...' or 'the law says that ...' they are making an internal statement of law that they accept as valid a law which they can identify by using the rule of recognition which holds the criteria of validity of all rules of the system. Judges are able to identify law through the rule of recognition, so as far as certainty in rules of a legal system is concerned the CLS position in undermined by Hart's legal positivism.

Perhaps the CLS claim that the law is indeterminate may find resonance in Hart's core and penumbra with respect to easy and hard cases. Hart says that in hard cases the law is indeterminate, open textured and inconclusive. Since this means there are gaps in the law, the judge will have to legislate during legal reasoning to fill the gaps in the law. This means that in Hart's legal positivism there is no pre-existing law in hard cases, rather the judge makes the law as he/she decides the case. The CLS movement will also have to acknowledge Professor Dworkin's theory which denies that the law has this character.

17 University of London LLB (External) 1996 Questions and Suggested Solutions

Assuming lawyers can use existing legal rules to argue for both sides in a case, does that diminish the law in any way so as to create a crisis of confidence in the legal institution? Law is an argumentative practice and lawyers will always feel able to argue for both sides in a case but that does not mean each side's argument is equally valid. The CLS movement in unmindful of the fact that claiming the law is indeterminate will mean that the parameters of lawful conduct will always be unpredictable; that judges will have unrestrained powers to do as they please when deciding cases.

We can use Unger's work 'The Critical Legal Studies Movement' as a benchmark to discuss whether there is any justification in the claim that the CLS movement's emergence in western countries has been influenced by a crisis of confidence in these countries because of loss of faith in western institutions, particularly the legal institutions. Unger criticises the objectivism and formalism in the law. He says that the law can be rightful and legitimate only if it embodies 'a coherent and justifiable view of human relation'. On objectivism, he targets the laws of contract and property as providing the core of the objectivist criticism. He says property law has an inbuilt legal market which is a constitutional interest with its own legal structure in a democratic society. He says that in reality the situation is more ambiguous and indeterminate because of some abstract concepts of rights.

It is difficult to understand what Unger is protesting about since property laws confer rights on people which are widely respected. It just is not the case that people in western countries complain about the unfairness and arbitrariness of property laws. Have people lost faith in property law in a country like Britain? The thriving property market does not in any way suggest that people have lost faith in property law. Prices of properties may be trapped in negative equity during a recession but that belongs to the realms of economics, not law. Rather than experience a crisis of confidence people in western countries have confidence in property law and the institution of law to protect their properties.

Unger also makes the claim that in the law of contract, the dominant principles of freedom of choice and terms are contradicted by other principles that say the freedom to contract is subject to a contract being for legally permissible acts that do not undermine the fabric of society. It is again difficult to see how this character of the law of contract has a destabilising effect on the legal institution so as to create any loss of faith in the institution. No one will say it is acceptable that the law recognises all bargains struck by people no matter how irregular and obnoxious they are. One would go further to argue that a contract that places a duty on a contractor to supply hard drugs for sale to children is one that can rightly be said to undermine the fabric of society and which the courts would refuse to enforce. Similarly, a contract that places an onerous burden on a person without capacity could also be said to be a grossly unfair bargain between people of unequal resources, and should not be enforced, since the law recognises that the vulnerable in society need the protection of the law. It is strange that the CLS movement fails to see the good sense behind such mechanisms in the law that balance and check the rapacious greed of some people. I believe the CLS movement is wrong to point to such countervailing principles in law to characterise the whole institution of law as contradictory.

On formalism, Unger's argument is that every doctrine must rely on some view of which human associations are 'right and realistic' in social life. The lawyer needs a theory as a guiding vision. This guiding vision is to prevent legal reasoning becoming a game of analogies. To Unger, analogy-mongering must be brought to a halt. His point is that it is possible to question some of the received wisdom as mistaken, and this in done by relying on a normative theory of the branch of law in question. This is drawing on Unger's 'deviation doctrine' which

223

only goes to demonstrate the CLS movement's nihilistic approach to law. He calls his position superliberalism. He says that his views push the liberal views about state and society, freedom from dependence and governance of social relations by the will

'to the point at which they merge into a larger ambition: the building of a social world less alien to a self that can always violate the generative rules of its own mental or social constructs and put other rules and other constructs in their place.' ((1983) 96 Harvard Law Review 602)

This is certainly a liberal view that says the self can always see itself with its present ends. However, in a democratic society where laws have been made by the established legislature it is doubtful if an individual or group of individuals must be considered 'deviationist' just because they seek to challenge the existing order or received norms. An agitation for law reform is in order where the existing legal order is inadequate or inefficient; however, Unger does not say anything to suggest that rejection of existing law is brought about by any crisis of confidence in western society, and more so by lack of faith in the law. Rather, he advocates resistance to the established legal order just because formalism is not necessarily a requirement of superliberalism.

The CLS movement proffers an instrumentalist view of law, which has a Marxist origin that sees law as an instrument of oppression. Horwitz in *The Transformation of American Law* (1992) argues that the law induces false consciousness in people who may feel they are benefiting from the law. Property law is given as an example of this false consciousness. Gramsci says that the concepts of property law, contract law and rule of law are used as smoke-screens for the domination of the capitalist class over the working class. I would argue that the CLS claims it alone has an insight into the make-up of human society and human nature. Can it not be argued that 'false consciousness' is an easy expression to suggest that other people have no backbone, autonomy or self belief?

The reason for the CLS movement's diatribe against the legal system is that the system protects landowners through the laws against trespass, which instil into people a general respect for property rights, thereby making it seem natural and desirable that a person should feel empowered to exclude others from a piece of land when necessary.

In response to the CLS criticism that the law is oppressive it can be said that the criticism is not about the idea or nature of law. The CLS movement presents law as something 'out there' imposing its oppressive burdens upon hapless citizens and people. This is a historical fact theory which can be contrasted with legal positivism. Legal positivism sees law as clear and ascertainable, it gives the virtues of clarity, objectivity, certainty and public ascertainability as reasons for this view.

Professor Hart in *The Concept of Law* says that legal positivism regards law as the demands of the state 'out there' which must be independent of our moral judgments. Hart's reason for making this distinction is to make people clear headed – the fact that something has been passed as law is not conclusive of the question of obedience. Indeed, the law can be evil but the person has to be clear about this. Legal positivism requires constant criticism of the law, thus ensuring that the law is morally improved. Legal positivism disproves the CLS movement's claim that law is oppressive.

If the individual is expected by legal positivism to constantly criticise the law which is a demand of the state 'out there', it is strange that the CLS movement can lay claim to any crisis of confidence in western society for its incoherent doctrine. How can one lose faith in law, which is the demand of a state 'out there'? After all, the moral conscience of the individual is always to be distinguished from the demands of the state in the law's name. When the CLS movement says the law is incoherent, the movement ignores Dworkin's theory that says the law is always coherent, justified, explained and underlain by principles of law. When a principle like 'no man should profit from his own crime' is used to deprive or disinherit someone who has murdered his benefactor, that does not show the uncertainty in the law or the indeterminacy of the law or the oppressive nature of law, but rather it demonstrates the moral worth and the background standard against which the wills legislation is interpreted.

The CLS movement developed a 'deviationist school' just to challenge the accepted norm; as Unger has said, the CLS movement has undermined the central ideas of modern legal thought. The movement is on somewhat shaky ground as it can only criticise but has no positive ideas to offer in place of the traduced legal order. The CLS movement does not provide any response to any crisis of confidence in the legal system, and it certainly did not emerge because of any lack of faith in the legal system. That the movement exists at all proves the democratic nature of western countries. Where liberal democracy is a way of life human ingenuity is allowed to flourish and is not crushed by dogma. This is why the CLS movement can thrive in western countries despite its being nihilistic about law.

QUESTION TEN

'While the specific predictions and empirical statements of Marx and Engels on law were rooted in the nineteenth century and have been largely disproved by history, many of the concepts and tools of analysis they created remain of vital importance for our understanding of law in society today.'

Discuss.

University of London LLB Examination
(for External Students) Jurisprudence and Legal Theory June 1996 Q10

General Comment

It is a big mistake to assume that the demise of communism in the former Soviet Union is synonymous with the demise of Marxist theory of law as a political tool. Think carefully about the theory. The predictive element in the theory may have been disproved by history but the theory itself is largely a powerful tool.

Skeleton Solution

Work of Marx and Engels – nineteenth-century observation – Marxist theory of law and society – relevance of theory to our understanding of law in modern society.

Suggested Solution

The work of Marx and Engels on law was influenced by Marx's observation of the harsh realities of life under capitalism in Lancashire cotton mills in the nineteenth century; this led Marx to conclude that capitalism was in crisis. This led to his 'historical materialism' theory which says that social phenomena do not exist in isolation; rather they are interconnected, and any analysis of institutions must be done to include looking at their historical developments and contradictions in order to reconcile them. Human relations in society must be approached in this light. The observations of Marx and Engels led to their work which is a critique of capitalism. It is a conflict theory of law.

The Marxist theory sees law as a superstructure imposed on a sub-structure; the human relations, in society. The law serves the interests of the owners of the means of production – the bourgeoisie. The workers – the proletariat – are exploited by the bourgeoisie, but this dialectic between the two groups will reach a resolution when the oppressed class overthrows the ruling class through a revolution to establish a dictatorship of the proletatiat, leading to a classless society. The state will wither away and there will be administration of things.

From the above, it is seen that Marxist critique of capitalism sees the exploitation in society that is based on the efforts of the bourgeoisie to earn profit from the labour of the proletariat. How is this done? Workers are employed by a capitalist. They produce goods and services that enable the capitalist to make a profit after paying the workers' wages. The profit the capitalist makes is the 'surplus value' of the workers' labour. The state is constructed to use the superstructure – law – built on the relations between the owners of the means of production and the workers, to control the proleteriat and maintain their dominance of the proletariat. The state is a creation of the exploiting class to facilitate this end.

The state is presented as a detached entity exposing the interest of the whole society, and law and the legal system are presented as being objective as described in the concept of the rule of law which says the law applies equally and is non discriminatory. The law is presented as seeking everyone's interests. This, in Marxist ideology, is to mystify the reality of law as an instrument of oppression in the hands of the ruling class. The Marxist view of law says that law is a means of social control used by the ruling class to dominate the working class. Two types of domination are isolated; one based on coercion and the other based on ideology.

Coercion is used through the legal system. The legal system relies on institutions like the police and the prisons to control the lower class and to protect the interests of the capitalist class – in particular, to protect the property of the capitalist class. Property is seen as a fundamental right, and there is a line drawn between lawful and unlawful acquisition or appropriation of property belonging to another. The criminal law is seen as an instrument used to facilitate this end.

The second function of law is ideological. The ideological nature of law is that it is supposed to be a matrix of complex values and beliefs. The values and beliefs are those of the dominant class, and they underpin the existing social order. Thus laws on private property, the employer/employee relationship and the institution of family are seen by the ruling class as a useful and productive unit for the worker, thus allowing the bourgeoisie to maintain their hegemony over the working class.

The Marxist view of law recognises that consent is likely to be achieved through ideological means, as greater coercion would mean a breakdown of the relationship between the bourgeoisie and the proletariat that may hasten the predicted revolution of the masses. To will the proletariat into false consciousness, the capitalist state constantly renews itself and undertakes law reform to forestall the uprising of the masses. The welfare state, for example, was established to guarantee the minimum subsistence which the state gives each poor person as a ploy to hoodwink the worker into thinking the capitalist society seeks his/her interests.

In Marxist analysis, therefore, the law is a bourgeois law. The concept of the rule of law is used as a smokescreen, to convey the impression of democracy where fair liberal values are promoted. In Marxist ideology this image of law is illusory and largely symbolic in its practice. Bankowski and Mungham (*Images of Law* (1976)) say that the welfare laws are still bourgeois laws promulgated to induce false consciousness among the proletariat. The law is always the superstructure that reflects the relations between the owners of the means of production and the workers.

The criticism of capitalist society by Marxist theory of law can be analysed by looking at a society like Britain to see whether there is some credibility in the theory. We can say that in a modern society like Britain the conditions that existed in the nineteenth century no longer apply. The welfare state has provided a huge cushion between the ruling class and the working class. We can also mention the property-owning democracy introduced by the Thatcher government in the 1980s where workers were integrated into the mainstream of the British economy. Then there is the share ownership in privatised utilities – employees own shares in their companies. This is a kind of 'stakeholding' policy introduced to make the worker feel part of the enterprise. Some miners have joined hands to buy out the collieries where they work. It can, therefore, be said that in modern-day Britain the distinction between the capitalist and working-class person is very much blurred.

It follows from the above that the Marxist theory of law presented as a conflict theory of law seems inappropriate in modern-day Britain, and that the theory is best understood in its historical context – as an observation on the nature of law as it existed in the nineteenth century under capitalism.

However, to understand the value of the Marxist theory of law we need to concentrate on the coercive and ideological functions of the law as espoused. For example, as long as the criminal law is used to regulated the activities of the lower class and the civil law is used to regulate the activities of the ruling class, a case can be made that Marxist of theory of law is useful in our understanding of today's society. For example, many poor working-class people are brought within the purview of the criminal law for stealing and possession, convicted and sentenced into imprisonment, whereas the civil law is used to regulate companies and their bosses, who may commit horrendous offences like environmental pollution and escape with a fine. Similarly the boss who installs unsafe machinery which kills workers also escapes with a fine.

The ideological nature of the law is that it seeks to establish values that are somehow seen as values of the elite. Parliament makes laws because Members believe they are needed by society to solve problems; some people may say Members of Parliament belong to an elitist class and that, therefore, they reflect the values of their class. Although the present trend in law reform has made Marx's prediction of revolution false, the theory itself has a core value which is helpful to understand the nature of relationships that exist in society. Our understanding of law in society today is immensely enriched by Marxist theory of law.

QUESTION ELEVEN

'Feminist jurisprudence does not so much claim that traditional jurisprudence was wrong, but demonstrates that women have been in a radically different social relation to the law than men.'

Discuss.

University of London LLB Examination
(for External Students) Jurisprudence and Legal Theory June 1996 Q11

General Comment

Since feminist jurisprudence is now a strong element in the study of law, questions on issues raised by the topic can be given the attention they deserve by the candidate. With many women now involved in the study and practice of law, there are bound to be critical questions asked about some 'received wisdom' and ideas about how the law looks at men and women. Attempt the question only if you are confident about the point which feminist thought about the law makes.

Skeleton Solution

Origins of feminist jurisprudence – description of feminist jurisprudence – the claim made by feminist jurisprudence – Lucinda Finley as a paradigm – summary and conclusion.

Suggested Solution

Feminist jurisprudence can be said to have developed from the general women's movement in the late 1960s and early 1970s. Ashe says the development of feminist jurisprudence was an inevitable 'extension of the engagement of female reflection and speech to one more area of discourse' ((1987) 38 Syracuse Law Review 1129).

From the latter part of the 1960s onwards many women enrolled on law courses, and questioned the neglect in law curriculums of issues of concern to women like rape, inequality in pay among the sexes, domestic violence, sexual harassment and sex discrim-ination. Feminist jurisprudence is a broad church and reflects different strands of feminist thought, but the unifying theme is that society and in particular the legal system is patriarchal. It is, then, an inquiry into the law's contribution to building, sustaining, underlying and embellishing patriarchy, and seeks to find ways whereby this patriarchy can be undermined and eventually eliminated. This aim is what distinguishes feminist jurisprudence from traditional jurisprudence.

Dalton ((1987) 3 Berkeley Women's Law Journal 1) says that feminist jurisprudence explores women's subordination, its nature and extent, and is dedicated to finding the how and why of this subordination, and to finding a course of action for change. Its methodology is to concentrate on the legal system. It is feminist because it is based on women's experiences, and it seeks through awareness-raising to achieve the goal of law revision. Wishik says traditional jurisprudence is patriarchal and has not the spaces within which to 'create visions of feminist futures' ((1985) 1 Berkeley Women's Law Journal 1), and Dalton opines that women cannot only learn about the effect the law and legal institutions have on the lives of women but also how to challenge the structure of legal thought which in a culturally specific sense is 'male' oriented and calls for radical changes. In other words, feminists have found the 'maleness' of traditional jurisprudence worrying and want a change.

Finley ('Breaking Women's Silence in Law: The Dilemma of the Gendered Nature of Legal Reasoning' (1989) 64 Notre Dame Law Review 886) concentrates on legal language, which she says is gendered, to prove the inherent 'maleness' of the law. She says this is seen in legal reasoning and its language of expression. According to Finley, throughout the history of Anglo-American jurisprudence, the primary linguists of the law have been almost exclusively male. She says the history of traditional jurisprudence is such that it has been shaped, defined, interpreted and given meanings consistent with men's understandings of the world and people who are considered different from them. Because of this, law has excluded or marginalised the voices of those 'others', who happen to be women.

Finley says the men of law have societal power and are oblivious competing terms; they are insulated from challenges to their language and have come to accept their language as natural, inevitable, complete, objective and neutral. Finley's work is an examination of the relationship

17 University of London LLB (External) 1996 Questions and Suggested Solutions

between language, power and the law. Her thesis is that legal language and legal reasoning is gendered and that this gender matches the male gender of its linguistic architects. Law is seen as a patriarchal form of reasoning as the philosophy of liberalism of which law is part. Finley's claim that legal reasoning and language are patriarchal has normative sense in that male-based perspectives, images and experience are often taken as the norm in law. It is instructive as Finley says that the law uses privileged white men as the norm for equality law, for assessing the reasonable person, the way men would react is the norm for self-defence law, and the male worker is the prototype for labour law. Legal language draws heavily on men's experiences and the powerful social situation of men relative to women.

According to Finley the fact that many women are trained lawyers and are adept at male thinking does not mean legal language is androgynous – it just means that women have learned male language. She stresses, however, that the claim that law is patriarchal does not mean women have been totally ignored by the law. Women are the targets or subjects of many laws, but the point being made is that women's nature, capacities and experiences are seen through the male eye, rather than women's own definitions informing law. Finley, therefore, argues that feminist jurisprudence does not claim that traditional jurisprudence was wrong but that women have been in a radically different social relation to the law than men.

She gives several examples drawn from mainstream law that prove that the law is defined by male experience rather than the woman's. The legal definition of rage is an example at male perspective. It is the male's view of whether the woman has consented that determines the issue of consent; it is the male view of what are force and resistance in situations other than rape that defines whether force has been used against a woman and she has resisted. As far as sex is concerned, it is the male definition of sex – penetration of the vagina by the penis – that is accepted rather than the woman's experience of sexual violation that defines the crime.

According to Finley, in order for feminists to use the law to agitate for change, women must be able to talk about the complex relationship between power, gender and knowledge. Feminists must accept this connection in order to demystify the 'neutrality' of the law, to bring an awareness to the law that women's definitions have been excluded and marginalised; this will show that the law's 'neutrality' is one of the tools for silencing women.

Is there any chance that when feminists speak of the connection of power, history and domination they are employing politics and passion not law? Consider this. In legal language, experience and perspective are deemed to be biased. Having no experience or prior knowledge of something is equated with neutrality. This is relevant to jury selection. A woman who has been raped is more likely to be excluded from jury selection for a rape trial, the assumption being that her experience will render her incapable of being objective. Can it be said that her experience, rather than making her vindictive and biased, will give her critical understanding, making her more able to challenge the male-created vision of the crime? Is it possible that her experience leads her invariably to think of legal language as patriarchal? Is Finley right that the woman with personal experience of rape is more objective? This is very doubtful and Finley is not convincing here. She has a point though in saying that legal reasoning is embedded in a patriarchal framework that equates abstraction and universalisation from one group's experiences as neutrality. In so doing, legal reasoning views male experiences and perspectives as the universal norm around which terms and areas of law are defined. This is what feminist jurisprudence seeks to change.

Touching on labour law, Finley says that the meaning of work is gendered to mean work done for usages outside the home. This focus does not take into account women's work at home as wives which is unregulated by law. Why not pay women for housework? Is housework not 'work' in the conventional sense because the male architects of legal language say so?

On tort law, Finley says that the law defines injuries and compensation primarily by reference to what has kept people out at work and what their work is worth. She says in this framework damages for non-economic loss, pain and suffering, and nervous shock are seen as marginal and expendable. The most obvious cases of nervous shock to be cited are *Bourhill* v *Young* (1943) and *McLoughlin* v *O'Brian* (1983). Did the court in these two cases think of the submissions of the plaintiffs as marginal and expendable because the law considers physical attributes of women as the same as men? This is a difficult point Finley makes. It is easy to dismiss the law on nervous shock as patriarchal because women consider nervous shock a crucial area of recovery. I do not think it is entirely correct to say if women are denied recovery for nervous shock it is because the law sees them as suspect and expendable.

Another area of the law on which Finley comments is the criminal law. The language of criminal law makes the paradigmatic criminal male. The female criminal is deemed doubly deviant, first for not conforming to the stereotypical view of the woman as a mother, and second for being a criminal (Chesney-Lind and Daly, 'Feminism and Criminology' (1987) 5 Just Q 497; Heidensohn, 'Models of Justice: Portia or Persephone? Some Thoughts on Equality, Fairness and Gender in the Field of Criminal Justice' (1986) 14 International J Soc of Law 287). This is about the conflict aspect of language. The language of conflict means there will be winners and losers, and in a patriarchal system, it will often be women and their concerns that are devalued, overlooked and lost in the race to set priorities and choose sides.

Similarly the law on provocation is seen from male experience. Because women do not react with a sudden white-hot rage they are denied the defence of provocation. The agitation of women for a change in abortion law is explained on the basis of the autonomy of the woman. Denying women a right to abortion is denying them rights over their own bodies, and this is seen through male eyes not the woman's.

Having considered the limitations of legal reasoning and the connection between power, gender and legal knowledge, feminist jurisprudence looks at the multiple experiences and voices of women as the frame of reference. It asks us to look at things in their historical, social and political context. It distrusts abstractions and universal rules because 'objectivity' hides biases; it questions norms and assumptions in traditional jurisprudence, questioning its content and pushing its boundaries. This is all based on the fact that experiences of men and women are many, different, and diverse but they also overlap, so difference may not be a relevant legal criterion.

To Finley, therefore, the answer does not lie in the French feminists' argument for creation of a new language (see Irigaray, *This Sex Which Is Not One* (1985)). Women cannot create their own separate legal language, but since their voices must be heard the only possiblility is to speak the same legal language as men in order to try to bring women's experiences, perspectives, and voices into law, and help to empower women and legitimate their experiences. She acknowledges that there has been development in language change. The term 'sexual harassment' is now in vogue, as is the term 'battering' used for domestic violence. The effect of change in legal reasoning and language has been felt in the United Kingdom. As the case of *R* v *R* (1992) shows, the concept of rape has been broadened to cover rape in marriage. On the law of provocation, the law has, as in *R* v *Thornton* (1992), recognised the concept of the 'battered woman syndrome' as an acceptable defence. This recognises that sudden loss of self-control is not in the make-up of women as it is for men, and the case of *Roe* v *Wade* (1973) shows the law recognising the autonomy of women over their bodies.

17 University of London LLB (External) 1996 Questions and Suggested Solutions

Feminist jurisprudence has made enormous strides. It has succeeded in pushing the boundaries of law and legal language to the extent that the law has now come to recognise that women in the past have been in a radically different social relation to the law than men. It is not that traditional jurisprudence is wrong and must be abolished. It is just that women's experiences and expectations were not sufficiently recognised by the definitions of law which traditional jurisprudence offered.

QUESTION TWELVE

'All theories of natural law have relied upon some thesis that value is inherent in nature. Since that thesis is plainly wrong, all theories of natural law are incoherent and illogical.'

Discuss.

University of London LLB Examination
(for External Students) Jurisprudence and Legal Theory June 1996 Q12

General Comment

The difficulty positivism has with natural law will continue to dog jurisprudence for a very long time to come. This is a straightforward question that invites you to consider the positivist position that natural law is illogical and whether you agree with that position.

Skeleton Solution

Positivism/natural law dichotomy – David Hume's is/ought argument – Kelsen's attack on natural law – difference between 'is' and 'ought' propositions – Finnis – conclusion.

Suggested Solution

Positivism denies any connection between law and morality, thus whilst natural law theories have relied on some intrinsic value of nature in discovering what the law ought to be, positivism refutes the illogicality of such a thought process, and claims all natural law theories are, therefore, incoherent and illogical.

The first positivist attack on natural law as made by David Hume in *A Treatise of Human Nature* (1874), who criticised the deductive fallacy of natural law philosophy. According to Hume, the starting point of natural law theories is human reality, particularly human nature, and then the theories derive value judgments from such starting point. To Hume this is illogical reasoning by which an 'ought' statement is derived from an 'is' statement. According to Hume, a deductive argument is invalid if it derives a conclusion based on a value judgment from premises which are facts. Instead of the valid connection between propositions being 'is' and 'is not', natural law propositions are connected with an 'ought' or 'ought not'. An example of such deductive fallacy is seen in the following syllogism:

Bettie is a cat

Bettie is black

therefore all cats called Bettie ought to be black.

The fallacy of this deduction is that an 'ought' conclusion is derived from 'is' premises.

This is better explained by Thomas Aquinas' use of natural inclination. In any system of morality, statements about human nature describe what people are and do. Men ought to behave in certain ways because that is the nature of things. It can be seen that statements which are prescriptive, evaluative and normative are derived from the empirical statements that say something 'is'. Hume considers this kind of reasoning invalid because the conclusion does not follow from the premises, and there are no 'oughts' in the premises either.

Hume's attack on natural law gains support from Kelsen. In his book *What Is Justice?* (1957) Kelsen attacks natural law from the scientific viewpoint. He says that natural law extinguishes the difference between the rules whereby natural science describes its objects and the rules whereby ethics and jurisprudence describe objects, namely, morality and law. In natural science two phenomena are connected to each other by the principle of causality – cause and effect. To use Kelsen's example, if a metallic body is heated it expands. The relation between cause and effect is not attributable to any human or paranormal powers. However, when we speak of morality or law we refer to rules prescribing human behaviour, rules which are the specific meaning of acts of human or superhuman beings. An example is the moral rule of Christ which says that a person has to be his/her brother's/sister's keeper, or a legal rule which prescribes punishment for stealing. Ethics describe the situation which exists under a moral rule: be your brother's keeper; jurisprudence describes the situation under the legal rule: if a man steals, he ought to be punished. It can be seen from this that the rule of morality, like the rule of law, connects the condition with its consequence. This follows the principle of imputation. Natural law, for example, is expressed as: if A is, then B is. On the other hand, the rule of morality, like the rule of law, is expressed in this form: if A is, then there ought to be B. The difference between natural science and morality or law is the difference between the 'is' of causality and the 'ought' of imputation.

To Kelsen, it would be better if a general norm was presupposed which prescribed a certain type of human behaviour so that any particular behaviour not in accordance with the presupposed general norm can be characterised as good, bad, or correct behaviour. These are recognised as value judgments and the term is used in an objective sense because the value is in accordance with a presupposed norm. Kelsen distinguishes a positive value from a negative one. A positive value is derived from a presupposed norm. A value which does not conform to a presupposed norm is a negative value. If an individual's behaviour is described as good or bad, this means that the person's behaviour is in accordance or not in accordance with a presupposed norm, therefore, the value judgment is expressed as: 'a person ought to or ought not behave in a certain way'.

Kelsen says that without presupposing a general norm we cannot make a value judgment in the objective sense that something is permitted or forbidden. According to Kelsen, value is not inherent in the object adjudged valuable but it is in the relation of the object to the presupposed norm. He asserts that value is not inherent in natural reality; therefore, value cannot be deduced from reality. This means that it does not follow from the fact that something is, then it ought to be done, to be, or not to be done. His example is that it does not follow that if in reality a big fish swallows a small fish it implies that the behaviour of the fish is good or that it is bad. The conclusion is that there is no logical inference from the 'is' to the 'ought' of natural reality to moral or legal value.

Furthermore, what under one system of morality is good may under another system of morality be bad; similarly what under one legal system is a crime may not be a crime under another legal system. Value, then, is relative. Natural law doctrine dwells on the point that value is inherent in nature and that this value is absolute; in other words a divine will is inherent in nature. Kelsen makes the point that only by presupposing that value is inherent in nature can natural law claim that law is deducible from nature and that this law is absolute justice. Kelsen's damning conclusion is that the assumption that value is inherent in nature is metaphysical and unacceptable from the scientific point of view. This being the case, natural law doctrine is based on an illogical fallacy, deriving 'is' from an 'ought'.

Kelsen says that the norms allegedly deduced from nature are tacitly presupposed and are based on subjective values presented as the intention of God – a supreme legislator. Kelsen's verdict on natural law is well worth quoting:

'Before the tribunal of science, the natural law doctrine has no chance. But it may deny the jurisdiction of this tribunal by referring to its religious character.'

This is a serious indictment of natural law. Does the theory falsely claim value is inherent in nature? Finnis, in *Natural Law and Natural Rights* (1980), says that it is not true that natural law theories entail the belief that obligations and duties of human beings are deducible from propositions about their nature. Thomas Aquinas has said that the first principles of natural law specifying the basic forms of good and evil can be understood by everyone of the age of reason and are not demonstrable. They are self-evidence, and are informed neither form facts, speculative principles, metaphysical propositions about nature nor what is good or evil. In short, they are not derived or inferred from anything. Principles of right and wrong are derived from pre-moral principles of practical reasonableness, and not from any facts, metaphysical or otherwise.

According to Finnis, when one distinguishes what is good to be pursued, intelligence operates in a different way yielding a different sort of logic form when distinguishing in a historical, scientific or metaphysical way, what is the case. Finnis does not see any reason for saying that there is a rational operation of intelligence in the historical or scientific case of intelligence. The basic form of good that practical understanding offers is what is good for human beings considering the nature they have. To Aquinas, practical reasoning takes place by experiencing one's reason from inside – by following one's inclination. These are not psychological or metaphysical judgments about human nature, and there is no process of deduction. People just do not judge that they have an urge to make some inquiries and conclude that knowledge per se is a good or a value to be pursued. On the contrary, people understand that the object of the urge they experience is an example of a general form of good for themselves.

Criticisms can be levelled at Aquinas' theory of natural law. D J O'Connor in *Aquinas and Natural Law* questions just how the specific moral rules which need to guide our conduct can be shown to be connected with allegedly self-evident principles. Finnis rejects any suggestion that Aquinas derived an 'ought' from an 'is'. He believes that the argument that natural law is based on value judgments is because the phrase 'natural law' brings an image that refers to the norms of natural law as being based on judgments about nature. In his ethics and theology Aquinas points out the analogies running through the whole order of nature. Human virtue is similar to the virtue that can be based on anything of nature which is good. To Aquinas, therefore, human virtue is in accordance with the nature of human beings. The opposite of human vice and criteria for conformity or contradiction to human nature is reasonableness. Reasonableness is an underived first principle which makes no reference to human nature but only to human good.

Finnis bridges the dichotomy between positivism and natural law with his seven basic goods which he says are self-evident. He does not start from any facts about nature or man so there is no derivation of an 'is' in Finnis' theory. What he says is that everybody can recognise that his seven basic goods – life, knowledge, friendship, procreation, practical reasonableness, play, aesthetic experience and religion – are aspects of human existence which as such are good, ie worth having.

Positivists mount a strong indictment of natural law but the important question is whether it is true that natural law derives an 'ought' from an 'is'. I agree with Aquinas that natural law is not derived from any fact about human nature. It is underived and therefore, there cannot be any fact of nature which imbues natural law doctrines with value. Saying that the criterion for conformity or nonconformity with nature is reasonableness is not the same as saying nature has an inherent value. It cannot be correct to say, therefore, that all theories of natural law are incoherent and illogical because they do not make the claim attributed to them. Since natural law is based on the principle of reasonableness which is underived from any fact, it follows that Kelsen's argument that natural law presupposes a moral norm from which it derives its subjective conclusions cannot be right either.

Using the Net for Research in Business, Law and Related Subjects

by Kevin McGuinness, Steele Raymond, Professor of Business Law
and Tom Short, Principal Lecturer and Researcher,
both at Bournemouth University

Using the Net is an essential guide for all lawyers and business people using the Internet worldwide. Starting with a general introduction to gaining access to the Internet, the book goes on to provide analysis of sites of interest under a series of subject headings. These include:

Advertising Law
Banking
Bankruptcy and Insolvency
Civil Procedure
Contract, Consumer and Commercial Law
Corporate Law and Securities
Expert Witnesses

Finance
Insurance
International Law and Relations
Law Practice Management
Negotiation and ADR
Newspapers
Patents and IP

For ease of use, a disk is included with the book giving direct access to 2,000 primary sites linking to 100,000s of specific sources of information.

This book assimilates a vast body of invaluable information for lawyers, business people, accountants and financiers and particularly for those conducting research in any of these fields.

For further information on contents, please contact:

Claudine Pryce
Old Bailey Press
200 Greyhound Road
London
W14 9RY
United Kingdom

Telephone No: 00 44 (0) 171 385 3377
Fax No: 00 44 (0) 171 381 3377

Published February 1997
ISBN 1 85836 072 2
Price £19.95   298 pages approx
E-Mail Address: hlt@holborncollege.ac.uk

2nd edition publishing January 1998

Law Update 1997

Law Update 1998 edition – due March 1998

An annual review of the most recent developments in specific legal subject areas, useful for law students at degree and professional levels, others with law elements in their courses and also practitioners seeking a quick update.

Published around March every year, the Law Update summarises the major legal developments during the course of the previous year. In conjunction with Old Bailey Press textbooks it gives the student a significant advantage when revising for examinations.

Contents

Administrative Law • Civil and Criminal Procedure • Commercial Law • Company Law • Conflict of Laws • Constitutional Law • Contract Law • Conveyancing • Criminal Law • Criminology • English Legal System • Equity and Trusts • European Union Law • Evidence • Family Law • Jurisprudence • Land Law • Law of International Trade • Public International Law • Revenue Law • Succession • Tort

For further information on contents, please contact:

Mail Order
Old Bailey Press
200 Greyhound Road
London
W14 9RY
United Kingdom

Telephone No: 00 44 (0) 171 385 3377
Fax No: 00 44 (0) 171 381 3377

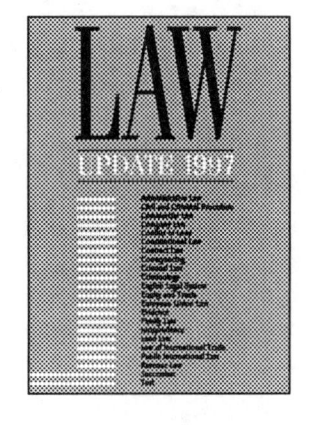

ISBN 0 7510 0782 X
Soft cover 234 x 156 mm
396 pages   £6.95
Published March 1997

Old Bailey Press

The Old Bailey Press integrated student library is planned and written to help you at every stage of your studies. Each of our range of Textbooks, Casebooks, Revision WorkBooks and Statutes are all designed to work together and are regularly revised and updated.

We are also able to offer you Suggested Solutions which provide you with past examination questions and solutions for most of the subject areas listed below.

You can buy Old Bailey Press books from your University Bookshop or your local Bookshop, or in case of difficulty, order direct using this form.

Here is the selection of modules covered by our series:

Administrative Law; Commercial Law; Company Law; Conflict of Laws (no Suggested Solutions Pack); Constitutional Law: The Machinery of Government; Obligations: Contract Law; Conveyancing (no Revision Workbook); Criminology (no Casebook or Revision WorkBook); Criminal Law; English Legal System; Equity and Trusts; Law of The European Union; Evidence; Family Law; Jurisprudence: The Philosophy of Law (Sourcebook in place of a Casebook); Land: The Law of Real Property; Law of International Trade; Legal Skills and System; Public International Law; Revenue Law (no Casebook); Succession: The Law of Wills and Estates; Obligations: The Law of Tort.

Mail order prices:

Textbook £10

Casebook £10

Revision WorkBook £7

Statutes £8

Suggested Solutions Pack (1991–1995) £7

Single Paper 1996 £3

Single Paper 1997 £3.

To complete your order, please fill in the form below:

Module	Books required	Quantity	Price	Cost
		Postage		
		TOTAL		

For UK, add 10% postage and packing (£10 maximum).
For Europe, add 15% postage and packing (£20 maximum).
For the rest of the world, add 40% for airmail.

ORDERING

By telephone to Mail Order at 0171 385 3377, with your credit card to hand

By fax to 0171 381 3377 (giving your credit card details).

By post to:

Old Bailey Press, 200 Greyhound Road, London W14 9RY.

When ordering by post, please enclose full payment by cheque or banker's draft, or complete the credit card details below.

We aim to despatch your books within 3 working days of receiving your order.

Name

Address

Postcode   Telephone

Total value of order, including postage: £

I enclose a cheque/banker's draft for the above sum, or

charge my   ☐ Access/Mastercard   ☐ Visa   ☐ American Express
Card number

☐☐☐☐ ☐☐☐☐ ☐☐☐☐ ☐☐☐☐

Expiry date   ☐☐☐☐

Signature: ....Date: ....